Protecting Children

A handbook for teachers and school managers

Second Edition

Ben Whitney

RoutledgeFalmer
Taylor & Francis Group

LONDON AND NEW YORK

First published 1996 by
Kogan Page as *Child Protection for Teachers and School*
Second edition published 2004 by RoutledgeFalmer
2 Park Square, Milton Park, Abingdon, Oxon OX14 4RN

Simultaneously published in the USA and Canada
by RoutledgeFalmer
29 West 35th Street, New York, NY 10001

RoutledgeFalmer is an imprint of Taylor & Francis

© 1996, 2004 Ben Whitney

Typeset in Times
by Keystroke, Jacaranda Lodge, Wolverhampton
Printed and bound in Great Britain
by TJ International Ltd, Padstow, Cornwall

British Library Cataloguing in Publication Data
A catalogue record for this book is available from the British Library

Library of Congress Cataloging in Publication Data
Whitney, Ben.
   Protecting children at school : a handbook for teachers and school managers /
Ben Whitney.—2nd ed.
      p. cm.
Rev. ed. of: Child protection for teachers and schools. 1996.
Includes bibliographical references and index.
   ISBN 0–415–34463–8 (pbk. : alk. paper)
   1. Child welfare–Great Britain. 2. Educational law and legislation–Great
Britain. 3. Child abuse–Great Britain. 4. Children–Crimes against–Great Britain.
5. Great Britain. Children Act 1989. I. Whitney, Ben. Child protection for
teachers and schools. II. Title.
HV751.A6W48 2004
362.76′0941–dc22   2003027643

ISBN 0–415–34463–8

For Lauren

Contents

Preface and guide to contents

This book is a substantially expanded, revised and updated new edition of my previous book, *Child Protection for Teachers and Schools*, published by Kogan Page in the Books for Teachers series in 1996. It is intended only for schools in England and Wales, as there are variations elsewhere in the law that I have not included, although the general principles should be much the same. (See, for example, *Protecting Children: A Shared Responsibility* [Scottish Office, 1998] in Scotland and *Co-operating to Safeguard Children* [Department of Health, Social Services and Public Safety, 2003] in Northern Ireland).

Since the mid-1990s there have been several key developments in child protection:

- *Childhood Matters*, a National Commission of Inquiry into the prevention of child abuse, which argued for a much broader definition of 'harm' (1997);
- *Working Together to Safeguard Children*, new government guidance for all agencies that creates the framework for local procedures (Department of Health [DoH] *et al.* 1999);
- the introduction of the Assessment Framework for Children in Need and their Families (DoH *et al.* 2000), which is intended to place greater emphasis on earlier intervention and on supporting 'children in need';
- the creation of the Criminal Records Bureau and new legislation designed to ensure more effective supervision of known sex offenders;
- a number of cases involving the abduction and murder of children, including Sarah Payne, Millie Dowler, Holly Wells and Jessica Chapman, that have received widespread publicity and prompted a national debate about the effectiveness of agencies in promoting children's safety;
- *Safeguarding Children*, a multi-agency report from the joint inspection services, including Ofsted (DoH 2002);
- the Laming Report into the murder of Victoria Climbié (DoH and Home Office, 2003) and the government's response in *Keeping Children Safe* (DfES 2003) and the Green Paper on the whole future of children's services, *Every Child Matters* (Chief Minister to the Treasury 2003), some of which is expected to go straight into legislation;

- the transfer of lead responsibility for children from the Department of Health to the Department for Education and Skills (DfES), together with the creation of a Minister for Children, Young People and Families.

No doubt things will have moved on again by the time you are reading this. Such is the nature of this kind of work: constantly evolving in the light of events. Alongside these general developments, child protection has also become a more prominent issue in education in particular, for a number of reasons:

- The case of Lauren Wright, a 6-year-old physically abused and finally killed by her stepmother and father in 2000, led directly to new legal requirements placed on schools, governors, further education colleges and local education authorities (LEAs) as a result of s.175 Education Act 2002. The publication of this book is timed to coincide with its implementation.
- Responsibility for early years provision has already been relocated into new services much closer to schools and LEAs than used to be the case. Education professionals are now involved with children at a much earlier age and when the child protection risks are statistically greater. Schools are likely to have an even greater role with families in future.
- The Victoria Climbié case has reminded us that there are children living in our community who are largely unknown to key agencies and who are therefore at increased risk of being harmed. Had she been in a school, or even known to her LEA, perhaps she might be alive today.
- Research published during the 1990s, which was highly influential in the development of the Assessment Framework, drew particular attention to the crucial pastoral role of teachers and to the fact that both they and other professionals were often confused about their contribution to child protection.
- Many teachers feel unsure about exercising reasonable force or physical restraint in response to challenging behaviour. Concern about false allegations has never been higher, yet many teachers are largely unaware of the guidance in this area, nor are they familiar with the procedure that would be used in the event of a complaint being made against them.
- National and international inquiries into child pornography and the Internet have identified a range of professionals, including teachers, among the suspected users. Some individuals in the education professions pose a significant threat to children's safety and well-being and, as by far the largest employer of those who work with children, educational organisations must be always vigilant.
- Children continue to be at risk of exploitation in the adult worlds of part-time employment and entertainments, where regulations designed to protect them are weak and frequently unenforced. New model by-laws were recommended in 1998 as a result of an EU Directive, but the core legislation is in need of substantial reform. This is a statutory area of responsibility for LEAs but

teachers often know about such activities and can help to raise awareness about the dangers they may involve.

All these changes provide the context for this new book. It contains considerably more reflection than before, as well as updating the factual information about the child protection process and the law on related child welfare issues. After almost thirty years of experience in social work, the voluntary sector and education, I am aware that the protection of children is often much more complex in practice than it looks on paper. It's all about people, not procedures. This is why things still go wrong, despite all the reports, inquiries and guidance. Learning *about* something is not quite the same as learning it.

Thankfully, child abuse does not need to be at the top of every teacher's list of daily priorities. Most of the time, our experience of children does not cause us to fear for their safety. Up to 30,000 children nation-wide will be on child protection registers at any one time, and many more will have been protected in other ways. These numbers are not insignificant, though for the individual school, to be involved directly in a serious case may be relatively rare. But every school needs someone with sufficient knowledge and expertise; every teacher needs a basic understanding of the issues. When it needs to be done, it needs to be done well, first time. Child protection is not an appropriate arena for well-meaning amateurs who don't know what to do. We may even become dangerous if we imagine that we can make decisions in isolation or that we know better than those for whom child abuse is a primary area of professional responsibility. We have to work together with others.

This book should be seen as a small contribution to that process of more effective partnership. It is not academic in tone, nor extensively referenced. It is essentially practical and anecdotal; intended to be read by busy teachers and LEA officers, not kept on a shelf for a crisis! I have tried to write about child abuse and child protection as they really are, not about how things would be in an ideal world where nothing ever went wrong.

It is aimed especially at:

- headteachers, designated teachers and nominated governors in all schools and colleges, who may be expected to have rather more knowledge and responsibility than their colleagues;
- other people working in education who have a particular concern for children's welfare such as LEA lead officers, education social workers, education welfare officers, early years staff and other pastoral workers in schools, special units and nurseries;
- teachers in training and newly qualified teachers as part of their induction process. Despite a recent commitment to increase the time given to child protection in initial teacher training, many new teachers will feel unprepared for these duties without further study.

Contents

After an Introduction that reflects on where teachers start in their response to child protection, Chapter 1 offers an historical and contextual review, drawing attention to key issues surrounding childhood and to the rediscovery of child abuse since the 1950s. In Chapter 2, I analyse some of the inquiries into child deaths and other incidents over the past thirty years and revisit an important publication from the Department of Health, *Child Protection: Messages from Research* (1995). I also examine especially the cases of Lauren Wright and Victoria Climbié, which have been crucial in bringing us to where we are today. What lessons have been learned (or not learned) that have influenced our approach to child protection in the early years of the twenty-first century?

Chapter 3 gives an inter-agency overview of definitions and understandings of 'significant harm', discusses the causes and effects of abuse, and outlines the responsibilities and roles of the various professionals involved. In Chapter 4, the focus is on the Children Act 1989 and the government guidance that stems from it. In Chapter 5, the current procedures are outlined in some detail as teachers are often not fully aware of them, but I have deliberately avoided giving large amounts of technical information that is relevant only to child protection specialists, such as details of specific offences, or statistics that would quickly become out of date. Information should be readily available locally if required.

Chapters 6, 7 and 8 are the heart of the book and develop the concept of the 'child-protecting school' by looking at a range of issues that need to be addressed in seeking to meet the requirements of the legislation and ensuring best practice. Chapter 6 includes reference to *Working Together* (DoH *et al.* 1999), the Education Act 2002, DfES circulars, Ofsted expectations, the role of governors and the LEA, and a step-by-step guide to the tasks of the designated teacher. Chapter 7 explores what actually needs to be done in practice in order to ensure that school staff play their full part in safeguarding children, and gives specific examples of where child protection issues may arise. Chapter 8 then examines some wider areas of child safety at school, such as bullying; using the curriculum; school websites; involvement with the media; videoing school events; and appointing volunteers.

Chapters 9, 10 and 11 deal with the part-time employment of children. I see this as an important safeguarding issue even though it is not usually recognised as such in local procedures. Chapter 9 outlines why this should be of concern to teachers, and how children's part-time work and their education may be related, and also covers children who take part in performances (film, theatre, TV, etc.) who may require time away from school to do so. Chapter 10 reviews the historical background to child employment and the current legal framework, as well as looking at the related issues of babysitting and work experience. Chapter 11 consists of a proposal for an entirely new regulatory approach, based on the protection principle, and is included here to promote further discussion about how the law might be reformed.

Chapters 12, 13 and 14 address the burning questions around allegations against teachers and other education staff in the context of procedures for dealing with 'professional' or 'complex' abuse. Chapter 12 is a description of three fictionalised cases, from the routine to the more serious, to show how the system actually works in practice. In order to try to reduce the danger of avoidable allegations, I offer some advice in Chapter 13 about school policy, staff standards of behaviour and an analysis of the potential risks inherent in the teacher–child relationship. The detailed procedure that is followed in the event of an allegation, both inter-agency and educational, is then examined in Chapter 14, in order to demonstrate how practice can best support the interests of *all* those involved.

In the Conclusion, I consider where services for children are going in current government thinking, and some of the possible implications for schools if they are to meet ever-increasing expectations in this complex area of pastoral care.

At six points in the text there is a Training Idea that is designed to encourage reflection and action on key issues. These are for individual or group use as appropriate.

Appendix 1 offers a school policy for child protection, based on the Staffordshire model, that expresses general principles in line with statutory guidance. Every school must have one, and publish it. It needs to be complemented by a detailed procedural document that can only be created by each individual school in the light of its particular size, circumstances, staffing, etc.

Appendix 2 summarises the private law aspects of the Children Act 1989 that relate to parental responsibility. This is a key definition of the legal rights of parents, knowledge of which is crucial for effective pastoral practice.

There follows a glossary giving definitions of some of the words and phrases commonly used by other professionals in child protection and which may not be immediately familiar to teachers attending multi-agency case conferences, etc. Other key terms are defined within the text itself as they arise. (Following this preface is a list of abbreviations and acronyms).

The book ends with a limited bibliography of relevant literature and an index.

Thanks are due to my wife, Julie, for her encouragement and insight, based on her own considerable expertise with children and young people. Also to my former employers in Staffordshire County Council, Education and Lifelong Learning, for giving me the opportunity to develop this project over the past two years. While I have drawn heavily on my professional practice throughout, the responsibility for the text is entirely my own. All examples cited are based on real cases, but key details have been changed as necessary to ensure anonymity.

Abbreviations

AALA	Adventure Activities Licensing Authority
ACPC	Area Child Protection Committee
ADHD	attention deficit hyperactivity disorder
AF	Assessment Framework
CAFCASS	Child and Family Court Advisory and Support Service
CAMHS	Child and Adolescent Mental Health Service
CAO	Child Assessment Order
CIC	criminal injuries compensation
CMO	Clinical Medical Officer
CMR	case management review
CO	care order
CPR	child protection register
CPS	Crown Prosecution Service
CPU	Child Protection Unit (usually in the police)
CRB	Criminal Records Bureau
CSA	Child Support Agency
CWU	Children's Workforce Unit (in DfES)
DfES	Department for Education and Skills
DoH	Department of Health
EC	European Community
EDT(S)	Emergency Duty Team (Service)
EPO	Emergency Protection Order
ESW	Education Social Worker
EU	European Union
EWO	Education Welfare Officer
FE	further education
FGM	female genital mutilation
FII	fabricated and induced illness
FPC	Family Proceedings Court
GAL	guardian *ad litem*
GCSE	General Certificate of Secondary Education
GMC	General Medical Council

GP	general practitioner
HO	Home Office
ICO	interim care order
ICS	Integrated Children's System
IEP	individual education plan (for a child with SEN)
INSET	in-service training
IP	injured party
IRSC	Investigation and Referral Support Co-ordinator
IRT	Identification, Referral and Tracking
IT	information technology
LAC	looked-after child
LEA	local education authority
MAPPA	Multi-Agency Public Protection Arrangements
MARAP	Multi-Agency Risk Assessment Panel
NAI	non-accidental injury
NCSC	National Care Standards Commission
NSPCC	National Society for the Prevention of Cruelty to Children
ODD	oppositional defiant disorder
Ofsted	Office for Standards in Education
PACE	Police and Criminal Evidence Act 1984
PCT	Primary Care Trust
PE	physical education
PEP	personal education plan (for LAC)
PP(O)	police protection (order)
PR	parental responsibility
PRU	Pupil Referral Unit
PSHE	personal, social and health education
PSP	pastoral support programme
PTSD	post-traumatic stress disorder
SATs	Standard Assessment Tasks
SCBU	Special Care Baby Unit
Sec.17	Child in Need
Sec.47	Child in Need of Protection
SEN	special educational needs
SENCO	Special Educational Needs Co-ordinator
SIDS	sudden infant death syndrome
SMT	senior management team
SSD	Social Services Department
SSI	Social Services Inspectorate (passing to Ofsted)
USI	unlawful sexual intercourse
YOI	young offender institution
YOS	Youth Offending Service
YOT	Youth Offending Team

Introduction: starting from here

- What exactly is child abuse?
- Is it true that children sometimes make it up?
- Why do so many cases go wrong?
- Do I have to tell someone if a child in my class has a suspicious injury?
- What do social workers actually do?
- Am I allowed to touch children?
- What if a child makes an allegation against me?
- Is child abuse really my problem?

Given the choice, I probably wouldn't start from here, but experience tells me that I need to. Many teachers are worried about child abuse; not just because they only hear about it when a child dies, but because they fear they could become the subject of an investigation themselves in circumstances that might end their careers. There has been a significant increase in the past few years in the number of allegations made against teachers by children. Everyone appears to know someone who has been affected, which seems to have generated the widespread perception that the best interests of children are being over-promoted at the expense of those who work with them, especially in education.

Such particular events only compound what is a more general unease about addressing the needs of children whose behaviour is problematic at school or whose lives are facing major disruption. We now meet the kinds of children we never used to. More teachers routinely see the extremes of family dysfunction and antisocial behaviour, perhaps in a way they had not expected. Put the two concerns together, and 'naughty children deliberately making trouble for their teachers' can become the immediate understanding of what is going on. Parents, even other professionals, often take the child's 'side' in such a dispute (as we all probably would if it involved our own child), even if there appears to be little basis to the complaint and they may not actually have all the information, only a particular view of it. This only sets up yet more barriers and increases still further the sense of a beleaguered teaching profession that nobody outside it really understands.

Some incidents in which teachers have used what they see as reasonable force in managing challenging children have become major news stories or even ended up in the courts. The media are always ready to blow things out of all proportion and to misrepresent the complexities involved. Such was the level of alarm among the professional organisations and unions that the Department for Education and Skills (DfES) appointed a network of Investigation and Referral Support Co-ordinators during 2001–2 to work with LEAs in ensuring that systems were working appropriately and that teachers' rights were being adequately respected. Interestingly, they have already found that their emphasis needs to be on the *whole* child protection system and on the pastoral practice of schools in general. The issue about allegations cannot be addressed in isolation.

Sometimes, months of suspension and stress have been involved, even for those who were subsequently proved innocent. That is a terrible experience for all those who have to go through it unnecessarily, and of course it is best avoided. I share on a regular basis in the frustration of having to wait for what seem like ever-slower procedures within the police and criminal justice systems that can leave everyone in wholly unsatisfactory uncertainty for months. Unfortunately, there is no alternative. Once a complaint of this kind has been received, the mechanisms of a formal investigation have to take over. That process is largely led by others, not by a person's employer. It is obviously bad news when someone has abused a child, but it is sometimes not much better news when they are found not to have done so.

We must, however, be careful not to let these cases lead us into a wider denial. They are not typical of child abuse and child protection as a whole. Most abuse is by parents and those within the child's immediate family, but some does involve teachers or individuals connected with the child in some other way. If you look carefully, there have been enough examples of real concern to at least make us stop and think, rather than immediately assuming they are all untrue. Children often have a genuine point to make, and deserve to be listened to, even if they do not always communicate in the ways we would prefer! Sometimes teachers have been insensitive, foolish or unprofessional, and the allegation could have been avoided by better practice. While not actually criminal, some behaviours are still unacceptable, or at least very unwise. A significant number of cases have involved physical or sexual assaults on pupils or the use of child pornography. It is a fact, not a conspiracy.

Finding a balance

As someone whose central concern is children's individual welfare, rather than having to manage a whole classroom full of them, I do try to appreciate the practical realities of the schools with which I am in daily contact. Perhaps, though, as a relative outsider, I can also see the issues more clearly than those who are most directly involved, and from all perspectives. Sometimes it sounds as though some education policy-makers and teacher representatives have begun to believe that children themselves are the problem, rather than those who have harmed them or abused their inexperience. Given our legal duty to promote children's welfare above all else, this approach can risk setting teachers somewhat apart from the other childcare professionals with whom they have to work, especially in this particularly complex area.

Distressing though unfounded individual incidents sometimes are, they cannot be permitted to influence our whole approach. The nature of the relationship with our pupils requires us to put their needs first, not our own, even if doing so is sometimes more testing than we would wish. Even if a child has made an allegation up out of nothing (and while I have known the odd example, it is rare in my experience), they are still the child in the situation. Children might be expected to behave in childish and immature ways from time to time. We might hope that school can be a 'safe haven', kept free from all the issues that affect the pupils the rest of the time, but that is no longer realistic. They are the same person in maths on a Tuesday afternoon as they are at weekends and in the evenings! Education has to engage with the whole child, not just part. Family life and its shortcomings inevitably spill over into school.

Equally, calls for pupils to be excluded because their parents are violent and abusive, for example, or because they have made a complaint about a member of staff, seem to me to be wholly inappropriate. Punishing children for the failings of the adults in their life cannot possibly be right. If the parents are violent to us, what must they be like to live with every day? A false accusation may still suggest an underlying problem of some other kind. Even violence by children has to be set in context. Many incidents would have ended safely if they had been handled differently. The damage done to some children by their upbringing, or lack of it, is frequently a factor, and one over which they can have little control. Some are suffering from a mental illness or a developmental disorder. Blaming the child for their problems doesn't usually take us very far.

Some teachers have become anxious about ever touching children, even out of friendship or to give reassurance, for fear that an innocent gesture might be used against them later. This reluctance across the board should not be necessary and is often a misunderstanding. Some touching is entirely acceptable. But there are, of course, children in our schools with psychological, emotional and behavioural difficulties, some of whose needs have never been properly assessed or met. They need to be handled with great care and sensitivity. Angry and abused children do not always behave well and are sometimes understandably suspicious of those trying to help them. If they feel adults have failed them in the past, they may assume it will be the same again this time, despite our very best intentions.

Recognising all these tensions and underlying feelings has never been more important than in the current climate of raising achievement by increasing inclusion. If we are to do something about breaking down the barriers that some children constantly face, and address their often generational underperformance, those children cannot all be hidden away in special schools, support units and children's homes, as some people would wish. We have to include them, with all their problems, in mainstream provision and expect to come across them in ordinary schools, just like other, less complicated, children. Otherwise they will become ever more marginalised and will pose even greater problems later. They will no doubt cause us all some difficulty along the way, but they are part of the wider community and so have every right to be there. Segregation is rarely appropriate in building a more cohesive society.

Children cannot always have what they want and must of course be subject to the necessary guidance and discipline of adults. But they are partners now in this process, not just passive recipients. We have a duty to consult them about their lives; they have a voice and will use it. In their own contribution to *Every Child Matters* (Chief Minister to the Treasury 2003), children identified 'being healthy' and 'staying safe' as key outcomes. So they must be given space to tell us what is happening at home if they want to, and the opportunity to use, for example, a complaints procedure or counselling service to draw attention to any failings on the part of those who teach them or any other adult in their lives who is abusing their trust. No one is above criticism any more. This must be a good thing. Children must have their views respected, even if they cannot always be followed. They have a right to a say in their own protection. But it's all about balance. Everyone deserves to be treated fairly; no one has the right to mistreat anyone else.

Coping with uncertainty

In my opinion, all these anxieties arise especially in education largely because of a wider insecurity about how we should relate to children and young people. Other professionals have largely moved on into a new kind of relationship already. Teachers are unsure of their role in child protection in particular, because they are unsure about their pastoral role in general. It's not that they are naturally any less sympathetic than others, but they do not want to be social workers. We have lost confidence in being *in loco parentis*, with all the personal authority that came with it, and we do not yet know what we can best put in its place. After all, the main job to be done in schools is teaching – delivering a National Curriculum and achieving improved results in literacy, numeracy and GCSEs – not making up for parental shortcomings or providing a family support service. Most schools do not have dedicated pastoral workers as well.

However, school staff have always been expected to take a certain stance on behaviour, discipline, etc., sometimes in a way that other agencies are not. This can put them in a much more vulnerable position. Headteachers have occasionally said to me that they fear to question classroom tactics that amount to little more than organised intimidation because without them, and in the absence of the well-aimed board rubber, there would be chaos! Children, many would say, need firm handling and clear instruction in school, even if these are missing everywhere else. But what if there is a conflict of values between home and school? Do those children no longer deserve to be there? 'Interfering' in a pupil's home life raises all kinds of potential questions about whether the teacher actually has any legal or moral right to do so. Whose children are they, after all? Despite the government's increasing reliance upon it, this whole pastoral area of school life is often left undiscussed and largely *ad hoc*, which is hardly an adequate basis for best practice.

When confronted by even the possibility of child abuse, we may feel reluctant to get involved, unaware of what to do or worried about having to take an unfamiliar step that we have never taken before. The stakes may seem unreasonably high. Parents may well be hostile to what we have to do and blame us personally. We may be justifiably frightened of them, or even of their child. Our actions are immensely influenced by these more affective factors, not just by our level of knowledge. Simply issuing guidance and procedures is not sufficient. If it were, nothing would ever go wrong. We may already know exactly what we *should* do; we may even have the necessary policies in place to tell us *what* to do, but actually *doing* it raises all kinds of questions, both personal and professional, that tend to get in the way.

Furthermore, one of the key findings of *Safeguarding Children* (DoH 2002), a joint report by all the inspecting bodies, including Ofsted, was that the working relationship between teachers and those from other agencies is often far from good. Proposed plans to place more social workers in schools might prove very interesting. My guess is that some would be excluded by lunchtime! Some teachers even went so far as to say that they would no longer make referrals to social services because of problems in the past. Faith in the system was often low, and teachers rarely felt sufficiently included in the outcomes of child protection cases to take adequate ownership of the issues. Social workers, in turn, often felt that teachers tended to be overly judgemental about families in difficulty and had unrealistic expectations of what they could be expected to achieve in the face of limited legal powers and even more limited resources.

These feelings of mutual uncertainty have to be acknowledged. Soon they may become less relevant if the kind of children's services reform now being suggested becomes a reality. But even if the structures change, children will still not be adequately protected if professionals do not trust each other, or do not have confidence in their own contribution to the process. In the face of so many other things to do, teachers could be forgiven for sometimes thinking that perhaps the tasks arising from both abused and abusing children are best left to others. Consequently, there can be genuine difficulties in building working partnerships, just at the point where we need them to be most effective.

Getting to where we want to be

I'm afraid I don't remember a great deal of what I learned at school, no doubt due entirely to my own failings. But I have always recognised the significance of Shakespeare's use in his audience of the willing suspension of disbelief. Of course it is obvious that there is someone standing behind the curtain or that the disguise of the woman dressed as a boy wouldn't fool anyone in broad daylight. Things cannot possibly be as they appear; there are far too many coincidences. But for the purposes of the plot, we agree to leave these misgivings on one side. I ask only for the same degree of co-operation throughout this book. There are many reasons why these expectations may be unreasonable and even unwelcome. But just for now, think as if it were possible and even desirable for it all to happen.

It is the clear wish of the politicians and the public that we all work more closely together across agencies to protect children, not be driven further apart. These mutual misperceptions and personal prejudices risk obscuring the essential vision of what is most important: the *vital* role of school staff within the network of caring agencies for protecting children. The job just cannot be done without us. More child protection referrals for children aged 3–16 come from schools than from any other source. The expansion of nursery education has added a whole new area of responsibility. Most children naturally look to their school for help if they need it. Prompt action by teachers and others saves lives and prevents abuse from happening.

It is important to recognise the very real worries with which I began, and not just to deal with these requirements as if each of us comes to such tasks without prior feelings, but they have to be kept in their place. Teachers sometimes seem to forget that *all* those adults who work with children have to deal with many of the same issues. Some of these may encounter far greater threats to their physical safety when visiting families in their homes or caring for those in specialist units, etc., as well as the risks attached to being alone with children, driving them to appointments, or just trying to get them to do things they don't want to do. It is rarely a teacher who has to deal most directly with a parent accused of harming their child, or seek to prevent a teenager from leaving their residential home at night, solely through the skills of perseverance and persuasion. We each have our own challenges to face.

Throughout this book I hope to offer a sensible and realistic framework within which schools can operate and play a small part in easing at least some of these concerns. Teachers are often asked to do things for which they have been neither trained nor properly empowered. Employers do not always seem to give school staff the structures and policies that are available to others. But we must keep a sense of proportion. Social workers and police officers must not see an abuser in every classroom or behind every allegation, no matter how unsubstantiated. Teachers must not allow themselves to become distracted from recognising the potential abuse in children's lives because of an overemphasis on themselves and their own uncertainties. The sense of personal discomfort is important, but it must not be allowed to dominate.

It is overwhelmingly children who are harmed by adults in our society, *not* the other way around. Usually they are harmed by the very adults who should be caring for them. Other adults are needed to do something to protect them. The Children Act is an excellent piece of legislation, still largely overlooked, not some charter for trendy 'do-gooders' and out-of-control children. We must know how to use it, and the procedures that arise from it, for everyone's mutual benefit. Few teachers know the child protection system as well as they should, but its framework of law and practice is an essential part of our involvement in pastoral care.

The Act does not lay down anything like the restrictions on adults that some believe it does, nor does it give children *carte blanche*, as they sometimes claim! Knowing what the system is, and being confident in our own particular role within it, provides not only full protection for children but also increased security for the teacher in doing what must be done. In fact, fulfilling this primary task properly also makes it less likely that false allegations will be made, because we will all become much more sensitive to the issues and far better prepared to recognise any potential problems before they occur. If we are genuinely committed to the task, we can make this work in the best interests of us all.

Caring teachers have nothing to fear from the child protection process. It will not always be easy, of course, and no system is perfect. Using it may risk our relationship with parents; people will make mistakes or let us down; things sometimes won't work out exactly as we would have hoped. Children are not always grateful. This is not about knights in shining armour riding over the horizon to put it all right again. Being abused is a mess. Doing something about abuse is often a mess as well. It may even cost us something personally, but it will ultimately be a job well done if it is done to the very best of our ability.

Chapter 1

From Poor Law to protection?

An historical perspective on children and their needs

Children in history

Acknowledgement of children as individuals and therefore with rights to life, dignity and respect is a very new phenomenon. Indeed, it could be argued that we have yet to accept it to its fullest extent. The UN Convention on the Rights of the Child (1989) presumably had to spell it out because it could not be assumed. The contrasting idea, that children are primarily extensions of their parents, part of their 'goods and chattels', has a rather longer history. Children have traditionally been seen as disposable assets whose 'ownership' might be the subject of dispute, much like property. In the context of divorce, for example, it took until the Children Act 1989 to try to change our thinking into something more child centred, though there is ample evidence that, even now, solicitors, courts and parents still see children as essentially something to be argued over rather than as persons to be valued.

In Aries' book *Centuries of Childhood* (1973, but now long out of print), the author describes the 'benign indifference' of parents towards their children in medieval times, and the sense that they should be treated with kindness but that no real emotional attachment was required. Aries acknowledges that others had seen the relationship as rather less than benign, with parents rapidly losing interest after the social significance of the birth had passed. Many, across the classes, seem to have abandoned the care and upbringing of their children to others, often taking little or no part in their life from then on.

In the distant past, children moved rapidly into the adult world, with few developmental stages between infancy and adulthood. In poorer families, they soon achieved the status of workers, while for the more wealthy, children were treated largely as ornaments, marriageable bargaining counters or masters-in-waiting. But as early as the seventeenth century, Aries reports that contemporary writers were complaining that parents had become over-indulgent. Theological understandings of children as unspoilt, and consequently closer to God than adults, fostered a climate of sentimentality in which children came to be seen as precious but fragile; at risk from darker forces and therefore to be kept apart and, in this sense at least, protected.

The innocence of childhood, at least to start with, was also a strong theme in the eighteenth and nineteenth centuries in, for example, the poetry of Blake and

Wordsworth. This verse is from a poem in Blake's *Songs of Innocence*, written in celebration of the annual service for charity school children held at St Paul's Cathedral:

> O what a multitude they seem'd, these flowers of London town;
> Seated in companies they sit with a radiance all their own.
> The hum of the multitudes was there, but multitudes of lambs,
> Thousands of little boys and girls, raising their innocent hands.

Yet typically, at the same time, in an increasingly urban society, the exploitation of children at work moved from being a rural, family-oriented phenomenon into an organised economic consequence of increased industrialisation (see Chapter 10). This led to the wholesale abuse of poor children for profit, including child prostitution on a scale that would certainly have been far greater than it is today, at least in the United Kingdom. (We have now found other children, further away, to abuse, via the Internet.)

More middle-class children, however, largely retained their place as valued objects and yet in need of moral restraint and discipline, contrasting images perhaps more prevalent in Victorian Britain than anywhere else. In school halls throughout the land at Christmas you can still hear:

> And through all his wondrous childhood
> He would honour and obey,
> Love and watch the lowly mother
> In whose gentle arms he lay;
> Christian children all must be
> Mild, obedient, good as he.
> (Mrs C. F. Alexander, 1818–95)

But in any society beset with high infant mortality, the sense of a child's distinct personality and identity was inevitably lost much of the time. I remember once seeing a gravestone in an ancient churchyard: 'Sacred to the memory of Florence——, who had several [unnamed] children, most of which died at birth'.

It has been compulsory to register births for only a century or so, in the aftermath of the Infant Life Protection Act 1872. Many children before then must have lived and died with scarcely anyone outside the family being aware of it. When that happens today, as it occasionally does, there is at least a public sense that it should not have been so. The 15-year-old who gave birth on her bed at home and then took the baby's body in a school bag to the local police station was, I am sure, given more care in 1999 than she would have been in 1899, but such sad events have not entirely gone away.

Social trends

My reading of the late twentieth century suggests a series of similarly conflicting images of childhood. We are still beset by contradictions. The range of statutory and protective arrangements has never been greater, as we shall see, but perhaps the risks have also increased just as much. The idea that other people might in some way be responsible for what goes on within family life has never received universal acceptance. The Englishman's (*sic*) home is his castle in many people's minds, not least where the social welfare services are concerned. Despite this, we still blame the agencies when things go wrong. We do not have a common view about the balance between the rights of the parent, child and state, or of how children should be treated, illustrated for me by a number of examples:

Liberated parents: independent children

Changing social trends in marriage and family life have primarily been driven by the rights of adults, with children's needs not the prime concern. Bringing up children has generally been relegated to a second-class activity, less important than economic productivity. Poor single parents in particular are expected to work, not to give their full-time attention to their children. For some potential parents at least, children represent an unwanted tie and a financial burden. Parenthood is no longer as significant in defining adult identity as it used to be, with even some signs of a return to our medieval indifference, as parents expect to have a degree of distance from the day-to-day needs of their children that recent generations would not have anticipated.

We have largely assumed that with the greater opportunities open to our children, they will be able to manage the emotional adjustments that are now required of them in order to cope with less stable parental relationships and the decline of the extended family. In return for adults' desire for greater self-fulfilment, children themselves also seem to want to get the whole business of childhood over with as quickly as possible. They are uncertain of their status as dependants and keen to establish their own views and perspectives, their own economic autonomy and space to be themselves, free from parental control. Sexual identity and self-expression are becoming issues at ever-younger ages. Despite this increased self-reliance, children and young people remain extremely vulnerable, often much more so than they realise.

Problem children: dangerous adults

Even though adults have encouraged this independence, at least in part, there is clearly a growing sense that such liberated children are a significant threat to our corporate well-being. Education in particular is beset by endless initiatives about dealing with bad behaviour, from truancy patrols to Anti-Social Behaviour and Parenting Orders and even fixed-penalty fines. Just being on the streets after a certain time as a young person is sometimes assumed to suggest a problem, and a few isolated examples seem to have tarnished the image of a whole generation. The spectre of 'truants' rampaging through shopping centres when they should be at school has been an enduring myth perpetuated by government ministers of both Conservative and Labour persuasion – this despite the fact that the reality consists almost entirely of perfectly well-behaved children out shopping with their parents, rather than running riot unsupervised.

The abduction of James Bulger in 1993 confirmed many stereotypical views about both children and their parents, and reveals a much deeper ambiguity in society's expectations. The widely publicised photographs of the two 10-year-olds who killed him created a climate of hatred and revenge that will live for as long as they do. The national desire for retribution was almost overwhelming. The earlier example of Mary Bell, an 11-year-old who killed two little boys, was exactly the same. Few saw either case as a tragedy involving *three* lost childhoods. The fact that the killers were so young somehow made them more guilty, not less, as all logic would suggest.

No one seemed interested in asking what influences the adults in those children's lives had brought to bear on them to make them as they were. Here, as elsewhere, we prefer abusers to be entirely different from ourselves: 'beasts', 'monsters' and 'perverts', with a clear division between 'us' and 'them'. In fact, with a few exceptions, they are likely to be much more like us than we might think – people whose life experiences contain both light and shade, if sometimes in highly unequal proportions. Abusers have mortgages and live down our road. They may have a professional job or even go to church. Their children go to our children's school. It is strangely comforting to focus on a few deranged individuals, but most abuse is much closer to home, and children are almost entirely the victims of it, not the cause.

To smack or not to smack

We are also far from clear or consistent about the boundaries of appropriate punishment by parents – still, after two hundred years, often the basic issue in cases of child cruelty. We are not always convinced of the value of child protection systems and what exactly we want as a society in this delicate area. Smacking is not illegal within the home and is actively promoted by some as an essential means of disciplining children, even in schools and day-care settings (where it has only recently been made universally illegal). Personally, I would very much prefer parents not to hit their children at all, and a change in the law to that effect has considerable merit as a defence of children's basic human rights.

But it is difficult to see how an outright ban could be enforced without overwhelming consent. A law might be applied in a very discriminatory fashion: only in the families where professionals can see what's going on, for example. Virtually all parents admit to smacking their children, so to use the word 'abuse' in such a context would be to deprive it of all meaning, which would not be helpful in identifying behaviour at the most unacceptable end of the spectrum. There is a strong sense in our society that parenting is essentially intuitive rather than something that can be inspected by outsiders according to a set of rules (which makes placing all the blame on professionals, when parents then misuse that freedom, somewhat unreasonable). Parents will always expect to make these choices for themselves. Of course we must provide every opportunity to help them to do it as well as they can, but I doubt we will ever be able to be overly prescriptive.

Control versus care

British culture generally emphasises toughness over sensitivity, and is a culture in which many people see force – personal or institutional – as a perfectly acceptable way of resolving conflict. Harsher regimes for offending or truanting children are regularly advocated by some politicians and even some teachers, even though we know they do not work. There are now even plans by the Home Secretary to reverse the whole thrust of the Children Act by forcing some children, and their parents, into new kinds of compulsory residential settings. The alternative suggestion, that most troubled children need the same opportunities, support, care and love as every other child because they have never known them, is easily dismissed as too soft. The heavy hand of the Poor Law is never far away (see p. 13).

'Pindown', for example, might have greatly exercised social work practitioners in the early 1990s as an unacceptable way of keeping children in residential homes under control, but I suspect the vast majority of the public neither knew nor cared. (Pindown was a way of restricting the liberty of children in residential care, subsequently discredited. See A. Levy and B. Kahan (1991) *The Pindown Experience and the Protection of Children*, Staffordshire County Council.) Despite calls for even more imprisonment, Britain already locks more children up when they offend than other, comparable countries, and is even quite prepared to expose them to the full glare of the national media and the adult court system rather than protect their anonymity. We are inconsistent in our definition of 'childhood' – at times seeing teenagers as still needing the protection of adults and the wider community, but at other times expecting them to be held personally responsible for their actions, old enough to stand on their own two feet and take the consequences, without any allowance for their immaturity.

It is no wonder that teachers are confused over what exactly society wants them to do about the children in their care; the wider society itself has no clear vision either. But despite this far from easy climate, we professionals have a *duty* to work together in their best interests. Out of what are now recognised as past disasters, there is supposed to be a new consensus based on a shared commitment to children's welfare. The individual child's well-being is intended to be our common focus. For teachers, whose main area of expertise is not in the field of social work and child protection, it may help to chart some of the key elements of children's

legislation in the recent past, in order to understand better how, and why, we have
come to where we are.

Public welfare provision

Child protection, if not child abuse, has had a relatively brief existence. The history
of any public policy to safeguard the interests of children goes back little further
than the Poor Law Reform Act of 1831. Like its much more modest antecedent,
the Poor Law of 1601 (the lapse of time shows how slow British society was to
respond to its growing understanding of its children's needs), this was at least
recognition that some families may need intervention from outside in order to
ensure a child's basic survival. But the Act was essentially punitive rather than
protective. Failing parents, invariably also the poorest, were seen as weak and their
children as in need of rescue so that, in the care of the state, they might learn to
work hard to overcome the inadequacies that had led their family into difficulty in
the first place.

A series of nineteenth-century laws created offences relating to direct physical
cruelty towards children. The threshold, however, appears to have been quite
high. In a celebrated case in 1847, *R. v. Renshaw*, a 10-day-old baby had been left
by its mother in a ditch, wrapped in a large piece of flannel. The baby was found
quite soon, evidently unharmed by the experience. The mother was acquitted of
attempted murder but then also cleared of even a common assault, as 'no actual
injury or inconvenience' could be proven. It is interesting to speculate, given
current definitions of 'significant harm' (see p. 57), whether the outcome would
now be any different.

The Poor Law Amendment Act 1868 made it an offence for a parent wilfully to
neglect a child's needs for food, clothing, medical aid and housing in such a way
as harmed, or was likely to harm, their health. Criminal legislation, to be enforced
against the parent, was the primary concern, rather than focusing on the needs of
the child. Some commentators apparently thought even then that the intervention,
which usually deprived the child of their primary carer and left them to be brought
up as a pauper in wholly unsatisfactory public institutions, probably did them more
harm than good!

The earliest concerted attempt to address what we would now call child
abuse followed the creation of the British Society against Cruelty to Children in
Liverpool in 1883. Many local societies of this kind merged to form the National
Society for the Prevention of Cruelty to Children (NSPCC) in 1890, which, by the
turn of the century, had set up a national network of inspectors. Much of the work
was commendably preventive: working with parents to keep families together as
much as protecting children by removing them from home and thereby 'relieving
the parents of their proper responsibilities'.

The Prevention of Cruelty to and the Protection of Children Act 1889, as its
cumbersome title suggests, reflected both emphases and was undoubtedly a
milestone. Despite the fact that many things still happened to children at home and

elsewhere that were clearly unacceptable, this was the first serious attempt to address the wider issues in a more proactive way. It not only made the ill-treatment and neglect of children an offence, but also made more thorough provision for the subsequent care of the child, if needed, by a 'fit person', though this did not always mean the kind of loving family that the child must have hoped for. Gradually the emphasis shifted from only the interests of the state and the punishment of the parents onto what might be best for the children. The Poor Law (Children) Act of the same year gave authority for the parish guardians to take over the parental rights of a child already in their care, if they were satisfied that the parents should not continue to hold them. The Prevention of Cruelty to Children Act 1904 first gave local authorities the power actually to remove children from their parents, including those who had not been convicted of any criminal offence, but where it was felt that the child's needs required it.

There has been a continuous debate ever since about the appropriate balance between the rights of parents and the powers of the authorities (though not so much about the rights of children until very recently), with the pendulum swinging between the two extremes. The Children and Young Persons Act 1933, still in force in part, and which first used the concept of 'the welfare of the child', erred on the side of intervention and removal. The Children Act 1948 placed more emphasis on supportive services and gave local authorities a duty to rehabilitate children within their family of origin if at all possible. The Children and Young Persons Act 1969 tended to increase the priority given to caring for children away from home again, though this may not necessarily have been its intention.

Even as late as the 1960s, Britain was still sending poor children halfway across the world to start a new life in Australia, even if they had living parents, with little or no knowledge of what happened to them when they got there. Others were placed in 'community homes', living and receiving their education entirely separated from their peers and families. Young offenders and those who failed to attend school could spend long periods in secure approved schools and borstals. Hidden away in the countryside there were villages and 'colonies' that were largely closed to the outside world, some of them as part of huge mental hospitals for those still described as 'subnormal'. (It was not until 1981 that all children received the right to an education, whatever their special needs or disability.) Children stayed in such places for years on end, simply because their parents had died, or were unable to care for them, or because they were thought to be morally inadequate. In my early days as a social worker I used to visit them, or those who were still living there as adults; it's that recent.

The Children Act 1989, which came exactly 100 years after the first attempt to legislate to any significant extent, is perhaps more in tune again with the approach of the 1948 Act. It will run throughout this book as an outstandingly humane and balanced attempt to resolve as many of the conflicts as possible in the best interests of children. Many of its provisions have still to make the impact they deserve. There has been continuing concern in some circles that too much emphasis is still being placed on investigation and response when something goes wrong, and not enough on family support and prevention. When a child dies, others might argue the opposite, and the uncertainty about what exactly we are trying to achieve continues to this day.

Child abuse rediscovered

Many writers would put 'rediscovered' in inverted commas at this point, as of course it never actually went away, but it is important to note that current systems date back no further than my own working life. Things before that were nothing like so organised. Parents went on being convicted of cruelty and neglect; offences of incest and abandonment were always on the statute book, but the emphasis still tended to be on the crime rather than on the child. Freud had reported that some of his patients claimed they had been sexually assaulted as children, though he later suggested that such accounts might owe more to hysteria than to reality. Much institutional abuse was simply ignored. The post-war years were generally optimistic, with a re-emphasis on the 'ideal family' that made the exceptions much more difficult to identify or to accept, even though they were certainly still there.

In 1946, John Caffey, a specialist in paediatric radiology in the United States, had first noticed that some injuries to the long bones of infants appeared to be caused by external action or trauma rather than by disease or accident. Silverman, in 1953, attributed such injuries to parental carelessness; Woolley and Evans in 1955 said they were caused by the deliberate actions of parents and carers. The growth in the techniques of radiology, and the extremely young age of the children being presented, gave the issue a new and a more public profile. Society often defines its problems not by what is going on, but by what it admits is going on. Suddenly, science was asking questions that forced others to respond.

It was Dr Henry Kempe, in a speech at the University of Colorado in 1962, who coined the term 'battered child syndrome'. He reported research by colleagues all over the United States, resulting, by 1967, in a network of registration and protection systems for children found to be at risk, or who had been injured. Kempe's terminology was quickly taken up in Britain. In 1963 Griffiths and Moynihan, two orthopaedic surgeons, and in 1966 Cameron *et al.* published papers on the issue, and a memorandum was circulated to all doctors for the first time. But gradually the 'battered baby' concept was seen to be too limited. The image of helpless babies, and the emphasis on particular acts of physical violence, was now complemented by more general questions about children's 'failure to thrive'. Sexual abuse remained largely unmentioned.

Although the first 'at risk' registers were set up in Britain during the 1970s, it was not until there was a series of public inquiries that the issue became a national priority. British social policy has tended to be highly influenced by particular cases, and it is to those stories over the past thirty years that we must now turn.

Chapter 2

Learning from our mistakes
Why things sometimes go wrong

An evolving process

By the late 1970s it was being recognised that child abuse, and therefore child protection, evolves. It is not a static process but contains several stages. For example:

1. There is a denial that physical or sexual abuse exists to any significant extent, and that which is acknowledged is attributed only to 'maniacs' and deranged individuals, etc.
2. The community pays attention to the more lurid forms of abuse or the 'battered child'. More effective ways of dealing with severe physical abuse are found, together with strategies for prevention.
3. Abuse is handled better by agencies; wider concepts such as failing to reach key milestones for no organic reason are included; more subtle forms of abuse are recognised.
4. Society acknowledges emotional abuse, scapegoating and patterns of severe rejection.
5. Attention is paid to the existence and needs of children who are being sexually abused and those adults with a past history of being abused as children.

This is not simply a progression over time. It is not that all is in order because we have reached stage 5, now that sexual abuse is much higher up the child protection agenda. Sometimes the basics aren't carried out correctly. Many people still retreat into denial. It happens much less often these days, but headteachers still occasionally tell me that they do not need to know about child protection because 'we don't have that sort of family in our school'. I do not share or respect their confidence. We know only what we are allowed to know, or are clever enough to discover, and I suspect we will only ever know about a minority of the abuse that children suffer. It is, by definition, a covert activity that is hard to detect. Research among adults would suggest that they did not receive, or necessarily seek, protection at the time, even from within the present system. Many factors will be significant in both understanding abuse and our effectiveness in responding to it.

Beyond Blame

Although it is, in one sense, now out of date as there have been other cases since, I have continued to draw on the insights contained in *Beyond Blame* by Reder *et al.* (1993). In another sense, this analysis of a series of child abuse tragedies between 1973 and 1989 remains extremely pertinent. As the title makes clear, the purpose of the book, and mine in referring to it, is to go beyond the expression of moral outrage or the allocation of blame, either to parents, professionals or 'the system', and to see what can be learned from the experience. It is perhaps because we rarely get past the headlines that we seem not to have understood exactly what is going on. I will later also consider other reports and analyses that post-date this research, but I believe that Reder *et al.* still provide a highly useful framework for our thinking, one that is simply reinforced by later incidents.

The 'social construction' of child abuse is rather like a spring – an evolving spiral of legislation, attitudes and responses that moves forward through time and within which three elements interact, each of which informs the others:

- social values about children;
- professional practice;
- theories and knowledge.

> As society progressively alters its attitudes to children and their welfare, expectations of parents are reviewed and refined. Unacceptable standards of care are defined, which warrant state intervention. Professional practice is itself sensitive to prevailing social beliefs and is guided by contemporary theories and knowledge, while new research is prompted by questions arising from professional work and social beliefs. From time to time, social attitudes become consolidated through political initiatives and legislation. At other times, social concern about state interventions leads to public inquiries, the results of which help to modify practice and may lay the groundwork for new legislation.
>
> (Reder *et al.* 1993, p. 6)

Some of the cases achieved more notoriety than others. Maria Colwell (1974) gained a particular status as the first child to be the victim of such an incident for some time, though there had been inquiries into the deaths of Denis O'Neill in 1945 and Graham Bagnall in 1973. But in the 1970s and 1980s, because professionals were now much more subject to the pressures of wider media scrutiny, there was an explosion of this kind of investigation. The cases of O'Neill, Colwell, Jasmine Beckford (1985) and Kimberley Carlile (1987) led directly or indirectly to new legislation, even if they were not necessarily typical of the issues as a whole.

The authors reviewed thirty-five cases, all but one of which led to fatalities. There were many other incidents during the review period, but not all the inquiries were made public. Not all the reports focused directly on the child concerned; one of them, that concerning Max Piazzani in 1974, does not even mention his age! Some were only concerned with the adults and how the criminal evidence against them had been collected. They varied from 13 pages to 585, and information was sometimes too sketchy on which to make a judgement. There was no common framework within which all the investigations had taken place, and there is no central register of all such reports that are published, so caution has to be exercised in seeing these as necessarily representative.

These cases all focus on children killed or neglected by those who were supposed to be looking after them. (Nationally, there are at least eighty to a hundred such deaths a year compared with a much smaller number, usually in single figures, involving strangers or random killings.) This is also the current emphasis of child protection procedures, and, although I will later argue for a wider definition of behaviours that put children at risk (see, for example, Chapter 9), it reflects the general thrust of our understanding. Abuse by people outside the family is far less common, but has a much higher profile when it happens. I saw for myself the literally world-wide publicity given to the picture of the two Soham schoolgirls in August 2002, whereas the killing of a child under other circumstances by a family member may not even make the news at all.

Oddly, we do not usually see this same process of detailed self-analysis and recrimination when a child is abducted and murdered. When there is an obvious murderer to blame there seems to be no need to turn on the professionals as well. But placing all the blame on parents and carers seems to be too much to handle. It is as if we feel that we should be able to prevent parents from harming their own children, and someone else must have been at fault if they do. Mistakes must have been made for such a thing to happen. Other situations are judged to contain too many random elements to make such a hope of prevention possible.

The findings

At the time of these cases, public concern was primarily about under-intervention and vulnerable children who had not been adequately protected, with regular calls for much greater action by the authorities. The primary problem then, as now, was perceived to be the failure of inter-professional communication. When you have a moment (and before you read Chapter 3), write down the names of all those agencies and individuals who might have some role to play in the protection of children. Anyone who has ever been to a case conference will recognise the problem; there never seem to be enough chairs! Reder *et al.* identify five key elements in this inter-relationship that directly affected the outcomes of the cases they reviewed:

1. *Professionals need to feel secure in their own work setting.* It is tempting to say that this point alone accounts for most of the shortcomings in every public service agency. Working with children is not a high-status occupation. Front-line social

workers are not well paid even by comparison with most teachers and many health workers; family support and residential workers earn even less. There are nearly always unallocated cases, staff vacancies and a high turnover, with major responsibilities sometimes being dealt with by underqualified or inexperienced staff. Like education, most caring professions have been in a constant process of reorganisation and increasing expectations for as long as anyone can remember. This is all highly unsettling for staff and inevitably undermines their confidence and job security, and reduces morale. Add to this the personal stress involved in such work, the general feeling that good practice often goes unrecognised, the pressure to achieve success in more measurable terms, and now even the prospect of being sued if allegations prove to be unfounded, and it is clear that there is still ample scope for individuals to fail to act as they should, when they also receive so little credit for when they get it right.

2. *Professional networks that are 'closed' tend to encourage fixed views and cut people off from information that they need to have.* Professional systems can become closed for a number of reasons: too much emphasis on our professional area as the most important; too much association with like-minded individuals who reinforce our own perceptions all the time; and stereotyped views of others that lead us to mistrust them or resist losing control to them. I have to say that in my experience, both social workers and teachers are frequently at risk of such weaknesses. The key is surely in enabling people to train more alongside each other and to establish personal contacts as an integral part of their working life. Professionals need to meet each other locally to share their individual perceptions on common tasks. It doesn't sound so difficult, but it rarely happens as it could. It will have to happen in future, whether we want it to or not!

3. *Children and families are given different messages by different people at different times.* The researchers suggest that this tends to happen unconsciously rather than deliberately. I would argue that it is largely caused by the legislative and philosophical frameworks within which people are required to work. There has been some progress recently in creating more integrated services for children. This will almost certainly become more commonplace in future if current government plans come to fruition. But the legislation is not joined up at all and is often based on very different understandings of children and their needs. Questions about school admissions, transport, provision for children with special educational needs (SEN), behaviour and exclusions are often dealt with without much consultation with other professionals involved with a family. Different agencies still use entirely separate processes of assessment, despite the existence of a new national framework (see Chapter 4). This can mean families having to repeat the process several times with different agencies, each operating largely in isolation from the other. Not all the assessments then necessarily reach the same conclusion.

4. *Child protection fails when more emphasis is placed on hierarchies of power*

than on individuals' knowledge of a particular situation. It is clear that for all the talk of inter-agency practice, which is essential, some professionals are given more status than others in child protection. This may inhibit team-working and the ability of junior staff to question decisions made by managers and other senior staff. Social workers, the police, doctors, the courts and many others all have highly influential roles, but teachers in particular often know more about the *children* than anyone. Despite this, key decisions can sometimes be made by people who have little direct involvement with the child and without much consultation with those who know them best. The culture of 'watching your back' has become very prevalent; professionals will often feel they must do what senior managers in their agency demand, not necessarily what they would wish to do for a particular child or family, without much opportunity to challenge or influence those priorities.

5. *Where professionals are confused about their roles, practice breaks down and children are put at unnecessary risk.* A health worker who acts like a police officer deprives the child concerned of both roles done properly. This can be very difficult for teachers, especially in the light of the previous point. They care very much about children and may have a clear view about what is best for them. They will often, however, have to hand the child over to someone else whose actions they cannot then control and who may have a rather different perspective. But that's the way the process works, and we have to live with it because, in the end, it provides the best safeguards that are available. It is tempting to think we can sort the issue out ourselves or just have a quiet word with the parent, thereby ruining the possibility of any proper investigation because we have contaminated the evidence. It might be nice to keep the issue 'just between the two of us', but we must each do our own job, not undo someone else's.

It was issues like these that influenced practice so heavily in the early 1980s as the new arrangements for protecting children took hold. As we shall see, these observations have, in my opinion, lost none of their relevance and have been given a new prominence by the Laming Inquiry (DoH and Home Office 2003). But when people ask why we seem to have left so many lessons unlearned – or, more accurately, why a few cases still go so badly wrong – they may be forgetting that the voices have not been all one way. There is another side to the coin.

Cleveland

Public and professional confidence in child protection took another major blow in the late 1980s, but this time not because of a lack of intervention, but because of a perceived excess of it. No one died because of Cleveland, but it came to dominate public thinking in an unprecedented way. Between May and June 1987, sexual abuse was 'diagnosed' by two particular consultants at Middlesbrough General Hospital in 121 children from fifty-seven families. Most of them were removed from their parents' care by court order as a result, some for considerable periods of time. The apparent high incidence of so much abuse in such a small area led to claims that the degree of actual evidence produced was limited and that the test of anal dilation that had been used was clearly unreliable. There was also a strong sense that the actions of the agencies, even if the children had been abused or were at risk, may have actually added to their problems rather than alleviated them, let alone the issues of natural justice involved. There were also other similar examples in Rochdale, Orkney and elsewhere at around the same time.

The inquiry that resulted did not lead directly to the Children Act 1989 (see Chapter 4). Much of the thinking had already been done (though it was mostly ignored), particularly in the Law Commission's *Review of the Law on Child Care and Family Services* (1987). But its analysis and conclusions were now quickly taken up as more in tune with the increasingly sceptical national mood. Cleveland led to an overtly political debate, partly under the influence of a prominent local MP, so that it became directly linked to the formation of new legislation and the practice arising from it. For a few, it represented a welcome opportunity to rein in the powers of social workers – a somewhat jaundiced interpretation of extremely complex issues. After all, social workers, and indeed the courts, only acted on information presented to them by others.

The actions of educational professionals were not a major focus of this inquiry. But Cleveland and its analysis, together with the national response to 'pindown' at about the same time, played a part in creating the context within which teachers and others would be asked to operate for the next decade and beyond. If the questions in the 1970s and 1980s had been about *how* we work together, the new concern was essentially about *why* we should be getting involved at all – surely the more fundamental issue?

Does our intervention achieve what is best for children, not simply what is best for the adults who live and work with them? Had it all become too much a question of following procedures rather than actually delivering an improvement in the quality of children's lives? Whether or not this new intention has been achieved is another question entirely, but the expectations became significantly different. Such was the report's influence that many of its recommendations will seem stunningly obvious to anyone who has been involved in work with children in recent years, but at the time it was a major shift in thinking. It was Cleveland, not the Children Act, that first identified the following:

1. *The child is a person and not an object of concern.* Children not only need professionals to explain to them what is happening, but also are entitled to participate in the decision-making and to have their wishes and feelings taken into account. They should have the right to put their views to a court that is deciding what should happen to them and not to be subjected to repeated examinations and questioning. It was this idea that led to the introduction of pre-recorded video interviews for court proceedings, and much of the same language is repeated in the guidance that accompanied the Act. Protection should have the child's needs at the centre.

2. *Parents are entitled to be treated with respect and to be kept fully informed by professionals, courts and agencies.* 'Partnership' became the buzzword of the 1990s here as elsewhere. Decisions should not be made without the implications being discussed with parents at every stage. They should not be left isolated and without support, and are entitled to have their rights fully explained, even if they are under investigation. If children do have to be removed into care, this should not necessarily mean that parents cannot have continued contact and the right to challenge the arrangements that others are making about their children, nor should it lead to the automatic loss of their 'parental responsibility', a vital part of the new Act's philosophy (see Appendix 2). They should have the right to attend meetings and case conferences unless their presence will seriously act against the child's best interests. All professionals should demonstrate this openness, including those in health and education.

3. *Statutory powers should be used only when necessary and last for the minimum time possible.* It is impossible to overemphasise the significance of this idea and its impact on subsequent practice. For example, the previous 'place of safety order', much discredited by Cleveland, was removed by the new Act and replaced with interventions that were much more short term and focused. Avoiding orders altogether is usually preferable and will probably be far better for the child in most situations, moving the emphasis away from the idea that in care proceedings or in divorce, orders should be made just as a matter of course. As one commentator said at the time, there should no longer be any examples of important decisions about children being made late at night by a single magistrate in their pyjamas!

Child Protection: Messages from Research

Even within a few years of the implementation of the Children Act in October 1991, reflection on experience was beginning to influence practice, just as Reder *et al.* (1993) had suggested it always should. Much of the analysis was collected together in a review of twenty different research projects published by the Department of Health in 1995 under the title *Child Protection: Messages from Research* (often referred to simply as *Messages from Research*). It immediately became important for local procedures to be evaluated against this document. Its intention was overwhelmingly practical, even including exercises that practitioners could do together in order to examine the quality of their own work, though I don't know if anyone actually used them!

These studies addressed areas such as what families considered 'normal' and 'abnormal' in child-rearing and found that many behaviours that might be considered an indication of abuse also occurred in families where there were no obvious concerns about the safety of the children. It is as much the *context* for the behaviour or action as the behaviour itself that may make it significant. Examples included children witnessing sexual activity or engaging in masturbation, which it would clearly be presumptuous to call evidence of abuse in all cases. Abuse is effectively a continuum, not an isolated event, with the intention as important as the action in determining the impact on the child. The emphasis in child protection should be on the *effects* of the abuse, on what is bad for children, even if no actual acts of direct assault take place, not so much on a list of actions that are abuse *per se*.

This reflects the Children Act's emphasis on the broader concept of 'significant harm' rather than on a list of circumstances that would automatically require statutory intervention (see Chapter 3). This is also where the idea of repeated or continuous exposure to maltreatment, even at a relatively low level, first became more sharply identified as carrying at least the potential for harm, in addition to actual acts of violence or sexual assault. Such children's needs are often known, especially to their teachers, but they are not necessarily referred for investigation. Indeed, they may not actually need such a complex process, but support and help for their parents should be provided in some other, less confrontational way. This insight was the basis of a new emphasis on emotional abuse, in addition to existing concepts of cruelty and neglect, as well as emphasising prevention as much as crisis intervention.

Controversially at the time, *Messages from Research* suggested that there was little factual basis to the widespread concern about 'satanic' or 'ritual' abuse. This had been an issue raised by some religious groups and inevitably taken up by the tabloid press, and had created a considerable degree of national interest. Occasionally there were elements of ritual in the way in which abusers sought to justify their behaviour, but even where claims had been made by individual paedophiles, the studies found that allegations about devil-worship, witchcraft and the use of sacrifice were unfounded. The emphasis in most of the studies was that abuse is only exceptionally an entirely irrational behaviour undertaken by those on the margins of society. Such extreme cases are not typical, and therefore a different kind of response may be needed in the majority of cases that still carry the potential for appropriate care.

As well as addressing these specific research areas, the projects also raised a number of wider points about the way in which the system was being applied by professionals and agencies:

- More than one project concluded that both teachers and others were often unclear about the role of educational professionals, in both schools and LEAs.
- The training of professionals was frequently insufficient for the responsibilities involved.
- Children and their families often still felt that important decisions were being made without their having any real chance to influence the outcomes. This tended to make those outcomes less successful than they might otherwise have been.

As we shall see, these insights paved the way for the Assessment Framework, which in turn became an essential tool for direct interventions in families. It has always been necessary for professionals to re-interpret their responsibilities in the light of greater understanding. It is, for example, a sign of how quickly things have changed that, just ten years ago, there was little consideration given to the role of the Internet in fuelling abusive behaviour towards children. A National Commission of Inquiry, *Childhood Matters* (1997), also tried to move the debate on to issues of prevention and to wider concepts of harm, but did not have the political impact that those who contributed to it must have hoped for. Yet again, public judgement on individual cases, rather than professional self-assessment, proved to be more influential in highlighting the perception that more significant legal and organisational change was needed. Two children, in particular, have to be mentioned next.

Lauren Wright

There is nothing especially unusual about Lauren's case, but she is a very important person specifically as far as British schools and their teachers are concerned. That's why this book is dedicated to her as a representative of all those children who have been through the same experience. If any good can come from the death of a child, at least staff in every school in Britain should now have a much clearer sense of their duty to protect children like her. Lauren died in May 2000 from a blow to the stomach and from the constant neglect she had suffered for months previously at the hands of both her stepmother and her father. She was covered in bruises, and her digestive system was in total collapse.

Of course it should not have happened; there were plenty of warning signs, and all the agencies were at fault. Lauren had at one time been abandoned by her natural mother in Turkey, being left to be brought home by the consular authorities. She was placed on a child protection register for a while. Then she was cared for by her grandmother and, now living with her father and his new wife in a small rural community, was the subject of regular concerns from those in the houses nearby. Many people had their suspicions, but they did not take sufficient personal responsibility for ensuring a response.

Lauren's stepmother was a playground assistant at her school, with her own children there as well. She deliberately set out to plant a false trail to suggest that Lauren's injuries were the result of accidents or bullying, as many abusers do. She even managed to mislead paediatricians and social workers, not only Lauren's teachers. But there were fundamental failings by the staff, as well as an understandable difficulty in believing that something so awful could possibly be true about someone they knew. Crucially, in my opinion, the school was very small. It did not have the necessary policy or procedures in place, despite the clear advice from the LEA that it should. No doubt the headteacher had a string of other specialist designations that went with the job, as well as that for child protection. But this role did not receive the attention that it deserved, and all the local agencies, as usual, resolved to do better in the light of this disastrous experience.

That might have been the end of it, had it not been for the fact that these events occurred in the constituency of a former Education Secretary, Gillian Shephard. Along with the NSPCC, she expressed public disappointment that there appeared to be no statutory basis to the school's responsibility and that consequently no direct disciplinary action could be taken against the staff concerned. She moved an amendment to the Education Bill then going through Parliament. It was accepted by the government and, as a result, s.175 Education Act 2002 is now in force, which makes it a statutory duty on all schools to safeguard and promote the welfare of their pupils (see Chapter 6).

The prospect that this will lead to teachers getting the sack if they do not act in such a situation in future, as the press have speculated, is extremely unlikely. The duty lies with governors and with LEAs, and witch-hunts against individuals are rarely helpful. Corporate responsibility is, however, significantly enhanced by this provision. The LEA's role is now much more than just advisory. Lauren's legacy is certainly that there is now no room for confusion about what we should be doing. Teachers *must* do whatever they can to protect children; it is part of the job, and not doing what you are employed to do may ultimately be a disciplinary matter. Senior managers must make sure that policy is in place; that staff are trained; that they act when required; and that responsibility is taken in accordance with local procedures.

The Laming Inquiry

Because of its tragic severity, timing and extremely wide significance, the national response to the death of Victoria Climbié must, of course, be included in this review. At a number of points in this book, the implications of the Laming Inquiry of 2001–3 will be relevant in informing practice. This was undoubtedly one of the worst cases of child cruelty that Britain has ever seen. In her final weeks of life, Victoria was confined to a bath; no part of her body was free from injury. But I am not personally sure that this lengthy Inquiry into her murder by her great-aunt and her partner tells us a great deal we did not know before. Most of the recommendations are things that should always have been done anyway, like passing on messages when staff are on leave or off sick, or ensuring that inexperienced staff are properly supervised. The services concerned were in complete crisis at the time and standards just fell apart. That does not mean that the standards themselves were inadequate.

There is a very real danger that one set of circumstances that were highly unusual and even coincidental when taken altogether might be seen as suggesting wholly new problems with an entire system that therefore needs fundamental reform. In the view of many practitioners and academics, this would be an unreasonable generalisation from a particular example and would suggest a widespread failure in the child protection system that is not borne out in the experience of thousands of other families and professionals across the country. At the more philosophical level, Laming has drawn attention primarily to issues about inter-agency working that are, in fact, almost identical to those already identified by Reder *et al*. ten years before. That said, Laming also identified some new questions, as all reflection on our experience must do, and this time there has been a political will to respond. In particular, it has focused attention on the quality of leadership and management of child protection services, rather than criticising only the front-line workers. This has already led to proposals that will be enacted in new legislation, probably during 2004 (see below).

As Victoria was not known to her LEA, the primary emphasis of the inquiry was not on education, but there are some points that should still be noted as relevant. It would certainly be helpful if children known by one agency not to be in any form of education were routinely reported to the local education service. There is no obligation on the parent or carer to make such reports. That alone might have saved Victoria's life. There should be a shared database of vulnerable children, held in common by different agencies and across local authority boundaries. The regulation of private fostering also requires a thorough overhaul, especially where children have come from overseas. Agencies often do not know exactly with whom some of the most vulnerable children in our society are living. Parents who place their children with others, or someone else on their behalf, should clearly still have some role to play in monitoring their continued well-being.

But the driving force behind the Laming Inquiry appears to have been more the need for some kind of public confession of collective failure, rather than suddenly being confronted with an example of abuse that was completely incomprehensible and for which British systems were wholly unprepared. It should have been obvious that Victoria was at risk, and the mechanisms to protect her should have been used. Managers failed to manage and workers failed to act. There was a reluctance to take responsibility for her needs, and any one factor that could have been done differently might have made all the difference. Taken together they spelt disaster. But the fact is, they *are* done differently, every day, most of the time, and children are protected as a result. The system usually works. It's just that nobody notices when it does!

So where now?

Child protection is changing. There is now a Minister for Children, Young People and Families, located within the DfES, not in the DoH, as part of a whole new children's division. There is to be a new Children Act 2004 in the light of the government's response to Laming in *Keeping Children Safe* (DfES 2003) and the Green Paper on children's services, *Every Child Matters* (Chief Minister to the Treasury 2003). Proposals, as indicated in the current Children Bill, are likely to involve an independent children's Commissioner for England (there is one in Wales already) and a clear legal duty to safeguard children placed on every relevant agency. Strategic leadership of local authority children's services at senior officer and councillor level will be expected and a lead professional identified for each case. New Local Safeguarding Children Boards are expected to take over the role of the current Area Child Protection Committees (ACPC), with essentially the same co-ordinating functions but at a more senior level and with greater powers to intervene and evaluate practice. Education services will be central in supporting families and may even be integrated with social workers into new kinds of children's departments, as has already happened in some areas.

There may yet be a variety of options from which to choose, according to local circumstances, rather than one system that is the same everywhere. We may see more multi-agency Children's Trusts, also incorporating health, though the pilot schemes have yet to receive a thorough evaluation. Apart from recognising these general trends, it has been impossible to anticipate the eventual outcome of all these proposals in detail before publication. But whatever happens, there will still be social workers and teachers and police officers and health professionals as before, if, hopefully, in better communication with one another. As *Keeping Children Safe* acknowledges, even if things change at a political or organisational level, the task of child protection will remain essentially the same. Structures come and go. The systems are not the main issue, and nothing of what follows in this book will go out of date in any crucial sense.

We can reform the management arrangements and still have all the same problems. We know what works; we do not need to re-invent it. Those who do the job certainly need better resourcing, not only financially but also in terms of status and training, and, sometimes, a greater sense of personal responsibility. The commitment of the Green Paper to raising the profile and expertise of those who work with children is most welcome. Services must be integrated, not separated, and information must be shared. There will still need to be a clear local procedure that involves all professionals co-operating. Even if child protection is not your core task, it is still part of the job for anyone in contact with children for other reasons. There is no other way to do it. It just needs to work better, every time, as far as we are possibly able.

There might be a case, as some have argued, for a more specialised body to deal with only the very serious and high-profile cases, or for those involving professionals or the Internet, but not for all the rest that are far more typical of abuse as a whole. The problem is, you don't always know which cases are which at the very beginning, where the intervention matters most. Abuse often hides behind other problems. Also, in households where parents are adept at keeping agencies at bay, especially those not customarily visited by social workers, a great deal of persistence may be required if it is to be discovered. Such a specialist agency would have to be at some distance from front-line workers and would still be dependent on them for its information. As the government recognises, most families with problems just need a bit of accessible help, not a hugely complicated structure to unravel that immediately puts them on the defensive. But some abuse is undoubtedly more deviant than local staff may be able to handle under normal arrangements.

In the end, *all* those who are involved with children must, individually and together, be constantly vigilant, caring, knowledgeable and responsive, not assume that it is someone else's problem. Every child is potentially at risk. Ultimately we can only try to learn from our mistakes, but the idea that no one will ever make one if we change the organisational framework is wholly unrealistic in such a complex area. Understanding the past always helps us to see where we are going, but the personal duty on each one of us can never change. Everything that follows must be understood in the light of it.

Chapter 3

Understanding and defining abuse

The four categories and their implications

Area Child Protection Committees

The protection of children is an inter-agency process from start to finish, in which every agency has its own statutory duty to fulfil. While some individuals will have lead responsibility, no one has sole responsibility, and all practice should reflect this emphasis. *Working Together to Safeguard Children* (DoH 1999), often referred to simply as *Working Together*, currently requires local authorities to establish joint arrangements for protecting children in their area and gives an indication of how this should be done. (Incidentally, the term 'safeguarding' is growing in usage as being rather more comprehensive than 'protecting', though the two are often used to mean much the same thing.)

For the past twenty-five years this has been done through the establishment of a local Area Child Protection Committee, involving representation at a senior level from all the member agencies. In larger authorities there may be more than one ACPC, each covering a smaller area. The Laming Inquiry suggested that such a body should become statutory, with a more formal system of accountability, as it has no real control over the actions of its constituent agencies. The government has generally accepted these criticisms. As has already been noted, this is likely to lead to new local Safeguarding Children Boards in the near future, but there will still be the same need for co-ordination between those with different areas of expertise. We may talk less of 'inter-agency' procedures and rather more of 'multi-professional' practice, but the point will still be the same. It is always going to be about 'working together' across different disciplines and professions.

Currently, an ACPC may have sub-committees, including, for example, a specialist interest group looking at education or health issues or facilitating dialogue on policy matters. There will usually be programmes of joint training and there must be some system for reviewing local practice, especially in response to deaths and serious injuries, and making recommendations for change. An ACPC's primary task is 'To develop and agree local policies and procedures for inter-agency work to protect children, within the national framework provided by this guidance' (*Working Together*, paragraph 4.2). All designated teachers in schools should have a copy of their local ACPC procedures, as these will determine practice in education just as much as in health, social services, etc.

The services primarily involved in child protection are:

- social services department;
- the police;
- health services;
- probation officers;
- education;
- day care services;
- the NSPCC;
- voluntary organisations;
- the community.

Social services departments

Social services departments (SSDs) carry the duty to 'make enquiries' or to investigate allegations of 'significant harm' (s.47 Children Act 1989) and to carry out assessments of 'children in need' (s.17) under the Assessment Framework introduced from 2001. ('Social services' is a generic term used throughout this book for the local authority department in which the social workers are employed, although it might actually be called something else or have other functions as well.) All other agencies have a duty to assist them. SSDs currently work with all age groups, not just children and families, and provide a range of other facilities, or purchase services from other providers. There may in future be a greater separation of these tasks.

Social workers take the lead role in managing child protection casework, from initial investigations, applications for emergency or longer-term court orders if required, through to the maintenance of the child protection register and the oversight of child protection and care plans. They also manage the calling and administration of child protection conferences, although these may now be chaired by a more independent person. Senior managers contribute to the work of the ACPC, and SSDs have a particular duty to make services known to the public and act as a first point of contact. Social workers' particular focus is the welfare of the individual child.

The police

The police are responsible for the protection of the community and the collection of evidence for the prosecution of offenders. Their role is primarily in the early stages, especially in the most serious cases.

Not all proven child protection incidents necessarily lead to criminal charges. In recent years, the police too have been required to pay attention to the welfare of the child, which may sometimes conflict with obtaining justice by prosecuting the offender. Specialist officers work with social workers in joint investigations and are primarily responsible for establishing the facts of any crime and securing the necessary evidence. It is the task of the police and the Crown Prosecution Service (CPS) to decide whether an individual should be prosecuted, on the basis of a balance between:

- whether there is sufficient evidence of an offence;
- whether prosecution is in the interests of the child;
- whether prosecution is in the public interest.

Health services

Health services include a very wide range of professionals, who may be working for different authorities/trusts within an ACPC area, both in hospitals and in the community. They have a major role to play in the protection of children, by virtue of their lifelong contact with families and their specialist expertise. It will be, for example, a paediatrician or a police surgeon whose opinion will be required about whether a child's physical symptoms indicate non-accidental injury or sexual abuse. Social workers (or anyone else making a referral) are not qualified to make such judgements.

Health services include:

- consultants and other doctors;
- midwives and antenatal services;
- health visitors;
- general hospital and acute staff;
- general practitioners and primary care trusts;
- school nurses and clinical medical officers;
- community child health services;
- child and adolescent mental health;
- physiotherapy and other support services.

Each health provider for children must nominate a designated doctor/nurse, and each trust must have a named doctor/nurse to co-ordinate child protection in its service. Child protection must be included in the contracts agreed with the commissioning strategic health authorities. Staff in private healthcare settings are also required to be aware of local procedures and should know whom to consult when appropriate.

Probation officers and the Youth Offending Service

Probation officers and the Youth Offending Service (YOS) are mainly involved in child protection through the supervision of offenders in the community, especially those on the Sex Offender Register and violent offenders. With the police risk assessors, they have a key role in alerting other agencies to any concerns, especially where children are living with or near known offenders, through a confidential process of local Multi-agency Risk Assessment Panels (MARAPs) and Public Protection Panels. Specialist juvenile panels also meet to consider children and young people who pose a risk to others. All of them will be engaged in active crime prevention programmes that are supervised through the YOS. In some areas, probation officers have also developed particular skills in working with adult abusers. The more we know about how they behave, the more effective procedures can be. Young people under 18 in young offender institutions (YOIs) should also have access to child protection services, though they are often not given the status afforded to other children under the Children Act 1989.

Education services

Education services, including both school staff and LEA officers (education welfare, youth workers, educational psychologists, etc.), do not constitute an investigation agency but have a vital part to play in monitoring the welfare of children. Teachers have more day-to-day contact with children than do any other professionals, and every educational establishment must have a written child protection policy and referral procedures, known to all staff, teaching and non-teaching, in line with ACPC procedures as a whole. Every school must have a designated senior teacher, whatever the school's management status, including schools in the private sector and colleges of further education. Each LEA must also have a designated senior officer with responsibility for child protection. In larger LEAs this role may be shared among more than one person. LEA staff also have key roles in providing information to the investigating agencies and monitoring children at risk. All educational establishments and employers, as with all similar agencies, must have procedures for trying to detect any abuse by staff and volunteers, and appropriate ways of responding to any allegations (see also Chapters 8 and 14).

Day care services

Day care services include nurseries, pre-school groups and childminders, most of whom are now more closely linked to education. They have a very important role both in helping parents under stress and in detecting concerns at an early stage, especially in young children. All staff should be aware of their role in local procedures, in both public, voluntary and private organisations and services. Carers such as childminders and playgroup leaders can be placed in a difficult position, especially where they live close to their 'customers', but should still have appropriate procedures in place. Day care services do not always receive the recognition they deserve within ACPC structures and committees.

The NSPCC

The NSPCC is unique as the only voluntary body empowered to apply for certain court orders and to undertake investigations, but only operates in some areas. The NSPCC also runs specialist support and training services, both nationally and regionally, and a national helpline for parents and children. It also has some specific projects that work therapeutically with the victims of abuse, or with young abusers and those who are displaying inappropriate sexualised behaviour at an early age, including young offenders.

Other voluntary organisations

Other voluntary organisations provide a wide variety of services to children and families, either locally or nationally. Examples include Homestart, Surestart, locality organisations with particular interests such as Mencap and SCOPE, and national groups like ChildLine, the Children's Society and Barnardos. The voluntary sector is in touch with large numbers of children, including those involved in uniformed organisations, churches, youth clubs, etc., and may be represented on the ACPC through an affiliated body. Those children who contact voluntary organisations for help will be referred, if they are willing to identify themselves, to their local SSD for a personal response.

The community

In addition, the community as a whole (as evidenced by the referrals that arise from neighbours, family or anonymously) is vitally important in the general protection of children. Many individuals are better placed than most professionals to raise concerns. There may be particular issues of confidentiality and reliability to be addressed when information arises from a non-professional source, and members of the public are entitled to greater protection of their identity than are professionals. The public's image of child protection from the media may be very misleading, but the wider the local awareness, the better children will be protected.

Training idea 1: Attitudes and feelings (individual)

TASK: This is not about being right or wrong; it's about how you feel. You do not have to defend your views to anyone else but may wish to reconsider later in the light of more information. On a scale of 1 (strongly agree) to 5 (strongly disagree), how would you rate your views on the following statements?

1. Our society is too soft on adults who harm children.

continued

2. Children are nearly always best brought up by their own parents rather than someone else.

3. Most people who abuse children are sad and inadequate individuals whom we should pity.

4. Social workers interfere too much in family life.

5. Child abuse is 'flavour of the month' at the moment and given too much prominence.

6. There is more sexual abuse of children nowadays than when I was a child.

7. Most physical abuse is carried out by men.

8. Children often make things up to get at their parents or someone else in authority, like a teacher.

9. If a child told me they were being abused I would instinctively believe them.

10. When a child dies, it's usually because social workers haven't done their job properly.

11. It's probably best if a child just accepts the abuse and waits for it to stop rather than telling.

12. Smacking a child is an abuse and ought to be illegal.

13. Children today have too much power over adults, especially since the Children Act.

14. The child protection system works pretty well in keeping children safe.

15. Children who are abused usually grow up to be abusers.

16. If anyone I knew well was harming their children I would know about it.

17. Children are sometimes abused by other children.

18. I would know what to do if a child told me that they were being hurt by someone close to them.

19. Most children already know the person who is sexually abusing them rather than the abuser being a stranger.

20. Things were better for children in the past than they are now.

What is abuse?

It is important to be clear that when professionals act in child protection, we act as our employing agency's representatives, not as individuals. This may legitimately limit our area of responsibility, but also places us under certain obligations. We may have all kinds of personal feelings about children, parents, families and relationships. We may have many concerns about acceptable standards of child-rearing or the kind of lifestyles that we individually consider to be appropriate. We may have certain political or religious objectives and ideals. But, while important, these judgements are not the basis of our activity in child protection (or they shouldn't be).

This is difficult when, for example, a teacher is unable to persuade a social worker of the need as they see it to take some action about a child or young person whom they consider to be 'at risk' but others do not. Or when a social worker insists on taking action but the teacher fears it is an over-reaction that will have damaging consequences for their own relationship with the family. 'Good enough parenting' may not seem good enough to the teacher concerned about a child who sticks out like a sore thumb relative to the general culture of the school, but who is quite normal from the wider perspective of the social services or the health visitor.

'Moral danger' as an interpretation of under-age sexual activity represents another common area of misunderstanding. For a teacher this may be a very significant concern, from the context of a duty to teach about personal relationships from within a certain framework of values. It used to be sufficient justification for care proceedings under previous legislation. But to the social worker, the phrase has no legal meaning, except where an assault is being alleged or there is a clear threat identified that places a young person at risk of 'significant harm' (see p. 57). 'Abuse' has to be more than a matter of personal disapproval. Similar issues sometimes arise over the abuse of drugs, alcohol and self-harm.

Some people question whether we should include other kinds of actions by parents and carers that are not currently reflected in local ACPC procedures. For example, I regularly see parents driving their children away from school or along a motorway without ensuring they are wearing a seatbelt. That is certainly putting those children at risk of harm. I am highly uncomfortable about a family I see in my high street; the children clearly have no choice but to stand there much of the day while their parents preach their particular version of religious faith to the passers-by, even being expected to join in themselves occasionally. Neither of these are abuse in the usual sense of the word.

There are wider issues concerning children's safety in employment and entertainments that I explore in Chapters 9–11. Children can legally drive tractors, mini-stock cars and go-karts, climb mountains, own air rifles and carry out countless other risky activities that child protection procedures do not attempt to control. Social workers do not normally investigate incidents of bullying (though anti-bullying strategies should still be part of the evidence of a 'child-protecting school'; see Chapter 8). About sixty children a year die from the abuse of solvents and gases. Many children smoke. This can all appear to lead to a double standard in which some relatively trivial incidents receive a great deal more attention than others. Even deaths and serious injuries in other contexts that are seen as accidental could often have been prevented and may involve some kind of neglect by adults. Too much emphasis on the 'normal' characteristics of abuse may mean that other kinds of situations are unwittingly overlooked.

There is, however, a more positive dimension to this requirement to work from common understandings. Although there has never been an absolute consensus over what is meant by child abuse, there is a general agreement among professionals about what kinds of actions towards children constitute the areas of most concern and, consequently, about what we must then do about them. Operating within agreed multi-professional roles and definitions, rather than feeling that this is something we each have to resolve for ourselves and in our own way, provides a considerable degree of personal security. It is immensely comforting to be able to shelter behind our agency's policies and procedures when parents or others object to what we have done, provided, of course, that we have been aware of them and followed them.

Article 19 of the United Nations Convention on the Rights of the Child (1989) gives an internationally recognised agenda both for abuse and for its prevention:

> States Parties shall take all appropriate legislative, administrative, social and educational measures to protect the child from all forms of physical or mental violence, injury or abuse, neglect or negligent treatment, maltreatment or exploitation, including sexual abuse, while in the care of parents, legal guardians or any other person who has care of the child;
>
> Such protective measures should, as appropriate, include effective procedures for the establishment of social programmes to provide necessary support for the child and for those who have care of the child, as well as for other forms of prevention and for identification, reporting, referral, investigation, treatment and follow-up of instances of child maltreatment described heretofore, and, as appropriate, for judicial involvement.

While, in the real world, these lofty ideals are sometimes honoured primarily in the breach of them, they do at least provide a standard within which to earth our own legal and procedural responses. They are behind the wording in *Working Together* about what constitutes abuse:

> Somebody may abuse or neglect a child by inflicting harm, or by failing to act to prevent harm. Children may be abused in a family or in an institutional or community setting; by those known to them, or, more rarely, by a stranger.
>
> (paragraph 2.3)

Similar definitions will be found in ACPC handbooks and will all have roughly similar characteristics:

- Abuse involves both the reality and the risk of it.
- It causes (or risks) harm to the child's health or development in a definable way and at a significant level.
- It primarily involves actions (or inactions) of parents, carers and others known to the child or in a relationship of trust.
- It occurs in all communities and classes.
- It relates to avoidable individual acts (rather than, for example, to the effects of poverty or poor housing).

The four categories of abuse

Recognition of what is going on in a child's life, often behind closed doors, is a major challenge in effective child protection, as abuse is rarely witnessed by a professional person at the time. Cases that have reached the national media, in which the sudden deaths of infants have been subject to differing explanations and professional opinions, resulting in last-minute acquittals and even agreed miscarriages of justice, indicate how difficult it can be to know exactly what has happened in a particular situation. Hopefully, we are also able to act to prevent abuse *before* it occurs, but serious incidents also occur in families not previously known to the agencies. We often have to work from the effects of any possible abuse some time after the event – for example, from presenting injuries or changes in behaviour, not from actual first-hand evidence of the abuse as such.

The child themself will therefore often be our main source of information, provided they can give a coherent account of how the incident or injury occurred. To a very large extent, except for very young children, the child protection system effectively relies on them to have the confidence to tell someone else about what has happened before anybody can do anything to help. Much will therefore depend on whether they see what has happened as abuse. This is why the more recent emphasis on being open with children about such things and encouraging them to be more aware of what goes on is so important. This is not about teaching children to be suspicious of adults, but if they do not see there is a problem, or attempt to conceal it as they think they are supposed to do, the abuse is likely to continue unchecked, perhaps for many years. This certainly happened in the past.

Although some practitioners have argued that it would better to classify our concerns by the motive of the abuser and the degree of harm, rather than by the type of injury, inter-agency procedures currently operate on the basis of the agreed definitions included in *Working Together* (DoH 1999):

Physical abuse

> Physical abuse may involve hitting, shaking, throwing, poisoning, burning or scalding, drowning, suffocating, or otherwise causing physical harm to a child. Physical harm may also be caused when a parent or carer feigns the symptoms of, or deliberately causes ill-health to a child whom they are looking after. This situation is commonly described using terms such as factitious illness by proxy or Munchausen syndrome by proxy.
>
> (*Working Together*, paragraph 2.4)

The smacking of children is not therefore automatically considered to be child abuse. Social workers do not need to be told every time a child has been physically punished, as some have suggested, but there are no absolutely accepted criteria about what turns legally permissible 'reasonable chastisement' into an abuse. Things may yet change, but although there is certainly a lively debate, the government has no plans at present to outlaw physical punishments by parents altogether (as has happened with teachers and childminders, and may soon happen for parents in Scotland, at least for children below a certain age). Similarly, all children have injuries, cuts and bruises from time to time that may have a variety of other explanations. Clearly, other factors have to be taken into account, including:

- the frequency with which the child presents as injured and the explanations that are offered;
- the likelihood of the injury being accidental;
- the past history of the child and parents in other settings;
- the context of the incident;
- whether the presenting signs are consistent with generally unacceptable behaviours such as biting and finger-tip bruising, deliberate burning, marks of a hairbrush or shoe, etc.;
- the age of the child (the younger the child, the more the injury should normally cause concern);
- the existence of other kinds of violence within the family – for example, awareness of domestic violence or parental behaviour associated with alcohol, drug abuse or mental illness.

These incidents are often the easiest to resolve in that there is some kind of objective evidence of what has occurred, in addition to the child's account, if they are old enough to give one. Physical injuries can be measured, photographed and judged to have been caused in a certain way. But whether a given behaviour will, on the day, be seen as appropriate may depend on a particular interpretation of the facts. The enduring legacy of nineteenth-century concepts such as the 'rule of thumb', about the size of the stick with which it was acceptable for a man 'to chastise his wife, children and servants', still means that professionals describing something as abuse may not be the end of matter.

A father was once prosecuted for repeatedly beating his young son with a heavy cane. The son had significant wheals and bruising to his back and buttocks when the case was identified. The father did not deny that he had frequently hit the child. The boy had serious behavioural problems and a learning disability. The jury initially acquitted the father on the defence grounds that, for such a 'naughty' child, such an excessive punishment was reasonable. The decision was overturned on appeal, but the case illustrates that even obvious presenting injury is not the only issue at stake in deciding what action should be taken in response.

As has already been noted in the review of agency roles, teachers are not expected to be experts at assessing situations like these; far from it. Even an experienced child protection social worker will not rely solely on their own judgement to determine whether a child has been abused. A professional medical opinion will ultimately be essential, especially in the event of any court action, but these are the kinds of issues that may help in deciding whether there is sufficient concern to merit further enquiry. If there is information to suggest that a parent or other carer may have gone beyond anything that might credibly be described as reasonable, then an assault may have taken place and the child must be referred immediately under local procedures. It will be for the investigation to determine what should happen next.

Emotional abuse

> Emotional abuse is the persistent emotional ill-treatment of a child such as to cause severe and persistent adverse effects on the child's emotional development. It may involve conveying to children that they are worthless or unloved, inadequate or valued only insofar as they meet the needs of another person. It may feature age or developmentally inappropriate expectations being imposed on children. It may involve causing children frequently to feel frightened or in danger, or the exploitation or corruption of children. Some level of emotional abuse is involved in all types of ill-treatment of a child, though it may occur alone.
>
> (*Working Together*, paragraph 2.5)

This concept is intended to identify those children who are not necessarily physically harmed but who are brought up in an emotionally bruising environment characterised by expressions such as 'low warmth/high criticism'. Note the strong emphasis on repetition. These children's reasonable developmental needs are met primarily with continual hostility, indifference or verbal abuse. The parent's emotional needs may dominate, rather than the child's. The child may be regularly ridiculed or shamed, subject to a humiliating role within the family or under constant threat of injury even if it never actually happens.

They will lack self-esteem, may deliberately self-harm and will often present with behavioural difficulties. They may, alternatively, be excessively well behaved, especially at school, always anxious to please adults for fear of the consequences. They may give hints of being locked in their room at home or left with a succession of carers. They may be weighed down with caring responsibilities of their own. They may be 'starved', not of food but of affection, and may be particularly clingy, especially younger children. Basic needs might be conditional on their behaviour, or one child in the family might be singled out as different and ostracised, perhaps where parental relationships have changed so that not all children in the family are seen as of equal status.

This may be a way of life that has lasted for many years across several generations and that is difficult to identify as deliberate abuse rather than primarily a consequence of 'inadequate' parenting. Many of these children will be a constant concern to their teachers, and there may be agency involvement from time to time under 'children in need' procedures (see p. 54), depending on how co-operative their parents are or whether the evidence becomes sufficient to allow intervention against their will. The threshold for unwanted agency intervention is still quite high and will always require some objective evidence.

Some parents find the emotional bond with their children much more difficult than others but are still doing their best in trying circumstances. All parents may sometimes need a cathartic opportunity to acknowledge that their child is not always emotionally rewarding; that does not mean they are an abuser. I was once stuck behind a mother with a toddler in a supermarket queue. As fast as she tried to put her shopping on the conveyor belt, he took it off again, screamed for a sweet, threw a tantrum, etc. Her patience was clearly exhausted, so she picked him up, held him close to her face and said, 'You are a little shit!', before composing herself again and, amid much embarrassment and with modest assistance from me, got on with paying for the shopping and attending to his needs. There was no genuine venom in her tone and I was confident that she did not call him names as a matter of routine. But if there is information that suggests that harm is being caused to the child's health and development by the parent's *repeated* emotional indifference, a child protection response should be actively considered and discussed.

Sexual abuse

Sexual abuse involves forcing or enticing a child or young person to take part in sexual activities, whether or not the child is aware of what is happening. The activities may involve physical contact, including penetrative (e.g. rape or buggery) or non-penetrative acts. They may include non-contact activities such as involving children in looking at, or in the production of, pornographic material or watching sexual activities, or encouraging children to behave in sexually inappropriate ways.

(*Working Together*, paragraph 2.6)

Sexual abuse is probably no more widespread now than it has ever been; we do not know. The stories now told by adults, even those in their seventies and beyond, suggest that it has been around all the time. But our perception of it has become much more informed in recent years. The youngest case I have ever known concerned a child of six months, which previous generations would have found unbelievable. We also know that both women and men can be involved, although the overwhelming majority of *known* perpetrators are men and older teenage boys. It involves both heterosexual and homosexual activities.

Sexual abuse essentially involves an abuse of the trusted status that an adult has in relation to a child and their developing sexuality. (For details of specific offences, see the Sexual Offences Act 2003, which has consolidated a range of existing and new provision.) Such offences now carry significant penalties, provided sufficient evidence can be presented in a way that is acceptable to the court system. This is often difficult, as most of those charged tend to plead not guilty as a matter of course. As with other sex crimes, this puts a burden of proof on to the child that can, in practice, mean that they (or their parents and social workers) then choose not to proceed because of the personal trauma involved. In an example known to me, it was proposed that anal abuse of a young boy that the abuser had videoed at the time would have to be replayed to the child in court so that he could indicate the precise moment at which penetration had occurred. As this was clearly unacceptable, only lesser charges could be proven.

Sexual abuse is not, however, always frightening or violent, contrary to the media image, based largely on the few untypical cases involving the abduction of children by strangers. Children usually know the person who is abusing them. They may even like them, and the abuse is often couched in language designed to tell them that it is acceptable. Children are taught to be victims, sometimes over a very long period and possibly long before any actual contact takes place, in order to minimise the risk of the offender being detected. Both boys and girls are involved, and the signs can be many and varied, from genuine and psychosomatic physical symptoms through to a mistrust of adults, or overly sexualised and inappropriate behaviour by the child towards other children.

Any concerns of this kind should be identified as a child protection issue and referred accordingly. Children very rarely invent such allegations, and if they do, there will frequently be a reason behind it. More typically, they often say things without realising the significance of what they have disclosed, or have little under-standing of what has occurred. Any such information requires an immediate response. However, sexual abuse in particular may not be disclosed until long after the event. It is not uncommon for someone to tell the police about events twenty or thirty years ago when they were a child but which they had felt unable to talk about previously. Perhaps they have been waiting until their mother died or have to face it now because their own children are the same age as they were when the abuse happened and they now want to sleep over at their grandparents'.

Sometimes a partner may know about the abuse but feel powerless to do anything about it. This may simply be because of fear of an abuser who is also harming them, but the reasons can be more subtle than that. A health colleague of mine who works with adult survivors of sexual abuse and their families has devised an extremely powerful monologue in which she describes what it is like to be the wife of someone who knows that her husband is abusing their daughter. In it she rationalises all the reasons for not listening to the child and denying what is happening: 'I must be useless in bed if he has to turn to her. What will my parents say? How will we live if I throw him out? We'd have to sell the house and move away. Everyone will know and they'll just blame me. Best to let things lie. It'll stop soon. Perhaps if I give him more sex he'll leave her alone.' We might think that if we were in that position we would immediately support the child and seek help, but the issues are often not that straightforward.

Things can also be complicated with adolescents aged about 13–16 who are engaging in sexual activity with someone who is significantly older than they are but who do not see it as abusive. They may refuse to co-operate in a referral and decline any opportunity to make a complaint. Such situations can be very frustrating for teachers whose own moral perceptions are that such behaviour is entirely unacceptable. But operating within the 'Frazer guidelines' (formerly

'Gillick competence') means that agencies may be unable to persuade the child to seek help, even if what they are doing poses some considerable risk for them. Advice should always be sought in such circumstances from health and other colleagues.

Neglect

Neglect is the persistent failure to meet a child's basic and/or psychological needs, likely to result in the serious impairment of the child's health or development. It may involve a parent or carer failing to provide adequate food, shelter and clothing, failing to protect a child from physical harm or danger, or the failure to ensure access to appropriate medical care or treatment. It may also include neglect of, or unresponsiveness to, a child's basic emotional needs.

(Working Together, paragraph 2.7)

Like emotional abuse, neglect can also be very ambiguous, and is often related to the expectations that agencies might reasonably have about how a child *should* be cared for. Television series like *The Life of Grime* (about the work of Environmental Health Officers) have revealed to a wider audience exactly how some people choose to live – what we used to call the 'sticky' families where you wipe your feet on the way out! Physical standards of care may vary enormously, and who decides what is acceptable? How closely should parents supervise their children? What is an adequate diet? How important is personal hygiene? What time are children supposed to go to bed? Neglect of a child's needs might be only the presenting problem, not itself the problem, if, for example, the parent is suffering from mental illness or has been left with the sole care of children in a crisis. This would not make them a deliberate abuser, but a sudden deterioration in standards might require an urgent response, especially with very young children.

As far as possible, judgements should be made against objective criteria such as growth milestones, weight, etc., or where an actual offence may have been committed through wholesale abandonment of all acceptable standards. Children who are frequently poorly clothed; inadequately fed to the point where they steal food from other pupils; who are effectively abandoned to care for themselves or other siblings; regularly unwashed or without proper provision for their wider sanitary needs, as measured against other children from the *same* kind of family and community – all might be seen as neglected. There was at one time a spate of stories about parents leaving their children 'home alone'. There are no specific definitions of what is unacceptable; it all depends on the context, but children who have no adult present overnight should certainly be referred, at least for discussion about whether a response is needed.

In effect, there has to be some potential identifiable risk to the child's health and development, not just a lifestyle that is considered to be different. All teachers will have come across grubby but perfectly loved and happy children at some time. General living standards have probably risen in recent years with improved housing and sanitation, etc., but there are always exceptions where parents may be unable to meet their children's legitimate needs. To be called abuse, the parents' failure to provide must be putting the child at risk of harm, or actually be causing it now.

In education terms this might also include a parent who has no appreciation of their child's special educational needs. The child's language or hearing might be significantly impaired without the provision of some service that the parent is failing to ensure that they receive, despite numerous offers of help to do so. At its extreme, failure to ensure the attendance of younger children at school could also be seen as neglect, alongside the normal powers of the LEA for such a situation. Social workers will often want to treat such wider concerns as children in need (see p. 54), but this is acceptable only if real progress in the best interests of the child can be made by consent, as a genuine and effective alternative to using child protection procedures.

New understandings

It is helpful to have general agreement about what we are trying to deal with, even if we must be constantly revising and updating our responses in the light of experience. There should be an emphasis on prevention, as well as intervening in a crisis. Things have moved on from battered babies and obvious presenting injuries, even though it must never be forgotten that these are major indicators of concern that should never be ignored. It is still absolutely vital to get the basics right. But there have been several additions to the child protection agenda in recent years:

1. *An awareness of the impact of drug and alcohol misuse.* The lifestyle and actions of the parents may be the starting point for assessing the child's needs, rather any direct evidence of physical harm. Substance misuse in pregnancy may affect the development of an unborn child. A parent's ability to understand or care for their child may be diminished or impaired. A few substance misusers may experience mental states that put their children at risk of harm or neglect, especially if their use is out of control and their lifestyle is chaotic. Needles and prescription medicines may be inappropriately accessible. This does not mean that parents who abuse drugs or alcohol are necessarily unable to care for their children, but extra vigilance and support may be required to ensure that standards of care are appropriately maintained.

2. *A response to child and adolescent prostitution that now recognises that the young person is not the offender.* Some under-age sex is prostitution, and it does not always involve those young people thought to be most vulnerable. Young people may be putting themselves at risk, but that does not make the abuse

their fault; the adult is still responsible. There may be warning signs that are apparent to school staff, including unexplained absences, changes in behaviour, running away from home, apparent promiscuity at a early age, etc., but this will not necessarily be so. A 14-year-old girl was found murdered in a Midlands city after she had been involved in prostitution without her family or her school suspecting anything. Friends may be aware of it, but they may not, or the young person may be deliberately isolated from their peers by the abuser. Some relationships described as boyfriend–girlfriend are in fact based on a coercive exchange in which sex with others may be required in return for money, drugs, accommodation, etc. Prostitution may also involve adults and children of the same sex, although there is less evidence for this. There will usually be a local inter-agency protocol for dealing with such referrals, and they will need to be handled very carefully, especially when it comes to gaining the child's co-operation.

3. *A greater understanding of the abuse of children with disabilities.* Disabled children are, statistically, at greater risk of abuse than the child population as a whole. There will be particular responsibilities here for staff in special schools and sometimes a need to get past the image of all parents as heroic and long-suffering. Some find the whole situation too much to handle, and some abusers deliberately target children with disabilities because they know that it will be more difficult to detect their activities since the child will be an unreliable witness as far as the courts are concerned. Alternative methods of communication may be needed for an investigation to take place, or the child may not be able to articulate what is happening to them at all. There is widespread agreement that, even with this increased understanding, the system rarely works to these children's best interests as it should.

4. *An acceptance that some abuse is carried out by young people and children.* Some abuse is being identified in which both perpetrator and victim are children. These examples tend to be not like the James Bulger case but primarily involve abuse within the family, both physical and sexual. Work with adult abusers has also shown that many began committing abusive acts during childhood and adolescence, as well as often being subject to the abuse of others. (There is not, however, an absolute correlation between the two in all cases.) Early interventions with such children may therefore play an important part both in protecting others and in ensuring the appropriate assessment of the child concerned. Inappropriate sexualised behaviour towards other children may be an important indicator, and I personally have known examples in children as young as 4. Child protection systems should now be much more sensitive to the complexities of such concerns.

5. *Greater awareness of the abuse of children involving the Internet.* The Internet, and other new technology such as digital cameras and mobile phones, have all created opportunities for the abuse of children that did not previously exist. A recent international investigation identified thousands of British users who had

paid regular subscriptions to access explicit sites (Operation Ore). Thousands of images can be stored on easily disposable plug-ins the size of a keyring. Child protection workers have had to develop new skills as a result, especially in the analysis of IT equipment, but there is some concern about the time being taken to deal with these investigations and the lack of any additional resources for the considerable extra work involved. High-profile failures to secure some convictions have also undermined confidence in the process, and many identified suspects still remain to be investigated. The police have to take the lead in these inquiries, and, although they will focus on seizing home computers, etc., there will often also be issues of risk to be considered relating to any children within the alleged perpetrator's own family, or any professional or voluntary setting in which they are involved. Concerns about anyone connected to education will normally result in a strategy meeting. (See Chapter 14. See also Chapter 8 for advice about school websites, etc.)

6. *A clearer focus on issues of adult mental health.* There are often professional and organisational barriers between those who work with adults and those with direct responsibility for children. Child protection may begin from an awareness that an adult poses a risk to children, not from any actual incident. For example, post-natal depression, psychotic episodes and delusions, feelings of wishing to attempt suicide, etc. may all be reflected in behaviour towards children and cannot be seen in isolation. From the mother who is unable to cope with the care of a newborn child to the parent who, in complete despair, kills their children and then themselves, there are clearly significant risks to be addressed. All those involved with families and parents need to be child focused. Again, there will usually be a local protocol between agencies about the sharing of relevant information.

7. *A revolution in our view of domestic violence.* We now know that there is a major correlation between violence against partners and violence towards children. This increased understanding has been especially true in respect of the police, where such issues are no longer seen as purely private matters between adults, and there is a requirement to assess the protection needs of any children who are identified in the course of responding to complaints and incidents. Children may be the recipients of physical violence themselves or may suffer emotional abuse from being in a violent household and knowing what is happening around them. The acknowledged existence of domestic violence as part of a child's pastoral context should be seen as a potential indicator of abuse and, at a significant level, be sufficient in itself for a child protection referral. Witnessing violence is now specifically identified as significant harm in the Adoption and Children Act 2002.

Effects of abuse

Until the 1970s there was an unspoken acceptance that children were sometimes harmed, but there was also a sense that as they grew up and the abuse stopped, its impact diminished. This justified not intervening, with all the consequent disruption to the child's life, except in cases of the most extreme violence or neglect where immediate protection was needed. We now know differently. I sometimes use in my own training an excerpt from a television programme in which the adult children of Fred and Rosemary West talk about their childhood hopes that the physical and sexual abuse that was happening to them would end once they were old enough to leave home. That is why they decided it was best not to tell anyone, in part hoping they could still keep the family together. The eventual murder of their sister Heather, and the obvious impact on their own lives as adults, makes it clear that such expectations are often misplaced.

Short-term effects of abuse may manifest in psychological and behavioural ways, as well as in immediately presenting physical symptoms. But research has demonstrated that the effects of abuse may last a lifetime. As well as the long-term damage that can be caused by some physical abuse, neurological damage and disabilities, etc., abuse may lead to difficulties in forming or sustaining close relationships or holding down a regular job, low self-worth and self-harm, mental illness, and extra obstacles in handling the skills that are required to be an effective parent. Those whose adult lives result in offending behaviour, long-term illness and social exclusion will be more likely to have been abused as children than the population as a whole.

As highlighted by *Messages from Research*, it is not only the abusive events themselves that are significant but also the context in which they take place. Coming to terms with the fact that your own parents harmed you, or your father used you for sex before you were old enough to have any understanding that it was wrong, can have a devastating effect on your view of yourself. Abuse is not over when it is over. It is this insight, more than anything, that has led to the culture of recognising what is happening *at the time* and empowering children to see that something can be done about it straight away. It is still too early to say, but the hope is that this will enable those who have experienced abuse to be able to move on into more satisfying adulthood, without all the baggage of the abuse still holding them back.

Causes of abuse

Why does child abuse occur? There are, of course, a number of possible answers. Many of the 'facts' about child abuse are capable of differing interpretations, depending on how we each perceive the issues. Victoria Climbié died because those who were supposed to be caring for her on behalf of her parents mistreated, tortured and ultimately murdered her. Is the answer to *why* she died to ask why they had become people like that? The Laming Report concluded that she died, in large part, because of incompetences and inadequacies among the professionals employed to protect children like her. It might also be said that she died because of major weaknesses in the private fostering system, or because there is no requirement to tell the education authorities of a child's existence, or because she happened to live in a community and a neighbourhood in which a child in such a parlous state could go virtually unnoticed.

'Explanations' can be about people, values or systems, and it is helpful to understand that our own interpretation of events may be capable of a number of meanings. My reading of the main approaches to analysing abusive behaviour is as follows:

Inadequate/deviant individuals

One perspective locates the causes in weaknesses and failings in the child's parents or carers, often on the basis of predisposing characteristics that make these particular people more likely to abuse. Theories of 'cycles of abuse' fit in with understandings like these, in which people who have been abused themselves are more likely to become abusers later, whether physically, sexually or emotionally. The focus is primarily individual, psychological and behavioural. Those who abuse children may be affluent, educated, even successful people in other areas of their lives, not only those with personal and social difficulties, but at this point they have an inherent weakness. They are just 'bad' or morally deviant when it comes to children. Some, however, who see abuse in this context would understand it more as a form of mental illness or personality disorder rather than as criminality, focusing more on the unmet emotional needs of the parent which make them unable to handle their responsibilities.

The key to understanding and preventing the abuse will therefore be in exploring the parents' own upbringing and the likelihood that they will look to their children to meet their own needs rather than being able to accept a caring role. The tension inherent in this situation, and in the likelihood of associated unsatisfying adult relationships, is likely to lead to violence or neglect against the child for failing to live up to their parents' unrealistic expectations. Alternatively, the adult may see the child as a source of comfort and reassurance and so be more likely to put them at risk of sexual abuse in order to make up for their own perceived deficit in appropriate sexual expression. Such understandings are likely to lead to legal, punitive or 'treatment'-based responses, which will need to be proactive and interventionist at an early stage and which are more likely to involve long-term alternative carers for the children involved rather than much expectation of rehabilitation.

Dysfunctional families

Another approach is more concerned with relationships than with the individuals within them. The particular emphasis is on the family. This is where the problem is; this is where the solution must lie, not in changing the personalities of the people concerned. Parents are understood as operating within 'systems' whose organic inter-relationships need to be understood in their context, both within the family itself and as a reflection of wider relationships outside. Each person within the system, including the child, both affects and is affected by the behaviour of all the others. Causation of abuse is circular, within the network. This is why virtually all abusers harm children within their own family, not random children, and such situations carry both positive and negative potential for change. This is largely the theoretical basis of the Assessment Framework (see p. 54).

Slightly more radical analysis would argue that systems need stability to survive and that the abuse becomes the means by which the network is maintained, protected and balanced. The key issue is the *function* of the abuse: 'How does abuse help to maintain the family's balance?' Abuse is the symptom of the family's dysfunction, not the cause of it. Indeed, abuse may be seen, even by the child, as the means by which the family continues to survive. A failed marital relationship may be sustained by scapegoating the child; a non-abusive parent accepts the abuse because the alternative is too much to handle; children collude with the abuse because they do not want to lose their home and their parents. This can become particularly acute in some cases of physical and sexual abuse.

Social pressures

A third view involves not simply saying that parents abuse their children because they have other problems such as failed relationships, debt, poor housing, poverty, unemployment, etc. Otherwise there would be an association in every case, which there clearly is not. But the focus here is on the factors *outside* the individuals that cause them to behave in certain ways in response to the pressure they are under, rather than on the family itself, either singly or as a unit. Situational stresses contribute to the actions of otherwise 'normal' parents who may lose control or be unable to manage the demanding role of parenting when there is so much else to cope with at the same time. Dealing with the underlying causes then becomes more important in protecting the child, rather than just responding to the presenting behaviour at the end of the chain. This understanding tends to lead to very practical responses such as supporting families financially or improving their access to services such as nurseries, family support, improved housing, etc.

Other analyses take a more structural and political view – for example, marriage and the family are declining, and ultimately unsuccessful, social phenomena that are sustained by outdated moral and religious ideologies. Abuse is therefore an indication of the inability of the institution to adapt. Or violence within the parent–child relationship may be seen as a reflection of violence within the wider culture, and cannot be understood in isolation. Supporting the individuals will never be sufficient alone without there being more radical social change to the nature of community and social structures.

Gender and power issues

A more recent area of thinking, but one that is crucial to a complete understanding, concerns gender and power issues. Abuse is 'gendered'. As regards sexual abuse, for example, the known perpetrators are overwhelmingly men and, although the balance between the genders is much more even in other forms of abuse, this is largely a reflection of the fact that many women are solely responsible for the day-to-day care, upbringing and, therefore, the disciplining of children. Relationships between the sexes are uneven, and, like domestic violence in general, the abuse of children is one inevitable consequence of this inequality. Dealing with abuse will be about empowerment of those who are primarily reacting to their own unreasonable oppression.

Questions of power have already been referred to as part of the basic definition of what constitutes abuse. If men, for example, expect or are given the role of being dominant, demanding, etc., this is more likely to lead to an expectation that the abuse of less powerful individuals within the family is acceptable. Much of this analysis, though not all of it, comes from within the feminist movement. The view of women as objects, and children as even more subordinate, inevitably creates a climate within which abuse can prosper. More equal roles and relationships, it is argued, in which stereotypes are resisted and every individual is given recognition as a valued person, are less likely to create potentially abusive situations. Unrealistic expectations of the 'perfect wife and mother', or indeed of the 'perfect dad', can lead to feelings of frustration and depression that simply reinforce a sense of failure which is then visited on the children.

Facing up to our feelings

This brief résumé of definitions and understandings is intended to stimulate thought, not to confuse or impress with a bewildering range of alternatives that cannot be reconciled! I find myself accepting some of each of these analyses, but not necessarily all of any of them. Trying to draw lines around 'abuse' and why it occurs is a process that is never complete. This chapter began by making it clear that we must act according to agreed criteria, not on our own judgements and values alone. But it is also important to reflect on where we are and why we are there. No one can approach the abuse of children without personal feelings. This work is not the same as taking a maths class or planning next year's timetable. Even getting this far may have raised all kinds of personal emotions, some of which may be very painful.

Most of us will experience a mixture of some or all of the following at some time or another:

- denial – because recognition may be costly and too difficult;
- guilt – because we all make mistakes;
- fear – that we won't know what to do, or for our own safety;
- anger – that people can do such things to children or to other adults;
- pain – at the recognition of abuse in our own lives;
- jealousy – when we have to stand back and let someone else take over.

Teaching is a stressful enough occupation at the best of times. Part of the stress inevitably arises from dealing with issues like these. Responding so intimately to children and their needs may not actually be what we had in mind when we chose to be a teacher. It will always help to step back and to analyse our reactions, and those who do this kind of work should be given much greater opportunity to do so than is often the case. For those whose own past experience, as a child or as a parent, has included the reality of abusive behaviour, there may be a particular need to seek personal support and even counselling in order to be able to act professionally. Asking for such help should never be interpreted as a failing. Neither should such experiences necessarily be seen as either especially equipping any particular individual for the task of child protection or effectively excluding them from it.

To do the job well, we will have to be prepared to understand ourselves a little more as well as understanding abuse; to approach ourselves critically and put our responses to the test. But teachers must also be knowledgeable and informed. It is now time to examine the law, and how it is put into practice, in order to be sure that we also have the information that we need to address these responsibilities as we should.

Training idea 2: Defining possible abuse (group)

TASK: Choose one of the following stories in each small group and discuss it:

1. What kind of abuse might be involved in each story?
2. What happens when you choose a different age and gender for the child concerned, e.g. 9 or 15, boy or girl?
3. Would you be more inclined to see each child as a 'child in need' or as a 'child in need of protection'? Why? What difference would it make?
4. What would be some of the factors affecting how you would respond if this story was told to you?

Share your insights with those who have looked at the other stories.

I've never got on with my dad. He's always preferred my sister. Every so often it all blows up and we have huge rows; usually it's about him saying I haven't done my share of jobs in the house, or my room's a mess. My sister can get away with all that. The other night he came into my room. He'd been drinking all night. There was some stuff on the floor – he just knocked me across the room with his fist. I hit my head on the cupboard and bruised my shoulder and arm. Mum tries to stop him but I think she's afraid of him.

I've always felt the odd one out in my family. Mum says that the reason dad left was because they were always rowing about me. I was the ugly one; the clumsy one. Simon was the one who always got the good report . . . one year my report was so bad I wasn't allowed to go on holiday with them. They make me feel so small I just want to hide away all the time. I don't speak to anyone at home any more – I just sit in my room by myself. Simon's got his own TV but they won't let me have one. Sometimes I wish I hadn't been born at all. They all hate me.

I never liked it but I didn't know what to do about it. It started when my mum got a Saturday morning job. I suppose it was my fault because I just used to lie in bed and not get up. My dad would come in. One morning I woke up and found him in bed with me. I realised I was being touched and started pulling away. And then I realised he was touching me down there. He told me I shouldn't kid myself because when I was asleep I was enjoying it. In the end I just got used to it. This was the closest thing I had ever experienced to love. The only physical affection that I can remember is these times with my father.

I'm glad my mum's got a boyfriend but I wish I wasn't left in charge so often. My mum works all hours so I have to collect my brothers from school and look after them till she gets in. Most weekends she goes to see her boyfriend. Sometimes she doesn't come back till late or forgets to leave money to buy food and there's nothing in the house to eat. Last weekend the littlest one was sick all night and I didn't know what to do. I'm always getting into trouble for missing lessons or coming in late, but I just feel so tired and dizzy and I can't concentrate.

Chapter 4

The Children Act 1989

A guide to key elements of the law

A new approach

Professionals always need to remember that they require a valid legal basis to their intervention into a child's or family's life; they do not have it just by virtue of their position. Parents and children may not easily appreciate that a school may also be involved in issues other than the strictly educational, so the underlying legitimacy must be clear to those who are asked to carry out these wider functions in case they have to defend it. Knowing the law is both empowering and enabling, but it will also be important in defining the boundaries. We cannot always do what we would like to do, or necessarily what others might expect us to do. The same goes for our colleagues in other agencies.

The basis for the protection of children is Part V of the Children Act 1989, implemented from October 1991. All work under the Act, which covers both 'private' law (such as divorce and separation) and 'public' law (care proceedings, etc.) for all those up to 18, is based on certain theoretical principles:

1. *The child's welfare is the 'paramount consideration'.* This is a clear reflection of the priorities also identified by the Cleveland inquiry. In practice, this means that intervention should always be based on what is in the child's best interests. If, for example, a child is at risk from an adult within their home, it would usually be best for the child to remain where they are with other trusted carers and for the alleged abuser to have to go elsewhere, rather than the other way round. Requiring the child to adapt to a new family or children's unit, possibly change school and be separated from their friends and siblings is not likely to be helpful and may even compound the effects of the alleged abuse. The Act allows for local authorities to assist an adult to find temporary alternative accommodation, even with cash if it is necessary. Much practice has changed to reflect this emphasis, but cases where other factors have obscured the centrality of the child's needs suggest that the lesson has still to be learned in its entirety.

2. *Delay is likely to be prejudicial to the child and should be avoided.* There is less evidence to suggest that this principle has been universally accepted, even

allowing for the fact that the guidance now contains much tighter timetables for decision-making. Care proceedings should, for example, be completed in no more than 40 weeks. Unfortunately, shortages of staff and other factors often mean that this remains merely an aspiration. Court processes in particular can still be painfully laborious in an attempt to balance the interests of all those involved. Owing to a shortage of guardians *ad litem* (see the Glossary) in some areas, cases can last up to two years, which is wholly unacceptable. Local procedures following a child protection referral should, however, move forward swiftly, and this may mean that sometimes little notice is given of important meetings such as an initial child protection conference, or there may be a tight deadline expected for producing a report.

3. *Courts should not make orders unless it is clear that to do so would be better for the child than no order.* In general, agencies will seek to meet children's needs by negotiation and agreement, using the powers of the law and the authority of the courts only when absolutely necessary. This has resulted in a significant change, though there are signs that after an initial period following the implementation of the Act, the use of courts is now much closer to what it was before. Applications for both emergency and longer-term orders have been creeping up again. This 'no order principle' will often mean that a social worker may appear to be going further than the teacher considers strictly necessary in trying to respond to their concerns by working with the family voluntarily. It is sometimes in conflict with the requirement to place the child's welfare at the centre. A reluctance to use courts, as a matter of blanket policy, without seeing that this may be putting a particular child at unacceptable risk would be a misunderstanding of this expectation and should be challenged.

4. *Decisions should be made in partnership wherever possible.* Agencies should create effective partnerships, not only with each other but also with families. Parents are of key significance, but other members of the extended family should be given the opportunity to participate in problem-solving wherever possible. Parents should have the opportunity to contribute to decisions that are being made about them. This is why they will often be present for at least part of a conference or core group meeting called to discuss their failure to provide adequate care, and why any reports or statements are usually shared with them. Working in this way may require new skills for teachers not always used to such openness.

5. *Children have a right to be consulted.* Children's views should be respected and children must be given every chance to be involved in discussing whatever changes are planned for their lives. The extent to which they can do this clearly varies with the child's 'age and understanding', but the idea should never be ignored. Even with quite young children, or with those for whom there are barriers to communication, it is often possible to be proactive in ensuring that they too can make an effective contribution to decisions being made about their lives – if

necessary, through a representative other than those who may speak for their parents. In legal proceedings, they may have their own solicitor or be supported by an officer of the court.

'Children in need' and the Assessment Framework

As well as influences of this kind stemming directly from the Children Act, and in the hope of creating a more seamless approach that combines both protection and prevention, social workers are now using a new *Framework for the Assessment of Children in Need and their Families* (DoH *et al.* 2000). This is a companion volume to *Working Together*, and the two should always be read together. They are intended to provide a response that is sympathetic to children's needs, by providing the minimum necessary intervention at the appropriate time. Child protection investigations should only be required in response to serious concerns or because other family support services are not suitable.

Section 17 and Schedule 2 Part 1 of the Children Act give local authorities a general duty to take reasonable steps to identify those children who live in, or are found in, their area and who are 'in need'. Schedule 2 also sets out the range of services that should then be provided to help these children and their parents – from support within the home, family centres, practical help, day care and counselling, to accommodation away from home on a voluntary basis, respite care and other temporary alternatives where the family cannot currently meet the child's needs effectively.

A child is in need according to s.17(10) Children Act if:

(a) he [*sic*] is unlikely to achieve or maintain, or to have the opportunity of achieving or maintaining, a reasonable standard of health or development without the provision for him of services by a local authority . . . ;

(b) his health or development is likely to be significantly impaired, or further impaired, without the provision for him of such services; or

(c) he is disabled.

These general concepts should be applied by all agencies, working together at local level, to particular groups of children who are identified as meeting the criteria for a response (effectively the same as those described as 'vulnerable' children elsewhere). As they are then entitled to a service, this definition may vary between authorities in the light of the level of resources available and the likely demand. The assessment process is applied both to child protection cases *and* to those children identified as meeting the 'in need' criteria. It is three-dimensional, child focused, should operate according to defined timetables and is intended to identify the family's strengths as much as their weaknesses by looking at:

- the child's developmental needs;
- the relevant family and environmental factors; and
- parenting capacity.

Carrying out this assessment has become a central role of social workers, in order to provide (or so they can ask others to provide) services that will be of most benefit to the family. Even where referrals are urgent, after the initial steps to safeguard the child have been taken, attention should soon turn to what needs to be done in order to improve the child's circumstances, and who will be involved in bringing such changes about (Figure 4.1).

There are up to 30,000 children on child protection registers at any one time (the numbers have fallen slightly in recent years), but it has been estimated that there are up to 800,000 children who may require some contact with social services and whose circumstances carry the potential to deteriorate to the point where they may need protection in the future (DfES, *The Children Act Report*, 2003). It makes obvious sense to try to identify and support these families *before* things reach a crisis. While social workers are responsible for initiating this process of support and ensuring that the assessment is undertaken within the defined timescales, they cannot do it alone. All agencies, including education, are required by s.27 to assist them in doing so.

The services that are needed might be to do with early years provision or the child's special educational needs, or relate to problems at school or with adult literacy, for example. Social services would therefore require others to support them in meeting the family's needs and minimising the risk of future harm, even

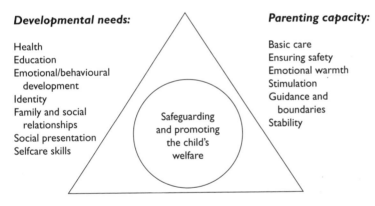

Developmental needs:

Health
Education
Emotional/behavioural
    development
Identity
Family and social
    relationships
Social presentation
Selfcare skills

Safeguarding
and promoting
the child's
welfare

Parenting capacity:

Basic care
Ensuring safety
Emotional warmth
Stimulation
Guidance and
    boundaries
Stability

Family and environmental factors:

Family history and functioning
Wider family
Housing
Employment
Income
Family's social integration
Community resources

Figure 4.1

if that child had not already been identified by the individual agency concerned as a priority. It is expected that there will soon be a common assessment tool routinely used by all agencies in place of the existing separation between, for example, social care, SEN and health procedures. This shared process is likely to follow the general structure of the Assessment Framework and will be a very welcome development, especially for families caught up in repeated assessments by separate professionals, though it will probably mean considerable change to current working practices for many of us.

In effect, the requirement to co-operate in this way, which pre-dated s.175 Education Act 2002 by well over ten years, already placed a duty on educational professionals to 'safeguard and promote' the welfare of children. Best practice since the Children Act would already have been to work together with other agencies in the identification and support of the most vulnerable children in the community rather than simply waiting for the child to present at school or elsewhere with an obvious injury or major crisis. The Assessment Framework was meant to herald a renewed emphasis on prevention. The reasons why this has not always happened as was hoped justify some further reflection.

1. *The Framework has not yet had the impact that was intended, even in some social services departments.* Social workers have been slow to introduce it in many areas, often because of chronic staff shortages which mean that cases requiring immediate protection still have to take priority. This is a major frustration for teachers and others who would like to see families receiving help at a much earlier stage. But in the light of constant and overwhelming public criticism if a child ever dies, social work managers are clearly unwilling to divert resources away from short-term crisis interventions and on to longer-term work in building the capacity of families to cope with their children more effectively. The two approaches are effectively in competition, which is completely against the intention of the guidance.

2. *The approach was at first rather cumbersome and bureaucratic.* An assessment under the Framework initially involved the completion of age-related booklets running to 25 or more pages (now somewhat reduced), but there has been a temptation for social workers simply to copy the pages headed 'Education' and send them to a child's school or LEA for completion. While this may provide information on, for example, SATs performance or attendance rates, it does not provide all the relevant information about parenting capacity or wider family relationships which teachers are likely to know a great deal about. It is also hardly in keeping with the spirit of the document, which is intended to facilitate 'joined-up' solutions to supporting families across agency boundaries. There should be face-to-face meetings about the *whole* child if the Framework is being used properly, and all agencies, together with the family, should receive a copy of the entire assessment at the end.

3. *Lack of awareness in schools and elsewhere.* While the DfES allowed its name to appear on the front cover of the Assessment Framework when it was published, virtually no work was done at the time to alert schools to its implications. In the early stages, LEA officers found themselves in multi-agency planning meetings with an expectation that they could commit school staff to changing their methods of assessment, providing time for the completion of the documents and attending all the consequent meetings. Teachers themselves had little or no awareness of what might now be required of them. This has led to a wide variety of practice, largely dependent on the willingness of individuals to provide the necessary time and expertise to make a realistic contribution. It cannot all be done by education social workers or those with a specific role in welfare-related issues, as it is the staff at the schools themselves who actually work directly with the child and usually know most about them.

4. *A family sometimes cannot receive an assessment unless the parents give their consent.* Other than in child protection settings, action under the Assessment Framework must be with the active support and co-operation of all those involved. This presents no problem for the parents of a child with a disability who are keen to access the services that may be available to help them. But it is a major obstacle to effective intervention in a family that does not see they have a problem and whose care of their children is not at a sufficiently alarming stage to justify action by agencies on a more compulsory basis. Teachers will know of many children who, they feel, need to receive services and assistance, but whose parents, or indeed the child or young person, do not want the social services involved. This is in part due to the historic perception of social workers as likely to be critical and over-interventionist, an image that social workers are desperate to lose. Despite the very best intentions of the Children Act, this dual task of supporting and investigating, placed on the same people in the same agency but at different times, appears to be increasingly difficult to achieve in practice.

'Significant harm'

Of equal importance to the concept of 'children in need' is the Children Act's definition of the grounds on which a local authority must intervene in a family even if the parents do not want it to do so. These are also the situations that *require* action under schools' child protection policies as actual or potential abuse and are based on the four categories outlined on pp. 37–43. Defining this threshold is never easy, and the Act moved away from listing specific situations or injuries on to more general principles (s.31). There must now be the reality or the risk of 'harm' and to a 'significant' degree.

'Harm' is defined as 'ill-treatment or the impairment of health or development', and the concepts of 'health' and 'development' are intended to be wide-ranging, including physical, emotional, social, behavioural and intellectual elements. Significance is determined with reference to 'what could reasonably be expected of a similar child'. This is intended to be realistic and to take account of what may be practically possible given the family's circumstances or the general culture of their community. What might be significant in one school might not therefore be significant in another. Various tests such as the standard of parental care, the care likely to be given in the future and whether the child is beyond parental control are then required.

All this can mean that *proving* that the requirement for unwanted intervention has been met is far from easy, and there may well be a difference of opinion on this issue among the professionals involved. Some situations are obvious, but might still need pointing out as such. Colleagues in other agencies who do child protection work all the time can get overly used to working in as low-key a way as possible. But the Act has, in effect, stressed that local authorities must justify their interventions far more thoroughly than used to be the case, as a protection for the parents against unwarranted interference. This may be the reason behind the apparent reluctance of the social worker to respond urgently to your concerns – not, hopefully, merely a lack of time or interest.

Statutory powers

S.47 gives social workers a duty to make inquiries into a child's circumstances where they have 'reasonable cause to suspect that a child in their area is suffering, or is likely to suffer, significant harm'. They must then take the necessary steps to ensure that the child's welfare is safeguarded and promoted and decide what action is now appropriate. Other professionals must assist them as required (s.47(9)). This is the problem with the suggestion that less emphasis should be placed on situations requiring immediate intervention; they have a duty to do it on demand and there is more than enough of it to do!

If needed, this is the point at which the inter-agency procedure will take over (see p. 62). But this process requires that social workers, the NSPCC or the police are given access to the child in order that these inquiries can be made. What if they are unable to do so? Most of the time the investigation takes place without much difficulty and with parental co-operation, but the lead agencies have certain powers available to them for the rare occasions when they are needed in the child's best interests.

Child Assessment Order (s.43)

The power to make a Child Assessment Order (CAO) was introduced during the passage of the Children Bill as a means of proceeding with minimal interference to the family – a kind of halfway house between voluntary and compulsory action. The idea was first mooted in the report *A Child in Mind* (1987), which examined the death of Kimberley Carlile. An application can be made by the social services to the Family Proceedings Court in order to obtain authority to proceed with an assessment of the child where parents have refused to co-operate. Orders are intended to promote a multidisciplinary assessment of the child's needs, though the emphasis is primarily medical.

The application in itself may be sufficient to resolve the impasse, but, if not, a CAO requires the parent to produce the child for examination. It does not entitle the social services to keep the child away from home, nor is there any change in parental responsibility. The order lasts for only seven days, and if the authorities then wish to remove the child, they must make further applications for other orders. The use of CAOs is infrequent, and is required only in cases when all those with parental responsibility are refusing to co-operate. Only the consent of one such person is required, as they each have the right of independent action under the Children Act.

They are mainly intended for situations where social workers or health professionals have been unable to see a child in person and where there are grounds for suspecting that the child may have been harmed or ill-treated. A CAO might exceptionally be used in connection with other kinds of assessment – for example, for a possible special educational need, where parents are refusing to consent – but this is even rarer. There are usually other ways to move such situations forward, but they probably carry some unused potential that should always be considered if appropriate.

There is an important legal point here that will crop up more than once in this book, about what happens if a child refuses to be examined. Even when a court has made an order, a child of 'sufficient age and understanding' (no particular age is specified) may not agree to be assessed. The court is no more powerful than a parent in overruling the child's objection. Most doctors would normally refuse even to consider examining a child who was withholding their consent. Doing so could be seen as an assault, and all professionals, including teachers, have to be extremely cautious about proceeding against the child's wishes in such a situation.

Emergency Protection Order (s.44)

An Emergency Protection Order (EPO) also requires prior application to a court. Although an order can be made *ex parte* (see the Glossary) without the parents present, they must be informed of the hearing. This is a more invasive intervention in that the applicant acquires parental responsibility for the child for the duration of the order and can therefore make parental decisions, including deciding where and with whom they will live. The application must pass the tests of significant harm and of being better for the child than making no order. In theory, anyone with an interest in a particular child's welfare can apply, though action by anyone other than a social worker is extremely uncommon. The order lasts for eight days, but can be renewed for up to seven more. Keeping a child away from home for any longer period would require applications for further orders such as an interim care order (see p. 61). These short periods are in marked contrast to the position pre-Cleveland, when twenty-eight-day place of safety orders could become almost permanent by frequent renewal.

Parents retain considerable rights during these proceedings. They may seek to have the order discharged or to obtain contact with the child. They do not actually lose their parental responsibility, though in practice it can be significantly curtailed. Parents must be told what is going on and, after no more than fifteen days, the authorities must be able to produce sufficient evidence to convince a court that the child is still at risk, or the child must be allowed to go home. There should no longer be any examples of children being kept away from their parents without justification, though some would argue that this approach has unintentionally led to the very opposite becoming true, so that children are not being removed when they ought to be.

Police protection (s.46)

It is often not appreciated that the police have far greater powers than social workers – not only powers of entry into people's property, but the right to remove any child from their home in an emergency without any prior application to a court. *Only* they can do this. The power is often referred to as a 'police protection order' (PPO), but no order is involved; that's the whole point. A 'constable' may, at any time, remove a child into police protection or, for example, prevent a parent from removing a child from a hospital. They can even use force to do so, though this is rarely necessary. This is the power used in high-profile incidents that get a great deal of publicity when they happen (but which are also extremely untypical). It enables a child to be removed when surprise is of the essence or when they are left at home alone, thought to be engaging in prostitution or arrive unescorted at a London railway station late at night.

The police must tell the local authority about the child and ensure that the child is removed into their care within no more than seventy-two hours (designed to cover a holiday weekend). In practice, this happens much more quickly, and the two agencies will usually act together if at all possible. If necessary, the social services can then apply for other orders if it is not safe for the child to return home or no other voluntary arrangements are possible. There are also powers under the Act (s.50) for courts to make a recovery order where a child subject to an EPO or care order has run away or gone missing.

Care orders

Only a social services department can normally initiate proceedings to put a child into care or place them under a supervision order (s.31). Only a court can decide that the grounds are satisfied, so in this important sense social workers themselves never 'take children away' from their parents. This is an entirely different decision from whether to 'accommodate' a child on a voluntary basis under s.20, and the two situations must always be carefully distinguished, even though both groups are included in the definition of 'looked-after' children or 'children in public care'. Only in the case of a care order does the local authority acquire parental responsibility; other arrangements are intended as a support to the family, not implying any sense that the parents are not appropriate to have care of the children. Care orders give the local authority power to restrict the extent to which a parent can exercise their own parental responsibility, though it is not removed from them entirely, as under the previous legislation.

The hope, in all but a few cases, will still be to rebuild the family relationships, not to end them. The child's own family is still likely to be the best place for them to be, unless there are very good reasons otherwise. Care orders can be made on an interim basis but only for a few weeks at a time before a longer-term decision must be made. As before, this is all designed to ensure that children can be protected if required, but that they do not stay away from their home any longer than is necessary. Eventually, courts may agree that family relationships have entirely broken down, though children are sometimes returned to the care of their parents while still under the order. A few will need to be placed for longer-term fostering, adoption or residential care.

Summary

It is important to remember that most of the time these legal powers are not needed. Most child protection work is still done by negotiation and agreement with families, but there are some situations that require a more formalised approach. Where reasonable inquiries are being frustrated and, most importantly, where professionals are being denied direct access to the child concerned, professionals must be prepared to take the difficult decision that compulsory intervention may be necessary. These are mostly decisions for social workers and their managers as the lead investigation agency. But the evidence of others may be crucial and, where concerns are known to another agency, they must be shared so that action can be considered. It is up to everyone in child protection, not just the social workers, to ensure that all the known facts about a child are passed on. If you think more formal action is required because you remain concerned about a child, share that concern with others, even if they do not agree. No one likes to use the courts, but sometimes it cannot be avoided in the ultimate best interests of the child. Nothing, and no one, is more important.

Chapter 5

The inter-agency child protection process

What social workers and others do to safeguard children

Responding to concerns

So what exactly happens if there is concern about a child who may have been abused or is seriously at risk? How are decisions made about how to respond and who is involved? The guidance, *Safeguarding Children: What to Do if You're Worried a Child Is Being Abused* (DoH *et al.* 2003), sets out the procedure you might expect to find in any local authority. (At least a copy of the summary should have been circulated to all key professionals, including designated teachers.) This document is helpful to teachers in that it describes what social workers and others should be doing, though some would argue that what it says is either obvious, unrealistic (if, for example, there are staff shortages as there nearly always are) or already set out elsewhere in local procedures. I have tried not to simply repeat the same information again, but to examine the process in a more analytical way. What *really* happens and why? This should assist the reader in understanding both what other agencies should be doing and why they sometimes don't do what you might expect!

Receiving a referral

The previous chapters should have helped to clarify the situations that are appropriately seen as child protection issues. If these kinds of circumstances apply, nobody can protect a child until someone picks up a telephone, talks to a social worker colleague or fills in a form. It seems mundane but it is essential. Someone has to share the concern and let the process do its job. If possible, even at this stage, action will still be taken under s.17, with the child being designated a 'child in need' and with the consent of the family, rather than under child protection procedures. This should be clarified at the point of referral to the social services under local arrangements. If there is any doubt about whether the threshold for a 'section 47 investigation' has been reached, the social worker may be reluctant to accept a referral without the knowledge and consent of the parent. This reluctance is appropriate if we are talking about children in need, but if the concerns are sufficient to suggest the reality *or the risk* of significant harm, parental consent is *not* always required. (See Chapter 7 for advice on making referrals, confidentiality and consent, etc.)

Investigation

Once a referral has been accepted, social services (or in some areas the NSPCC) are responsible for 'making enquiries', either by themselves or, if criminal offences may be involved, jointly with the police. This investigation has several functions:

- to ascertain the facts about any situation which has been referred and to decide on an appropriate response;
- to establish a permanent record of the allegations being made or the evidence which is being presented – that is, what abuse has occurred, over how long a period, etc.;
- to make an initial assessment of the current level of risk to the child; and
- to establish whether there are continuing grounds for concern and whether child protection procedures should be invoked or other services offered.

The first concern is not solely to identify the alleged abuser and to deal with them. This will be the principal role of the police in a joint investigation if appropriate. The aim of the social services will be to concentrate primarily on the needs of the child. This will normally involve a social worker making contact with a parent or carer in order to acquaint them with the concern if they are not already aware of it, and then with the child (in person) if this has not happened first, as well as contacting any other key individuals in the child's life. It may also be necessary to consider the needs of other children within the household or to contact parents currently living apart from the child.

If it is decided to accept the concern as a child abuse referral, rather than dealing with it in some other way or taking no further action (and this decision should be made within one or two working days), the social worker will then undertake what are usually called 'lateral checks'. These involve a series of telephone enquiries to other professionals, and into past records, in order to establish what is already known about the child and the family. This is a crucial reason why referrals can never be about unnamed children and why *only* social services and the police can undertake these enquiries.

Under child protection procedures, agencies must make information about the family available, even if it would normally be confidential or require the individual's consent first. GPs and hospitals, for example, must disclose patient records about a child if asked to do so in connection with an investigation of this kind. School staff should do the same. Checks will also be made against the authority's child protection register (see p. 68) and the police national computer and sex offender register to establish whether any of the individuals in the family is known to have a past history that would influence the level of concern in this particular case.

If there is an immediate need, a medical examination will be arranged that will require the consent of both parent and the child, if of sufficient age. Whether this is necessary, and the timing of it if so, will depend on the nature of the referral, whether there is likely to be any medical evidence to be gathered or whether the child requires urgent treatment. Clearly, some injuries may require immediate action, or it may be necessary to ensure that a serious bruise, burn or other wound is seen by the relevant professional at an early stage as an 'expert witness' before it becomes ambiguous and a judgement about its possible cause becomes much more difficult.

Listening to the child

As has already been noted, listening to the child is a crucial part of the process, and the Laming Inquiry specifically drew attention to the fact that it does not always happen as it obviously should. This was one of the key aspirations of the Children Act in the early 1990s, and there is no excuse for its not being routine. Children over the age of about 5 are usually able to describe what may have happened to them and will have a unique perspective that may be completely different from that of their parents and carers, especially if the adults have been trying to conceal vital information. Of course, not all children are fully able to understand their experiences, and their version of the events may not always be the whole truth. Professionals will have to use their judgement and experience as well, but the *opportunity* for a child to share what they know should be axiomatic.

Ideally, a child should tell their story in full only once, though more informal conversations may take place with a social worker in the early stages if there is a need to clarify the nature of the concern. A parent would normally be present unless the circumstances are exceptional, and an alternative 'responsible adult' may sometimes be necessary, which could be a teacher. Formal joint interviews by a social worker and a police officer are increasingly being recorded on video in order to obtain evidence for any subsequent court proceedings, either civil or criminal. Interviews take place in specialist centres that are as child-friendly as possible and according to a strict code of conduct that ensures the questions are appropriate without leading the child or interpreting what they say.

This way of working avoids the need for the child to repeat their story again in court, perhaps many months later, but they may have to be available for cross-examination, if via a remote video link rather than actually having to be in the courtroom. The impact of all this on a child who has been seriously assaulted, but who may be the only source of information about the event, is clearly never less than stressful, requiring a great deal of skill by those involved in supporting them. Unfortunately, the judicial process in particular can sometimes be highly unsympathetic, though there have been some improvements in recent years. This is, however, still one reason why even very serious allegations sometimes never come to court, as it would be too distressing for the child to proceed in the face of a hostile defendant intent on making them prove every last detail of the allegation.

Initial assessment

Most of the time, children will remain living at home during these enquiries, but should the need arise, immediate steps should be taken to protect them, nearly always on a voluntary basis. This may involve placing the child elsewhere within the extended family for a while or, better still, encouraging the alleged abuser to leave the home for the time being. (This is sometimes a consequence of bail conditions where charges have been brought.) In some cases it may be necessary to apply for the orders outlined previously, but this is uncommon. An initial assessment under the Assessment Framework should be undertaken in order to identify the child's needs more fully.

From the first day, the police and the social workers will be talking to each other in a strategy meeting or discussion, if only on the telephone or in the car on the way to a home visit, in order to ensure a co-ordinated approach. Other professionals should also be consulted as required, and many referrals do not need to proceed beyond this point. Parents may agree to receive advice and support; services are provided to try to address some of the problems that were the basis of the concern. Other agencies are asked to assist; assurances are given about giving children better care in the future or making changes in behaviour which will ensure that the identified risks are removed or reduced.

This process of risk assessment may involve formalised models or may be more *ad hoc*. At its best, this will be a multi-agency process, not something undertaken by social workers alone. In many ways this is the nub of child protection, and is where things are mostly likely to go wrong if decision-making is not sufficiently well managed. How do we know what the risks are to this child? What influences the decision about how agencies should respond? But how can anyone predict the future? It is all too easy to be critical with hindsight. What the social workers should be doing is gathering all the necessary information that enables them to make an informed judgement, and then acting upon it, including, for example, the following questions:

- What are the risks posed to this child? Do they meet the criteria of 'significant harm'?
- What are the factors that increase this child's vulnerability, such as their age, individual needs or the past history of the people they live with?
- What would make the risk of significant harm more or less likely, such as a change in the family's circumstances and behaviour? How likely are those changes?
- What are the strengths and weaknesses in this child's situation and what is the balance between them? Does the risk 'score' outweigh the status quo?
- What do other professionals who know this family have to say?
- In the light of all that, what now needs to be done?

Following this assessment, the involvement of the social services may go no further. If so, they should let the referring agency know that the case has now been closed or referred elsewhere. If, however, the immediate assessment indicates that further risks to the child remain, or if parents are not responding to advice and offering their full co-operation, an initial child protection conference should be called, involving all interested agencies.

The child protection conference

Conferences are not a forum for deciding whether a child has been abused and, if so, by whom. That is a matter for the courts, if appropriate. The issue is about whether or not there is a *continuing risk* to the child and whether the child should be placed on the child protection register because a longer-term child protection plan is required. *Working Together* recommends that an initial child protection conference should be held within fifteen days of the first strategy discussion/ meeting, but this is not always possible. Reviews should be held within three months and then six months, if the initial conference decides to register the child. Social services are responsible for arranging them, though they are often chaired by an independent person not directly employed by any of the participating agencies.

A conference, either an initial conference or a review, should be called:

- when there is evidence, or strong suspicion, that a child has suffered, or is likely to suffer, significant harm; or when there is doubt about the situation and more information is needed to make a decision;
- when a child is known to be living in a household that contains an adult with a previous conviction for offences against a child (known as a 'Schedule 1 offender') or other adult known to pose a threat to their safety;
- when there is a new concern about a child in a household where another child is already on the child protection register;
- when there is a new concern about a child currently on the child protection register;
- when a child on a child protection register elsewhere moves into the area;
- when there are problems or disputes about the implementation of a previously agreed plan for a child already on the register, or major changes in a child's circumstances, such as a change of carer;
- when a conference is requested by an ACPC agency because of concerns about the child's safety or care;
- in relation to a perceived risk of harm to a child who has not yet been born;
- when it is proposed to remove a child from the register.

Conferences require a minimum range of agencies to be present, usually three, before decisions can be made. Attendance should be a high priority for anyone invited to take part. The key decision to be made is whether a child needs to be on the child protection register and, if so, what provision is needed for their continued protection. Of course, just putting the child's name on a list does not protect them. What matters is the action, or the plan, that is then agreed as a result of that expression of concern.

Parents will normally be invited to attend, at least for some of the time, or be given the opportunity to express their views through a representative. This should also be true of children who are old enough to do so. Invitations should be circulated to all agencies in writing, but often arrive at very short notice. Anyone unable to attend should submit a report, in writing if at all possible.

A conference can be expected to last anything up to two hours. Minutes are circulated and must be regarded as highly confidential, and to be shared only with those who need to know the information.

The following checklist is recommended in the Department of Health publication *The Challenge of Partnership in Child Protection* (1994) as the information that is required in advance for all those who are invited to a conference. This probably rarely happens in all its details, but it provides a useful reference point if there are problems about procedure that teachers wish to raise:

- the name of the person chairing the conference and relevant information about his or her task;
- the concerns that have led to the conference being called;
- general information about child protection conferences, including their legal and procedural basis;
- the task to be accomplished and the decisions to be made;
- what the consequences of the conference might be;
- how the conference will be organised;
- information about the categories of abuse that are the criteria for registration;
- any other relevant information about ACPC procedures;
- information about any exclusions from any part of the conference and the reasons (*sub judice* evidence, etc.);
- who will be present and in what capacity;
- where and when the conference will be held and how to get there;
- a copy of the agenda.

This list is in the context of the information required by parents in order for genuine partnership to be reflected in the way in which the agencies are working. It is expected that all of this will be explained to them before the meeting. However, the guidance also says that all participants, especially those not routinely involved or experienced in such meetings, will also need this kind of information in advance in order to be able to make an informed contribution. This may be especially true of a teacher. I would argue that there should at least be an indication of why the conference is being called and which agencies are crucial to effective decision-making in this particular case. This may well help in making a rational decision about what to do in the event of conflicting priorities of time, which is impossible if there is little more than the child's name and address to go on. It is clearly inappropriate for someone to attend just as a matter of routine and then to feel that they have no meaningful contribution to make, but there is sometimes value in having people there who can bring an element of objectivity to the process.

Conferences should now operate according to a standard agenda. This is roughly what you would expect to find:

- introduction of all those present (chair, family, representatives, agencies, etc.);
- identification of any key people who are absent/apologies;
- an outline of the context, purposes and aims of the conference;
- the 'ground rules' (confidentiality, etc.);
- clarification concerning any missing information;
- reports about the incident/area of concern and the result of the initial assessment/investigation;
- additional information from all other agencies;
- comments by the family/child (if appropriate);
- consideration of the degree of continuing risk (to each child individually if more than one is involved);
- the decision as to whether to place the child's name on the child protection register;
- recommendations for future work and the child protection plan;
- appointment of keyworker and core group members (see below);
- date for review.

The child protection register

Children judged to be at continuing risk once all the relevant information has been shared will be admitted to the local authority's child protection register under the relevant category of abuse, or more than one category if necessary. Only a fully quorate conference can make this decision, and *all* professionals present can expect to be asked for their view. It is always preferable to secure a child's safety without need for registration, and numbers on the register nationally have fallen slightly in recent years as the criteria have become more sharply defined. It is not good practice to put a child on the register 'just to be on the safe side' or because there is anxiety about the impression that might be given by not doing so. But if there is clear evidence of unresolved risk, children should be given the protection that registration brings, provided it is then followed up by the necessary action. Registration is only the beginning of the process, not the end.

The register provides a central record of those children in the authority's area currently known to be at risk so that professionals who are concerned about any given child can confidentially check their status. Theoretically, this should never be necessary for an education professional working with the child as, if the child is on the register, they should be aware of it already or have been told by the keyworker. But it provides a way of checking past history and an important safeguard, especially for agencies such as hospitals that are presented with a previously unknown child in suspicious circumstances.

Access to the register is restricted to senior agency officers, including head-teachers and senior LEA/welfare staff. Enquiries are dealt with on a 'call back' basis to ensure that confidentiality is maintained. The register itself is held on computer by the social services department on behalf of the whole ACPC. It should indicate under what categories the child has been registered and who the keyworker is. All enquiries to the register should be logged so that a pattern of concerns from individual agencies might become apparent to the custodian or keeper of the register. Following initial notification, if there are any changes to the child's address, school, etc., it is essential that the data are amended and lead agencies informed. This updating process does not always seem to operate as efficiently as it should. Procedures will also exist to deal with what happens when a child on the register goes missing or moves to another local authority, or when there is a significant change in the level of concern.

It is possible that in future there will be no specific child protection register as such. The problem with the current approach is that this is a stand-alone list of children, rather than being a means of highlighting those children known to be at risk from within the wider population. Not being on the list may be misunderstood as meaning there are no concerns. The alert only works if people specifically access the register to find out whether there is any current or past concern. The development of Identification, Referral and Tracking (IRT) and the Integrated Children's System (ICS) should mean that vulnerable children can be made known to all agencies via a shared database, ideally across local authority boundaries. This system could then contain common indicators of concern, and a child pro-tection register would not be needed as well.

There are, however, major legal, technical and data protection issues to be over-come before this level of shared information could become a reality. There are several existing systems in individual agencies that would need to be harmonised, including the Unique Pupil Number used in education. All children would also have to be known to the authorities so that they could be included, which some would see as a significant issue of civil liberty and an infringement of individual freedom. It would also be essential that information was kept up to date, which might be more of a challenge once agencies' own internal systems were not the focus.

Core group

If there is a need for continued action to protect the child, the conference will appoint a small group of professionals under the leadership of the keyworker, who is always a social worker. This group will be responsible for ensuring that two vital tasks are accomplished:

- the completion of a core assessment under the Assessment Framework – a much more thorough process than the initial assessment, and one that takes considerably longer if it is done properly;
- the drawing up of a 'child protection plan' in the light of this assessment, which sets out how action is to be taken to support the child and address the family's identified needs.

While the social services should take the lead in facilitating the work of the group, every professional is responsible for ensuring its effectiveness. The group should meet for the first time within ten days of the conference and then as necessary to ensure the achievement of the identified objectives. Written notes of the meetings should be kept and circulated. Parents may also be invited to the meetings but are not actually members of the group. According to *Working Together*, the aim of the child protection plan is to:

- safeguard the child from further harm;
- promote the child's health and development, and
- (provided it is in the best interests of the child) support the family and wider family members to promote the welfare of the child.

The plan should:

- describe the needs of the child and what therapeutic services are required;
- include specific, achievable, child-focused objectives intended to safe-guard the child and promote his or her welfare;
- include realistic strategies and specific actions to achieve the objectives;
- clearly identify roles and responsibilities of professionals and family members, including the nature and frequency of contact by professionals with children and family members;
- lay down points at which progress will be reviewed, and the means by which progress will be judged, and
- set out clearly the roles and responsibilities of those professionals with routine contact with the child, e.g. health visitors, GPs and teachers, as well as any specialist or targeted support to the child and family.

(Paragraphs 5.81 and 5.82)

This guidance places teachers as absolutely central to the continued protection of a school-aged child, and this responsibility must be reflected in the level of commitment to the core group and its work.

Reviews and de-registration

Review conferences must be held as required to reformulate the child protection plan or to decide that the child can now be de-registered. Again, at least three agencies must be present for such decisions to be made. A child's name may be removed from the child protection register if:

- the risk of significant harm to the child has diminished as a result of the action taken or a change in the child's circumstances, or because a reassessment now indicates that a plan is not necessary;
- the child and family have moved permanently to another local authority area (in which case, the receiving authority must convene its own conference within fifteen days);
- the child has reached the age of 18, died or permanently left the United Kingdom.

It is important to stress that a child whose name has been removed from the register might still require the services and support of the constituent agencies. All those working with the family should continue to exercise vigilance and may even want to continue meeting. It is not necessarily appropriate to close the case entirely just because the level of risk has diminished, although this often seems to happen. The keyworker should discuss with the parents and the child what services might still be appropriate, but they would now have to be provided on a voluntary basis. Agencies should be notified when a child is de-registered if they were represented at the original conference, and if further concerns arise, a re-referral should be made as required.

Since the Laming Inquiry there has been a significantly increased level of inspection of casework practice, including the examination of individual files, in order to ensure that children at risk are not being overlooked and that procedures have been followed correctly. This is likely to be even more significant in future as the new Safeguarding Children Boards are developed, and will also be a feature of Ofsted inspections of both local authorities and individual establishments. Representatives of all agencies, not just the social services, can therefore expect to receive some external scrutiny of their actions. LEAs and schools may find themselves having to account for their practice during an inspection of the social services department, and vice versa. Ultimately, such inspections will be fully multi-dimensional across all the professional services involved.

Serious case reviews (Part 8 reviews)

Additional procedures exist for those cases where there have been deaths or serious injuries, together with incidents that arouse major public or media concern, such as abuse within a care setting. These comprise a review of all agency involvement with the child and family concerned, including, for example, the parents of an injured child where they themselves have recently been in the education or care system. Following a particular tragedy or an example of poor practice, individual headteachers and governing bodies, as well as LEA officers, will need to be aware of the significance of this process if they have been in any way involved or have information to share.

School records must be secured immediately if a request by a senior officer is made in connection with such a review. A report on each case is sent to the DfES, and there will currently be a process within the ACPC for examining any conclusions or implications for future practice. A tragic example from my own experience concerned a change in school, education welfare and health procedures where a teenage girl was thought by school staff to be pregnant but was denying that she was, subsequently followed by the death of the child when she gave birth at home with no medical support.

Summary

These, then, are the general inter-agency procedures and the legal frameworks within which educational professionals are expected to operate in protecting children. Change in the future is inevitable, but it will still be essential for every children's agency to be confident of its own role within the process. In the light of this wider context, it is now time to turn to the guidance on the specific responsibilities of teachers, governors and LEAs, and to a range of related issues in ensuring that ours is a 'child-protecting school'.

Chapter 6

The child-protecting school

A summary of policy issues, inspection standards and the role of the designated teacher

Working Together to Safeguard Children

The work of LEAs and schools in child protection is governed by a collection of procedures and guidance documents, both local and national. Some are specifically aimed at educational professionals, such as DfES circulars and Ofsted expectations; some include guidance for schools within wider procedural advice, such as the inter-agency handbook for each local authority. The best way to approach this mass of information is from the general to the particular. Readers need to ensure that they have all the current documents to hand, as there may have been additions since the publication of this book. Again I have tried not simply to repeat them, but to analyse their implications.

This chapter begins with the parts of *Working Together* (DoH *et al.* 1999) that are addressed to the education services, alongside other agencies. This advice is not new, but, because it was made available primarily to LEAs rather than to individual schools, many headteachers and governors may not be aware of it. This document must form the background for any other, more local guidance, and the language will normally be reflected in ACPC procedures. In that important sense, the necessary actions for teachers are the same as they are for any person in any other professional capacity, but will need to reflect their particular context in addition.

> All those working in the education services can contribute to the safeguarding of children and child protection processes. All schools and colleges have a pastoral responsibility towards their pupils. They can play a part in the prevention of abuse and neglect, through their own policies and procedures for safeguarding children and through the curriculum. All schools and colleges should create and maintain a safe environment for children and young people, and should be able to manage situations where there are child welfare concerns. Children can be helped to understand what is and is not acceptable behaviour towards them, taught about staying safe from harm, and how to speak up if they have worries or concerns. The curriculum can also play a preventive role in developing awareness and resilience and in preparing

children and young people for their future responsibilities as adults, parents and citizens.

Through their day to day contact with pupils, and direct work with families, education staff have a crucial role to play in noticing indicators of possible abuse or neglect, and in referring concerns to the appropriate agency, normally the social services department. When a child has special educational needs, or is disabled, schools will have important information about the child's level of understanding and the most effective means of communicating with the child. They will also be well placed to give a view on the impact of treatment or intervention on the child's care or behaviour.

Staff working in the education service will on occasions be asked by a social services department for information on a child about whom there are concerns about abuse or neglect. The education service itself does not have direct investigative responsibility in child protection work, but schools and other maintained establishments have a role in assisting the social services department by referring concerns and providing information for s.47 child protection enquiries.

Where a child of school age is the subject of an inter-agency child protection plan, the school should be involved in the preparation of the plan. The school's role and responsibilities in contributing to actions to safeguard the child, and promote his or her welfare, should be clearly identified.

Throughout the education service:

- all staff should be alert to the signs of abuse and neglect, and know to whom they should report concerns or suspicions;
- all schools and colleges should have a designated member of staff with knowledge and skills in acting upon child protection concerns. He or she should act as a source of expertise and advice, and is responsible for co-ordinating action within the institution and liaising with other agencies;
- all schools and colleges should be aware of the child protection procedures established by the ACPC and, where appropriate, the Local Education Authority;
- all schools and colleges should have procedures for handling suspected cases of abuse, including procedures to be followed if a member of staff is accused of abuse;
- staff with designated responsibility for child protection should receive appropriate training;
- the school health service has a vital role to play in promoting and maintaining the health of school children and in safeguarding and promoting their welfare;
- school governors should exercise their child protection responsibilities, in particular in response to allegations against headteachers, and in ensuring that there are school child protection policies in place;

- in every LEA a senior officer should be responsible for co-ordinating action on child protection issues across the Authority;
- all schools should have an effective whole school policy against bullying and headteachers should have measures in place to prevent all forms of bullying among pupils;
- where a state school is concerned that a child may have 'disappeared' or about any aspect of a pupil's transfer which gives rise to concerns about a child's welfare, it should report its concerns to a person specified in ACPC guidance or to the LEA designated officer for child protection;
- corporal punishment is outlawed for all pupils in all schools and colleges, including independent schools;
- teachers at a school are allowed to use reasonable force to control or restrain pupils under certain circumstances. Other people may also do so, in the same way as teachers, provided they have been authorised by the headteacher to have control or charge of pupils. All schools should have a policy about the use of force to control or restrain pupils.

(Paragraphs 3.10–3.14)

(Note: The wider issues towards the end of this extract about staff are dealt with in Chapters 12–14.)

The Education Act 2002 and related guidance

As mentioned in Chapter 2, s.175 of the 2002 Act was a direct response to the case of Lauren Wright. The Act requires that governors and LEAs 'shall make arrangements for ensuring that their functions . . . are exercised with a view to safeguarding and promoting the welfare of children'. In the case of schools and FE colleges, this duty relates to all those under 18 who are registered there. (Despite their inclusion in Circular 10/95, Ofsted has been slow to recognise that FE colleges are covered by child protection requirements, not just schools and LEAs, and to include this issue specifically in the relevant inspection framework.) Not only must there be child protection policies, in line with local inter-agency arrangements, but they must also be published in order to meet the requirements of the Freedom of Information Acts. The LEA's duty is somewhat wider, including, for example, when it is exercising its functions in relation to children educated at home by their parents, and those who are excluded or not being educated at all, an important response to the Laming Report.

All these same requirements also apply to independent schools (specified in s.157 of the Act) through the Independent Schools (Standards) Regulations, applicable from 1 September 2003. There has always been some confusion over the extent to which LEAs have any right to be involved in child protection practice in the independent sector, but the schools themselves are expected to follow exactly the same standards and will be inspected accordingly. *Working Together* places the main responsibility with the ACPC and the SSD, if in partnership with the LEA. Practice varies across the country, with some LEAs being more proactive than others in offering training, etc., but the same expectations apply to each individual educational establishment, however it is managed and maintained. There is a sense in which the LEA is responsible for all the children in its area, but the individual schools' governing bodies are each responsible for ensuring their own compliance and are accountable for their practice only to the external inspectors.

The same obligations do not specifically apply to settings other than schools where children may be receiving all or part of their education, such as a vocational centre or other facility, though of course they still have a general duty of care. But foundation schools, church schools, specialist schools, city academies and Pupil Referral Units *are* all included. Other settings such as work experience and post-16 centres are now likely to find that they are expected to meet the same standards, at least for any children of compulsory school age, on a good-practice basis, as a condition of contractual arrangements between themselves and schools or LEAs.

S.175(4) requires all those concerned to 'have regard' to any guidance issued by the Secretary of State (see the DfES Circular due to be issued in June 2004). The new circular is not expected to be significantly different from its predecessor, Circular 10/95, but the emphasis is now more on ensuring effective outcomes for children rather than prescribing detailed procedures. Best practice since 1991 has always been much the same, in line with the previous edition of *Working Together*. As is noted by Blyth and Milner (1997) in their brief summary of the role of schools in child protection, the Education (School Teachers' Pay and Conditions of Employment) Order 1987 already included a requirement to promote the 'well-being' of children by co-operating and communicating with persons and bodies outside the school when necessary.

The Children Act 1989 spoke only of the duty of education authorities, not schools (another example of how government departments have tended not to communicate with one another). But its implications for schools were obvious at the time. These are not recent extras in the teacher's workload. The fact that the duty is now more sharply defined, and that at least the possibility has been raised of disciplinary action in response to negligence in carrying it out, should, however, act as a renewed incentive to ensure that everything that is now required has been done.

Ofsted guidance

The quality of a school's practice in child protection should be evaluated in the context of how well the school cares for its pupils overall (Inspection Judgement 6). The 'child-protecting school' will be doing much more than carrying out its functions under local child abuse procedures, and some of these wider issues are considered in Chapter 8. Previous Ofsted guidance offered a helpful set of key tests about child protection in particular, most of which are essentially practical and evidence based.

Inspectors must evaluate and report on the steps taken to ensure pupils' welfare, health and safety, including the school's arrangements for child protection. In determining their judgements, inspectors should consider the extent to which the school ensures the health, safety, care and protection of all pupils (and students).

The school's care of its pupils cannot be satisfactory if it does not take reasonable steps to ensure the care of individual pupils and minimise the possibility of significant harm.

You should check whether:

- staff are aware who the designated member of staff responsible is
- the school policy is in line with local procedures
- staff are aware of what to do if they suspect, or have disclosed to them, that an individual child may need protection
- the designated member of staff has detailed knowledge of local procedures
- staff know who the responsible LEA officer is
- staff have knowledge of the possible signs and symptoms of child abuse
- new staff are informed about what to do as part of their induction
- all staff receive in-service training to maintain and update their knowledge and understanding of procedures.

In recent years I have noticed a significant increase in the profile given to child protection in both inspections and reports. The inspectors may not be completely familiar with the issues themselves, though they should have had some training specifically for this area. Schools should be active and forthcoming in drawing their attention to any examples of best practice. At the very least, the inspectors should establish that there is a policy and that every member of staff knows what to do in accordance with local inter-agency arrangements. They may also simply ask a selection of staff who the designated teacher is. In one inspection reported to me, seven different names were given!

The role of the designated teacher

Designated teachers for child protection are not expected to be experts at everything, but they are expected to take responsibility for a range of important tasks. They are pivotal to the whole process. Everyone in the school community – teaching staff, non-teaching and peripatetic staff, parents and pupils – should know who to talk to if they have a concern. If there is more than one person in the role because the school is large, or there is a deputy for when the designated teacher is absent, that must also be clear to everyone. The designated teacher should be a senior member of the staff, with some opportunity to influence both practice and policy within the establishment, but need not necessarily be the headteacher, provided they are given the authority they need to carry out their role.

The task of the designated teacher can be summarised under five 'p's':

- practice;
- policy;
- procedures;
- professional development;
- partnership.

Practice

Designated teachers must make sure that individual cases where children are suffering or may be at risk of significant harm are dealt with appropriately by all staff (teaching and non-teaching) and that the school meets its legal requirements. In particular, this means:

- making sure that concerns are raised by staff when necessary;
- discussing those concerns as required with outside agencies;
- completing all necessary paperwork and correspondence, and maintaining appropriate records;
- ensuring that the school is represented at case conferences and core groups;
- ensuring that school staff act appropriately when a pupil is included on the child protection register;
- keeping the school's governing body, senior management team (SMT) and the LEA informed about child protection issues as requested;
- arranging the efficient transfer of information when a pupil changes school. (The best place for a child's *whole* child protection history is with the designated teacher in their current school. This can save a great deal of time if concerns arise later on.)

The designated teacher does not necessarily have to do all the casework themself, but must make sure that it is done by the appropriate person as required.

Policy

Although it is the governing body's responsibility to ensure that the school has a current child protection policy, and publishes it (see Appendix 1), the designated teacher should check that the governors are aware of its significance and monitor its implications for day-to-day practice. The policy should cover all the circumstances in which child protection issues may arise, including:

- casework and referral issues;
- the distinction between 'children in need' and 'children in need of protection' and the duties on staff arising in each case;
- the role of external agencies such as social services;
- the boundaries of prior consultation with parents by school staff;

- a statement about confidentiality;
- a recognition of child safety issues and the school's 'duty of care', including, for example, where children are off the school premises but under the school's supervision (e.g. trips or swimming);
- a restatement of the prohibition of corporal punishment;
- the school's use of control or restraint;
- procedures for dealing with allegations and complaints against staff;
- the recruitment and supervision of volunteers and helpers;
- the name of the designated teacher and designated LEA officer.

Policy may also include, or be linked to, wider policies such as those concerning behaviour, anti-bullying, health and safety, use of the Internet or social inclusion. Parents should be routinely informed of the existence of the school's child protection policy and what it means in practice, both on admission and subsequently. An actual copy should be made available if requested. It may also be helpful to include a summary of the school's responsibilities in the governors' annual report or on the school's website.

Procedures

Practice varies over whether the LEA will recommend 'in-house' procedures that would be appropriate for all the schools in its area, bearing in mind the wide range involved in terms of size, age group, staffing, etc. This issue must be clarified at the local level, and there may be agreed inter-agency arrangements that apply equally to schools and to everyone else. Whatever the appropriate systems, designated teachers should ensure that:

- Concerns from individual staff are written down and kept safely in a way that is confidential but accessible when required. This would normally be in some kind of 'incident book' or 'at risk' folder. (It is best not to describe this as a 'register', or it may cause confusion with inter-agency colleagues.)
- Written accounts of any incidents are available when making a referral, together with any past history.
- Staff are informed as appropriate of conferences, reviews, core group meetings and of children on the inter-agency child protection register.

Professional development

Designated teachers are responsible for both their own and their colleagues' professional development in this area, in partnership with their Professional Development Co-ordinator. The LEA may provide trainers or support training, through both its own and local ACPC programmes, but bearing in mind the number of school staff who may need to respond to a child protection concern, it is likely that much of this expectation for 'Level 1' training will be devolved to individual school level. Small schools might be best advised to try to co-ordinate such events, or they could be open to all staff in a pyramid or cluster. Designated teachers could, for example:

- provide a briefing for all staff at least annually to update them on the importance of child protection and the school's procedures;
- check that all newly appointed staff, teaching and non-teaching, are given information about the school's child protection policy and training in the local procedures as part of their induction;
- arrange for colleagues to attend more specialised training if required.

Partnership

One of the best sources of advice and information for the designated teacher is another designated teacher! This kind of work is always best done with the support of others, not in isolation. Designated teachers in a local area should plan to meet each other on a regular basis, to share experiences, plan policy and train together. It is always helpful if such opportunities can also provide a forum for getting to know colleagues from other agencies and developing local multi-professional partnerships. People tend to work together far better if they have actually met before. An hour spent here may save several more somewhere else.

Although the guidance says there must be 'a' designated 'teacher', in larger schools the tasks will need to be shared between a number of key pastoral staff. It might even not be a teacher who fulfils this role, but whoever does so must still be a senior member of staff with access to SMT. In smaller schools it might make sense to consider whether a shared approach across a cluster might make the role more meaningful. In the Lauren Wright case, for example, because there were so few staff, child protection was only one of the numerous designations that went with the job of the headteacher. Given the likely rarity with which action would be needed in such a setting, it might make more sense for one of the heads to take on the role for a group of local small schools, in return for similar support in a different area of expertise provided by someone else. This would enable them to give a reasonable amount of time to the tasks of child protection, inform the practice of a number of schools at once, and relieve headteachers of the mutual burden of having to carry so many responsibilities at the same time.

The role of governors

S.175 Education Act 2002 places the duty on governors and the LEA rather than on the headteacher. Again, the full implications of this have yet to be worked out in practice, but I assume it is meant to stress that professionals are accountable to their employers for their actions and that the governors must therefore take the ultimate responsibility in this as in other areas. This emphasis can in no way be interpreted as suggesting that the headteacher, SMT or teaching staff can distance themselves from the school's role in child protection. But the governing body is responsible for ensuring that the necessary policies and procedures are in place for the staff to follow, and would carry corporate responsibility for any failings. Including governors in the line of accountability makes failure to act appropriately in accordance with those procedures rather more than just a matter of bad practice.

I have some misgivings about any suggestion that governors should be more involved than this, beyond the personnel, management and policy issues. A designated person may be helpful, though it could just be the chair *de facto*, but governors should not take an active role in any casework relating to the pupils, other than that involving any complaint against the headteacher. Many governors are parents too, and confidentiality could easily be compromised. It is helpful if governors, or a least a sub-committee, receive regular reports about the work the staff have been doing in child protection, without identifying individual children, so that they can maintain an informed awareness about whether or not these various requirements are being met. An Ofsted inspection should check whether this happens in order to ensure effective governance. Not being able to demonstrate that the governors know what is going on can be classed as a 'serious weakness'. Where the designated teacher is not the headteacher, they may want to meet with the headteacher directly on occasion.

The role of the LEA

As is mentioned in *Working Together*, every LEA must have a designated officer at a senior level with oversight of all the schools maintained by the authority. This officer will have a key role where child abuse allegations against staff are concerned, both school staff and those in any other position within the local education service that brings them into contact with children, such as outdoor education centres, youth workers, music services, etc. Their advice should always be sought in response to any complaint of alleged abuse made to a headteacher, chair of governors or education manager (see Chapters 12–14). In larger authorities there may be a need for more than one person.

Education welfare officers and education social workers may also have a role in their own right under local procedures, or be involved in training and policy formation, but often cannot provide detailed knowledge about children's needs, knowledge that is unique to those who work most directly with them. In most cases that will now be school staff, even if assisted by Education Welfare Officers (EWOs) and others on occasion. The LEA's role is likely to be increasingly strategic and, in particular, may involve more representational and developmental functions, building links with other agencies, writing procedures, etc., rather than direct involvement with individual children.

The status of the LEA in the management of child protection has sometimes been unclear, as the title of a recent report indicated, namely Baginsky's *Responsibility without Power?* (2003). LEAs should give schools a lead in how they must exercise their duties in such a complex area, building on examples of good practice and sharing the wider perspective that specialist staff will have. The new DfES guidance gives them a stronger role in monitoring and ensuring compliance than before. But officers with responsibility for child protection do not actually run the schools they represent, or manage their staff. Baginsky's research, following up a previous survey a few years earlier, drew attention to the changed nature of the relationship between schools and the authorities that maintain them, but it could be argued that this distance is not reflected adequately in *Working Together*, the Children Act or even 'Every Child Matters' (Chief Minister to the Treasury 2003).

The level of child protection support to schools has risen dramatically since the mid-1990s, and schools generally greatly welcome such advice. The Ofsted contribution to *Safeguarding Children* (DoH *et al.* 2002) concluded exactly the same. Overwhelmingly, LEAs were providing the information that staff would need, in documents, websites, casework advice and training programmes, but they were not always in possession of effective measures of the *outcomes* of such resources. Mechanisms did not always exist for recording access to training or which schools had adopted a policy and when they last reviewed it. But even where such arrangements were in place, LEA officers were not always confident that all schools chose to pass the information on when requested to do so.

There was, for example, some feeling that training tended to be accessed most by the schools that had a greater understanding of their role and that were already more experienced in child protection casework. The schools that most needed to send someone for training in order to update their knowledge, or where the designated teacher had recently changed, sometimes chose not to do so. LEA officers rarely felt that they had the right to insist, given the emphasis on local determination of budgetary priorities. The removal of additional funding that previously enabled training to be provided free of charge to schools was also a major concern that not all LEAs had been able to address.

Similarly, in many schools, some LEA officers were also juggling their child protection responsibilities with several other duties, rather than having the time to be as involved in school practice as they would wish. Some felt that such diffi- culties might seriously undermine the very good intentions of the new legislation and were concerned about who would be held accountable in the event of bad practice. Who exactly would be responsible if there was a major failing in the school's procedure or if there was no policy or designated teacher, despite the LEA's advice that there should be?

There is clearly a new focus at governmental level on local multi-agency joined- up services for children in which schools are central. LEAs will be expected to make sure it happens and inspected to that standard (Inspection Judgement 5.5). But what can an LEA (or even a Children's Trust or a Safeguarding Children's Board) do if the governors and headteacher of a given self-managed school choose not to follow the advice they are given? Many maintained schools no longer see being part of a local authority structure as a crucial part of their identity. Is child protection seen as a way for local councils to increase their influence again? Some headteachers seem to fear so and may react accordingly. But can it all be left to individual discretion? Clearly not, as universal legal duties are involved. These are all crucial, and so far unresolved, questions that will need to be addressed with the benefit of experience and any relevant case law now that the new section of the 2002 Act is in force and once the government's plans for the future are clearer.

The DfES has recently enhanced the status of the child protection information that is available to schools via www.teachernet.gov.uk/management/childprotection. This provides a forum for sharing experience, including the work of the network of Investigation and Referral Support Co-ordinators and the support provided by individual LEAs. Copies of national circulars and guidance should also be obtainable via this route. However, many LEAs already operate electronic systems for providing information about procedures, and schools will usually find it more useful to ensure that they have also accessed all the local sources of advice that are available, especially that provided by the ACPC. National educational documents always need to be supplemented by local multi-agency arrangements.

It may be difficult for some heads, colleagues and governors to accept that their school or college needs a child protection policy, or they may not wish to make its existence very obvious. They may fear that it sends a signal to parents or to the community that the school admits 'problem' families, or there may be some fear of reprisal or embarrassment where individual parents object to the actions that staff may be required to take. But the policy provides an essential safety net for all concerned, and staff are entitled to feel they have the backing of their managers in carrying out their duties. Managers must be helped to resist any such negative pressure and try to make it clear that evidence of the school's awareness of its role in child protection is a sign of both a good and a caring school. No one knows in advance which children are at risk, and all children are entitled to attend establishments that are alert to these issues. It is as much a right as education itself.

Chapter 7

From theory to practice

Referring concerns and making the system work for our pupils

Professional competence

All the information in the previous chapter – legislation, guidance and inspection standards – is vital and must be familiar territory for any school seeking to take its child protection duty seriously. There is enormous danger in school staff rushing into action without sufficient thought about the limits to their role, or believing that they alone can resolve the problems of a child alleging abuse. We must always act within the guidance, so we must know what it says. My first advice to a designated teacher who is unsure how to proceed is sometimes to tell them to do nothing – for five minutes – and *then* to read the procedures and decide what they have to do, having distanced themselves slightly from the situation and thought calmly about it first.

Prior preparation and some formal training will certainly be required. I have been heavily involved in both devising and delivering training for teachers in recent years. But simply finding the time is a major challenge. Who will cover the class while the designated teacher is away on a two-day course? Is 4.00 really the best time of day to start thinking about issues that are both complicated and personally demanding? Can child protection wait twelve months until we have a free slot in our INSET days? Shouldn't all training involve those from other agencies as well, not just other teachers? I have yet to find the best solution to all these genuine difficulties. Most of the time it's about making the most of whatever is available.

But training, guidance, even legislation, are still not enough. Most of the skills required for child protection cannot be explained in a book; even a procedural manual is only of much use when actually followed. There is no substitute for real casework, provided it does not merely reinforce bad habits! The key word is 'competence'. Professionals are expected to know how to do their job and then to do it as required. This section of the book is only a partial substitute for proper training and, ideally, should be complemented by it. My comments reflect what I have seen for myself, and what teachers and others have said to me during the hundreds of presentations I have made during the past fourteen years. It is not intended as a replacement for actually attending such events if you can possibly do so.

Identifying abuse

Identifying abuse is probably the area that causes most concern – square one! This is natural enough. The price of getting it wrong may seem frighteningly high, and there can be no certainty that we will always get it right. I do not always know whether a child is being abused from the information that I have available. I find that teachers are immediately reassured by this admission. Individuals sometimes imagine that they are the only ones who find this difficult, but even specialist social workers do not rely on their own judgement alone. It may take some time for a general concern to become specific enough to require an immediate response. When faced with a child who *may* have been abused – and it is often not much more than that – what realistic criteria can be applied that will at least ensure a reasonable level of confidence in the decision that must be made?

As in Chapter 3, I have avoided reproducing here a detailed checklist of signs and symptoms. These may be available in local procedures in order to give some common understanding of significant harm, but there is always a danger with lists. A child might score very highly on the various elements without there being any real evidence that abuse is the issue, and professionals might then be persuaded into responding inappropriately. Indicators can never prove abuse, and may be given too much status because we are all busy looking for certainty in order to reassure ourselves that we are doing the right thing. I prefer to recommend that we rely more on a combination of three things:

- experience;
- evidence;
- empathy.

As with all the available documents detailed elsewhere in the book, all these must be held together; none is sufficient on its own. They depend on *the* most important thing in child protection, reiterated by Laming: a quality relationship between the child and a trusted adult – someone in the child's life who will put them first when required. There is no chance of a child feeling confident enough to disclose, or of anyone feeling able to act on a concern, if the two people involved are strangers to one another. Other people unknown to the child may be important later, to bring a dispassionate approach to the investigation. But at the beginning, referrals grow out of relationships, not out of an indifferent judgement that certain criteria have been met so it must be child abuse.

It's about an encounter between two individuals, both of whom have something to gain and something to lose by giving a name to what might be going on. Sadly, children sometimes do not see their teachers in these terms, and, if they are to trust anyone, may be more likely to turn to some other adult within the school community or outside, especially as they get older. But school is where the help starts for many, and this must be good news, not a burden we would rather have avoided. Otherwise, the child will soon spot our ambiguity and decide to keep quiet after all.

Not, of course, that there is no element of objectivity; there must be. I am always rather worried by the teacher who says they want to pick the child up and take them home, understandable though such emotions might be in the heat of the moment. But recognising children who are at risk, who are being abused at present or who have been abused in the past is not about how sorry we feel for them or how much they may invoke our compassion. Some desperately abused children will neither thank nor value us for what we have to do; but we still have to do it.

Set against this context, our experience, both of this particular child and family, and of the child protection process, will enable us to be sensitive to those who may need us to act on their behalf. Of course, there is also the element of evidence, and being absolutely clear about what we have seen, heard, etc. that has prompted our concern. But the empathy is paramount at this stage; the ability of the teacher to enter into the child's experience and to feel what they are feeling. This is not the same as 'sympathy'. It's about being there with them, 'walking in their moccasins'. My principal advice to a teacher who is not sure whether a child is being abused – and we rarely are – is to get to know them better. Maybe the bruises or the story will make more sense then. The classic signs can be learned; the empathy has to be part of us.

Sadly, the signs of abuse are sometimes misinterpreted, and not primarily in the sense that physical injuries are too easily accepted as accidental. If anything, the reverse may be true, so anxious are we not to miss anything. I was once asked for advice about a 7-year-old boy with straight bruises across the back of his calves. It looked for all the world as if he'd been hit with a stick, and he wouldn't say how they had occurred. It had to be referred, and the investigation easily uncovered the truth. He'd been riding his big sister's bike, which he wasn't allowed to do, and the pedals had swung round and hit him! The teacher felt they had made a mistake, but they acted entirely correctly. That is good child protection practice: acting on concerns and making sure that all the facts are uncovered by those whose job it is to do it.

What worries me more is that a child's behaviour in response to abuse may be misunderstood as only a disciplinary issue, as attention-seeking or as 'typical of that family'. The child displaying inappropriate sexual behaviour that an adult has taught him is acceptable when they are alone together is perceived as a threat, not as the victim of the threats of another. Abused children may misbehave and not show the respect and obedience towards adults that we would wish. Why should they, bearing in mind what other adults have done to them? This is where empathy should come to our rescue. We do not have to *like* the children we work with; but we have a duty to protect them. We need the skill to see the bad behaviour as a symptom of the problem, not as the problem itself. Not, of course, that all children who misbehave are abused or that all abused children misbehave. But empathy will help us to act as required, even when our other instincts tell us something else.

Consultation

If you are presented with possible abuse as outlined in Chapter 3, but unsure whether you have the basis of a referral, talk about the evidence with someone else, within the context of appropriate confidentiality. There should be advice available for any teacher within their school, and, if necessary, from the LEA. Another designated teacher in another school may be available and it should be possible to ring the local social services, even if you are unclear about whether it is definitely a child protection issue. Part of any sensible consultation procedure is to be sure that referrals cannot be dealt with more appropriately as 'children in need'. But do not try to make such a decision alone.

If the query relates to a particular situation, it will usually be necessary to identify both yourself and the child to the duty officer in social services. The response to your concern might be very different if this is the third enquiry this week about the same family, each raised by different professionals, rather than a child and family who are previously unknown. If the query is of a more general procedural nature, it may be possible for the social worker to assist in clarifying what needs to be done, before you have to make a specific decision on this individual case. When in doubt, ask someone else; share the concern. This sounds obvious, but it often doesn't happen. Just making a note in your diary, or going home and not sleeping, will not help the child (or you the teacher).

Teachers are often worried that by raising their concern with someone else they will start some unstoppable machine that will ultimately result in the police turning up outside the child's front door with blue flashing lights and smashing it down at break of dawn! This will not happen. Probably, if anything needs to be done at all, the parent will receive a low-key visit and will then invite the social worker in for a chat and a cup of tea. They may even be glad that someone else has taken the responsibility for doing something about what they knew was going on but were afraid to do anything about themselves. We tend to assume a hostility that does not always exist.

It is never a good idea to sit on the bit of information you have, for fear of doing the wrong thing just by doing something. There may be other pieces of the jigsaw, entirely unknown to you, and which only other people can put together. Someone has to start the chain. Above all, resist the temptation to leave talking to anyone else until Friday afternoon and doing so then, just so you can clear the desk before you go home! That just puts everyone else under impossible pressure, and it will probably be too late to do anything constructive with your information anyway.

On a more structural level, the schools that are best at recognising and responding to abused and at-risk children also have effective pastoral systems, open and affirming contacts with parents, well-trained and motivated staff, clear and purposeful policies, etc. Child protection has to be part of a package, reinforced by the general climate that prevails in dealing with similar issues. All schools claim to be caring communities, especially in their mission statements pinned up in the reception area. But ideals needs clear evidence that they are actually true, and for *all* children. An absence of an agreed procedure for dealing with your concerns will make it much more difficult for the individual teacher to act as and when required.

Such schools have staff with time for one another when something needs discussing; children who are encouraged to be sensitive to the needs of other children and who know who to talk to; and space within the life of the school for promoting personal development by addressing the varied and individual challenges that the children pose. The whole ethos is child centred *and* supportive of the staff in making it happen. Some schools show this by setting counselling time aside for their staff; some have systems of peer support and mentoring; some use specialists or volunteers. As we have seen, when we act in child protection, we act as our agency's representative. Our agencies must therefore give us the help we need to do it.

Listening to children

Much of the time, our first source of information about possible abuse will come from the child, as well as from our own observations. Even quite young children may feel sufficiently confident in their relationship with a teacher, classroom assistant or playground supervisor to say something to them. Older children may be either more articulate or even less willing to put what they want to say into words! Embarrassment is likely to be a greater obstacle for the teenager than for the 6-year-old. Children with special needs, including those with linguistic and sensory disabilities, may require particular skills from staff who are able to pick up on non-verbal cues.

Opportunities for children to speak to you; room within the day for sharing; doors that are open when someone is there to listen – all these will help the child who is wondering whether you are the right person and this is the right time for them to talk about what has been on their mind for weeks. Dealing effectively with the little problems that children bring will make it much more likely that they will then trust you with a bigger one. They may even be testing you out. If we cannot find the time for something trivial, then they may assume that we will be far too busy to deal with something more significant and decide to keep it to themselves (as they may have already been told to do).

> ### Training idea 3: Listening to children (individual/group)
>
> TASK: Read the following handout and then discuss it together:
>
> 1. How would I feel talking to a child about issues like these?

2. What do I need to be aware of or change about my own behaviour?
3. What procedures are in place for me to follow?

Child abuse concerns relate to one or more of the following:

- physical abuse;
- emotional abuse;
- sexual abuse;
- neglect.

Many school staff are concerned about how to speak and listen appropriately to children who may have a need for child protection services. This is understandable, and it is very important to get such conversations right. Incorrect action may contaminate the child's evidence or lead to accusations of 'coaching'. It is essential that staff are aware of the distinction between:

- making 'friendly enquiries' in order to gain sufficient information to make a decision about what to do next; and
- interviewing the child about the alleged abuse (which is not the school's responsibility).

Children should never be undressed, examined, photographed or have detailed drawings made of their injuries. It is appropriate to record what is seen in the course of normal activity (including whenever a child is undressing themselves) and to ask only open questions. If the answer is a clear allegation of abuse, there is no need for any further questioning. Contact the designated teacher immediately, who will decide whether consultation and/or referral to the social services is now appropriate.

All such initial enquiries should be recorded in writing, even if the decision is made not to consult or refer at this point. Do not keep concerns to yourself or act alone. Always consult others in confidence.

If the child makes a clear disclosure, and the parents do not know they have done so, do not contact parents until you have taken advice from the social services or the police. It may be appropriate, but not if it will put the child at increased risk or compromise a criminal inquiry.

Do not ask 'leading questions' ('Was it your father who hit you?') or put ideas into the child's mind ('Did he use a belt?'); it must be the child's own story. Do not seek any more clarification than is absolutely necessary at this stage. You are not deciding whether the child has been abused and, if so, who by. That is the job of the investigating agencies.

continued

- Listen more than you talk.
- Act on the information you receive, but do not act alone.
- Record what you have seen, heard and done according to your school's internal procedures. Use the child's own words wherever possible (including any words used for sexual activity or private parts).
- Watch your body language. A child may be checking to see whether you are the right person to talk to. Sit at the same height as the child, and not behind a barrier such as a desk. Give encouraging signs that you are listening, not shocked, and that you know what to do.

At the point of disclosure or when our own concerns are raised, the alarm bells should start ringing in our heads. If the child has said something or asked for help, think about *why* they have disclosed and try to understand their perspective on what they want you to do. What is different because this is a child protection issue as opposed to all the other things that they may want to share? The child will probably not appreciate the crucial distinction, but the teacher must. Of course we want the child to talk to us; but we do not want to interrogate them, nor put at risk the potential investigation and even criminal prosecution that may lie ahead. At the beginning we do not know where it will all lead, so every situation has to be treated as an example of the best possible practice.

The usual advice is about boundaries. If you are trying to find out who abused the child, when, where, how and what 'really' happened, etc., then you have gone too far. As has already been said, teachers are not responsible for carrying out investigations, and the fewer times the child has to repeat their story, the better. The details must come later. The teacher's task is to obtain sufficient information to make a decision about where to go next. It may be obvious: 'My mummy's boyfriend has got a big snake that spits at me when I'm in bed. It always happens when she's out and I'm not allowed to tell her about it.' There is no need for any more discussion with the child; just comfort and care until the next stage of the process. It may be less clear: 'I don't like my mummy's boyfriend. He makes me do things I don't want to do.' Like tidying her bedroom or brushing her teeth – or not, as the case may be.

Common sense is a valuable ally, but not to be trusted entirely. Do not ask the child to change what they have said unless you do not understand and need them to put it another way. Never suggest that what they are saying could not possibly be true and that they must be making it up. The primary aim of this kind of encounter is to give the child space, not the teacher. It is best not to interrupt, nor to seek too much detail unless it is absolutely necessary in order to decide what to do. The adult should say as little as possible. It must be the *child's* story with no grounds for anyone to claim later that the child was led into saying what someone else wanted them to say. All you are doing is gathering what you need to know: listening and then responding to what you hear.

Writing things down

In very exceptional circumstances, the person who first hears the child's story may be asked, perhaps up to a year later, to give evidence in a civil or criminal court about what was seen or heard at the time. A defence barrister may try to find inconsistencies or accuse the teacher of deliberately misunderstanding what the child said. Or a child may be seriously injured and, as a result of the investigation, the child maintains that they did tell a teacher weeks before about a similar incident, but that nothing was done about it. Or a child dies and the LEA is asked to produce a report about all past involvement by the school and whether there were any previous concerns. The teachers involved cannot quite remember; the designated teacher has retired; the child has changed schools in the meantime. Endless variations are possible.

All these situations can be handled professionally only by the keeping of adequate written records. Again, as we can never know which cases may end up in this way, records need to be kept as a matter of routine. This is also essential if you decide not to make a referral at this time, which is a perfectly acceptable response if the circumstances do not warrant it. But the 'argument from silence' is never a strong one. The absence of records will rarely be sufficient to prove that action was not required. It is essential to record the fact that a concern was raised, a discussion held, advice sought and a decision made that no further action was required. I have come across staff in several schools who, when faced with a sudden crisis, fell into a complete muddle about what had gone on before or, worse still, contradicted each other and the child about what had happened previously. Sometimes a teacher feels that recording a decision to do nothing might be used against them in future, but *not* recording the decision to do nothing contains far greater potential for criticism in the long run.

The mechanics of record systems are for individual schools to determine according to their own internal procedures. But it is wise to have a process that involves asking a colleague to witness that what you have written is contemporaneous – that is, written at the time – and accurate. This record should then be signed and dated, and a copy kept by the designated teacher for future reference. Scribbled notes on backs of envelopes are not an acceptable alternative! Obviously, any record system must be confidential. If anyone else discussed the child with you, ask them to keep a record too if possible.

This will then enable a decision to be made about whether referral is needed without having to retrieve details from people's memories later, *and* provide a record of the actions taken in accordance with procedures. Someone should be in a position to spot trends if, for example, a child has given three different teachers grounds for concern in the past ten days, even though none of them has spoken to the others. Make brief notes of any meetings, telephone calls or related information. Part of the job of the designated teacher is not just to receive the reports and then file them away, but to determine any action that arises as a result of them, so they must be provided with everything that they will need in deciding what to do next.

Making a referral

It does not necessarily have to be the designated teacher who makes all the referrals. If this post is held by the headteacher by default (often not an ideal arrangement), they might not always be available when required, and someone else who has had direct contact with the child would have to do it. Whoever is making the referral, they must be clear which category, as defined by *Working Together*, is the basis of the concern. Even if we are not sure there has been abuse, we must be clear that we are talking about something which, if true, would amount to physical abuse, emotional abuse, sexual abuse or neglect, or the real risk of them, not some other kind of issue.

Referrals, usually made over the telephone to a duty officer in the social services and then confirmed in writing according to local procedures, will need to contain certain basic information:

- the child's full name (and any previous names or aliases), date of birth, address, ethnic and religious group;
- details of any other members of the family, as known, and anyone else who lives with them (this is one key reason why data collection systems need to be kept up to date);
- details of all those with parental responsibility for the child, including any such person known to the school but living at a different address (see Appendix 2);
- name and telephone number of the relevant GP and any related health information;
- details of any other professionals currently involved with the child and family;
- whether there are any current or past court orders that relate to the child (including section 8 orders [see the Glossary] under the Children Act 1989);
- details of any previous child protection history;
- where the child is at present (if relevant);
- where the parents are at present (if known);
- exactly what the concern is and on what it is based;
- how the referrer can be contacted; and
- any other information as requested by the agency receiving the referral.

Referrals need to be made at the right time; not too early, when there is no real basis for the concern, and not too late, when the information has already been known for some time. This also applies to the time of day or day of the week. Particularly with younger children or with more urgent referrals, the earlier in the day the referral can be made, the more time other agencies then have to make a response either while the child is safe at school or before there is a risk of having to extend their day unreasonably with late interviews or hospital appointments. Telling someone after the child has left the premises, or just as the office is closing for the weekend, is particularly unhelpful and should always be avoided if it is possible to do so. This is one reason why it is vital not to wait for the designated teacher if they are away from the school and action is required in their absence.

Local procedures usually include some acknowledgement of the referral and written advice as to its eventual outcome. If this is not forthcoming, raise the matter with the relevant social worker or their manager. It may be some time before a response is made; not all referrals need immediate attention. If the child appears to be at risk when visiting their grandparents, for example, and they are not going for another month, the necessary investigation may wait while more urgent matters are dealt with first. Allocating priorities is part of the job of the social services, not the person making the referral, painful though this sometimes is. But it is always helpful if the referrer is aware of the likely time when a visit will be made or when the parent will be advised of the concern if they are not already aware of it. This should always be discussed at the time, not left unclear.

Parental consent, sharing of information and confidentiality

The government has indicated that it intends to review the legal basis for sharing information as part of its response to the Laming Inquiry, and there are a number of related and complex issues here. Professionals and agencies cannot work together if they must each keep the information they have to themselves. But it is always best practice in pastoral work to liaise as closely as possible with parents about their children, not simply to take over from them. The Cleveland principle still applies. Normally it is not appropriate to discuss the needs of a family with someone else outside the school, without their prior knowledge and consent.

School staff have not always been very careful about ensuring appropriate agreement by parents, rather than just assuming that the staff may discuss the pupils' needs with others, as and when they feel it is necessary. Most other agencies will now insist on it. But in child protection the emphasis is on the *child* and their needs, not on the parents' rights, even if it is sometimes a difficult balancing act in practice. Social workers will usually ask whether the parent has agreed to the referral or is aware of it, but the fact that they do not know about it is *not* grounds for refusing to respond as requested if the child is at risk. It will usually be preferable to proceed with parents' consent, but it is not a requirement.

Some situations are clearly inappropriate for prior discussion with the parent for fear of contaminating the subsequent enquiry. If a criminal offence may be involved, be extremely cautious. For example, I am aware of a case, referred by a school, where the child had talked about a video that clearly contained explicit sexual material. This seemed to be more than just exposure to an adult film, that might be the subject of a pastoral conversation with a parent under other circumstances, as the child appeared frightened and distressed by whatever they had seen. On further investigation it transpired that boys were being brought to the house and abused while being filmed. This child, while not directly a victim, was nonetheless aware of what was going on. Any advance warning to the parent would have resulted in the immediate disappearance of the evidence and a possible threat to the child.

But in other situations one parent may have asked the school to pass on information on their behalf, perhaps about a violent partner. Some referrals arise out of other casework, and it is reasonable to tell the parent before you make the referral that the concerns are now such that contact must be made with an external agency in accordance with the school's published policy. However, if the concerns relate to child protection rather than to children in need, there should be no reason why a referral cannot be accepted even if parents do not know about it. If your professional judgement is that disclosure to parents will increase the likelihood of harm to the child, or a criminal investigation may be compromised, then do not tell parents until you have clarified the position with the social worker first. If there is still a dispute, I would always advise the school to send the referral anyway, provided it is for an appropriate reason. This does not infringe anyone's human rights.

The government booklet of advice given to all practitioners in 2003 provides a useful synopsis, effectively saying that while concerns about infringements of parental rights are reasonable, they should never stand in the way of acting on a genuine concern in the greater interests of the child:

> You may be anxious about the legal or ethical restrictions on sharing information, particularly with other agencies. You should be aware of the law and should comply with the code of conduct or other guidance applicable to your profession. These rarely provide an absolute barrier to disclosure. You should be prepared to exercise your judgement. A failure to pass on information that might prevent a tragedy could expose you to criticism in the same way as an unjustified disclosure.
>
> The key factor in deciding whether or not to disclose confidential information is **proportionality**: is the proposed disclosure a proportionate response to the need to protect the welfare of the child? The amount of confidential information disclosed, and the number of people to whom it is disclosed, should be no more than is strictly necessary to meet the public interest in protecting the health and well-being of a child. The more sensitive the information is, the greater the child-focused need must be to justify disclosure and the greater the need to ensure that only those professionals who have to be informed, receive the material.
>
> (DoH *et al.* 2003, summary, pp.15, 19)

It is best to make it clear in both the school's child protection and data protection policies that information may be passed on to other professionals without parents' consent, but *only* in the specific circumstances that the policy covers. This will include providing information in connection with referrals that have arisen elsewhere but which involve pupils at the school, as part of the lateral checks. One reason why a school collects data is so that staff can use those data if required – if, for example, a child is unwell or in an emergency. It is to enable us to carry out our duty of care. Although they will rarely think of it in this way, by enrolling their child at your school, parents have already agreed that you may take any action that you consider necessary in order to safeguard and promote their welfare – even, if necessary, to protect them from those same parents.

As has already been noted, there may be a need to discuss concerns with other colleagues, and this must be done responsibly. Schools are often large communities where controlling the flow of information can quickly get out of hand or, conversely, small communities in which everyone knows everyone else. Either way it is often difficult to keep things secret. This must not be left to chance and needs to be consciously managed. Gossip is clearly unacceptable in such a context, but there are number of less obvious issues that require a little more elaboration:

1. *What if the child doesn't want me to tell anyone else what they have just told me?* This will depend on a number of factors: the age of the child, what they are telling you, etc., but in general there can be no assurance given of absolute confidentiality. You cannot promise not to tell anyone else before you know what the child is thinking of telling you. If they then make a disclosure about abuse, you have a duty to pass it on. You can promise not to tell anyone without the child knowing who you have told, or not to pass the information straight to their parents. But you cannot promise to keep it to yourself. Hopefully, the child can be reassured about whatever it is that is causing them to be concerned and that you will stay with them and support them. This is another point at which our personal and professional feelings may have to be distinguished.

Difficulty might again arise with older children who are considered of 'sufficient age and understanding', according to the Frazer guidelines, to have some control over the outcome of the process. Their co-operation will, as we have seen, be essential for any action to be taken. It may be possible to negotiate some agreement about who is going to be told what that recognises the child's legitimate misgivings. This should at least ensure they continue to work with those who are available to help them. But the stakes may seem very high to a child. They may well get cold feet at the last minute. It may be necessary to tell them that you have listened very carefully to what they have said, and that they will be able to exercise some influence over what will happen next, but you still have to pass the information on to those whose job it is to protect them, even if they do not want you to. You cannot protect them yourself.

Children might be willing to talk about the reasons for their uncertainty and to see, for example, that taking no action may mean that other children are put at risk, perhaps a younger sibling. Would they really want to feel in any way responsible for something terrible happening in future because no one was able to do anything about it this time? It may seem a little harsh, but if they are old enough to want some influence, they must also be old enough to think through the implications of what they are asking you to do. Always keep a confidential written record of any conversation of this kind, even if no action results.

2. *What about teenage sexual activity?* It is essential to distinguish child protection concerns from what might be considered conventional sexual activity that is within the young person's legitimate power to give consent. I would argue that *any* evidence of sexual activity involving anyone younger than 13 should always be considered a child protection issue in the first instance. Not only is this below the age when reasonably informed consent could normally be given, but it also means that additional offences may have taken place, which may not be the case for a child aged between 13 and 16. While there may be rare examples where such behaviour would be seen as non-abusive, this is much less likely to be the case than with older young people.

Surveys suggest that increasing numbers of young people under 16 have engaged in some kind of sexual behaviour with those of roughly the same age, most of which will not be abuse within the *Working Together* definitions, even if parents and teachers do not approve of it. This kind of activity should probably be kept confidential if a teacher becomes aware of it, though some schools may have a policy, approved by the governors, that requires staff to disclose any such concerns to parents. If this is the case, be careful also to consider any child protection implications that may arise once the parents have been informed. If they are likely to react with violence or neglect of the child's needs, or if the pupil is fearful of the consequences, further action may be needed to safeguard their interests, especially if they are thought to be pregnant.

Information relating to sexual *abuse*, as opposed to sexual activity, should, however, always be passed on to the appropriate agency. Again the consent of the young person will be an issue in determining what can be done about it, but even if they are being uncooperative, they should not be criticised. There may be many hidden reasons why what looks like their willing consent to the activity is actually something else. For example:

- actual or possible sexual relationships with family members or anyone else in a position of power (even if the child is aged over 16), or which are exploiting the young person's immaturity;
- where the age difference effectively results in an adult having sex with a child and is manifestly outside the range of conventional teenage behaviour;
- situations that may involve coercion, exploitation or threats, even if they are described as 'boyfriend–girlfriend';

- any sexual relationship that appears to have a basis in financial or other reward;
- where the young person has special educational needs or is at particular risk of exploitation because of their vulnerability, such as a breakdown in their family situation.

This whole area is one for seeking advice and operating as far as possible by locally agreed inter-agency protocols.

3. *What about access to records?* Under normal circumstances, parents (and pupils who can demonstrate a responsible understanding) have the right to inspect any records held by the school, not just their educational/attainment records, and to control the use that is made of them. But the regulations specifically exempt information about child protection from having to be disclosed to parents in this way. Any such material could legitimately be removed from a child's file before it was handed over. There is no obligation to produce the records on demand (see DfEE Circular 0015/2000, *Pupil Records and Reports*). This is not always the end of the matter, and parents may still wish to dispute what teachers have written about them or their child in curriculum or educational records, multi-agency minutes and reports, or argue that information that has been collected is incorrect. Clearly, they have a right to do this, so great care must be taken to ensure the accuracy of all material that is kept in this way. However, the school is entitled to keep its own internal communications confidential if kept solely for use by the staff.

Attending a child protection conference

As has been outlined already, child protection conferences, both initial and review, can be an essential part of planning the response following an allegation of abuse. For any school-aged child, teachers and other educational professionals are central to the implementation of a child protection plan. The DfES guidance draws particular attention to conferences and the need for designated teachers and others to be clear about the contribution they can make to them. (It is also important to make a similar contribution to any assessment or plan agreed with parents on a voluntary basis as an alternative to formal registration.)

There are real tensions here: pressures on staff time, cost implications, training, etc., as well as some conflict between the ways different agencies operate, which can sometimes result in a feeling that 'we' always have to fit in with what 'they' expect us to do and that it never works the other way around! Other people at such conferences often seem to attend them so frequently, and to know each other so well, that a teacher for whom this is not a normal part of their job may feel disempowered and de-skilled. But although you may not always feel you have a major contribution to make, each child's school should be represented if at all possible.

Each participating agency is responsible for:

- Preparing and presenting their own contribution to understanding the child's needs, including any direct evidence about any incidents, as far as possible in writing. (A report should be sent if the person concerned is unable to attend.)
- Being clear about what contribution their own agency can offer to the child's future protection. (This may include direct commitments about what the school will do and assistance in seeking additional services from LEA colleagues as required.)
- Contributing to the assessment of risk, both actual and potential.
- Contributing to the decision about whether the child should be placed on the child protection register. This is expected of every participant, even those whose direct involvement has been limited, in the light of what they have heard at the conference.

Reports submitted to a conference must be based on objective facts, not expressions of personal opinion. Professional judgements are appropriate, based on experience of similar situations or similar children in the past, but they should be rooted in fact. Reports should give a rounded picture and comment on strengths as well as weaknesses. Parents will normally see what you have written, so you must be prepared to defend it if needed. For example:

> In my professional opinion, while these parents obviously care deeply about their child, his educational and social development have been seriously delayed by both his poor school attendance (64% this year) and the parents' repeated failure to ensure that the speech and language exercises were actually carried out as agreed at the meeting on 3 May last year. This is evidenced by [test results, changes in performance and behaviour, etc.]. He has also missed three appointments at school with a speech therapist although we sent a reminder to his home each time.

As opposed to: 'These parents have completely failed to work with the school and are generally uncooperative'!

It is best if the person attending the conference is personally knowledgeable about the child. This usually means the class teacher or the headteacher in primary schools and the tutor or year head in secondary schools. It does not have to be the designated teacher every time; indeed, it is usually better if the expertise is not confined to one person. It must be clearly understood by whoever is attending that this is only the beginning of a process and that further action may be required of them on behalf of their agency. Anyone attending should feel that they have been given the authority to make such commitments as are reasonable and the space to carry them out in the future as necessary. Membership of the core group (see the next section) is particularly important.

There may be some dispute between professionals about whether a conference is needed. There may be problems over allocating social workers or having to deal with other priorities first. This is sometimes the background to the cases that go wrong, where one agency has raised a concern but it never quite gets accepted as requiring any action until it is too late. If, having made a referral with no obvious response, *and your concerns remain or the situation deteriorates*, then make a further referral and follow the issue up immediately with a senior manager in the social services. If you are concerned that a child is still at significant risk of harm, then demand an initial conference, as senior agency representatives will normally have the right to do under ACPC procedures, or, if all else fails in an emergency, call the police. This is a power that should not be misused, but where there are genuine and urgent concerns, do not assume that someone else must be dealing with it somewhere. This prevarication in getting the issue to a conference was effectively what led to the death of Lauren Wright. If you have vital information to share, keep pressing until there is a forum for sharing it.

Core group working

Following the conference, the school should be informed in writing by the social services whether a pupil has been registered and who the keyworker is. The membership of the core group should already have been identified and the first meeting fixed. It will be for the designated teacher to clarify who the school's representative will be; it does not have to be the person who attended the conference. If the school was represented, it should already be aware of this information; if not, it is essential to respond at this point by offering a suitable member of staff to join the group. Having a child in your school who is on the local authority's child protection register involves certain responsibilities. Not everything needs to be done by one person, but it must be clear whose jobs these are:

- sharing the new status of the child within the school's pastoral system on a 'need to know' basis and advising staff of its implications;
- liaison with the keyworker, especially about continuing help/therapy for the child, future contacts with parents, what to do if the child is absent, reporting any change in circumstances or further concerns, etc.;
- providing information for the core assessment under the Assessment Framework, which should be completed in the early stages following registration;
- receiving information about changes to the child's legal status, care proceedings, change of carer, etc., and updating school data systems accordingly;
- liaising with other educational professionals who are working with the child such as education welfare officers, educational psychologists, behaviour support, etc.
- monitoring the child's general well-being, appearance, general progress, etc. and producing reports as required;
- attending the core group meetings and the review conference.

On the whole, this process is very effective and it is rare for a child to be killed or seriously injured while on the register. That means that for all the cases where systems and individuals fail, there are thousands more children, already identified as being at high risk of abuse, who are effectively protected. This is clear evidence that appropriate interventions can help to minimise the long-term effects of even serious abuse. What professionals do makes a real difference to the lives of countless children. This is a massive achievement, and it comes about not least because of the contribution of schools and teachers, especially here. Core groups can sometimes lack direction, or the commitment of members may wane over time. But they are where we do the real work, if mostly unnoticed.

It is often tempting to see other things as more important or to feel that cases still in their early stages deserve the highest time commitment. But turning up to core group meetings, implementing the protection plan and, hopefully, seeing the family through to de-registration again can be a highly satisfying experience, well worth the work involved. Make sure your school's SMT knows about it. Even if the names of children cannot be made public, headteachers and governors need to know what has been done on their behalf in order to ensure their continued commitment to doing it in future. After all, 'Feedback is the breakfast of champions!', as an American management guru once said to me (on video) in all seriousness.

Post-abuse support

Post-abuse support has always been an area of some concern, where agencies have felt unable to work with the child as they would wish for fear of damaging their status as a witness in criminal proceedings that may be many months later. This can appear to leave children unsupported at a critical time, especially where there has been serious sexual abuse. If the child is still attending school, staff may want to demonstrate their care for them by providing one-to-one support and counselling. Teachers and others may be unclear about to what extent they can discuss the abuse with the child or allow them to talk about it. These issues should be clarified with the child's social worker in individual cases. In general, there has been some recognition of the fact that work may need to be done with the child before the case reaches court, but in a way that will not contaminate their evidence. It is now more likely that this will be able to happen than used to be the case, but it may have to be handled by external specialists rather than by school staff themselves.

Other child protection situations

Finally in this chapter, some brief advice about the role of schools in specific child protection responsibilities that may crop up from time to time and which pose particular issues that will have to be addressed as required.

Sex offenders

It is possible that a school's involvement in a child protection issue comes about because one of its pupils is identified as displaying inappropriate sexual behaviour, or even becomes a registered sex offender as a result of a conviction, caution or formal warning if aged over 10. This sounds very worrying, and the immediate response may be a reluctance to continue having the child in the school (though exclusion could only be appropriate if the offence involved the jurisdiction of the school in some way as a breach of discipline). This concern is understandable among those with little previous experience in this area, and it is sometimes not appropriate for young people who have committed a sex offence to remain in mainstream education, but such a response should not be assumed in all cases.

News tends to leak out even though procedures are supposed to prevent it. Parents may give information to the school in advance of the official process of disclosure. The young person may therefore be at some risk themselves and move away, but of course that then transfers the responsibility to another school, with which there should be clear and honest liaison. Some young sex offenders will be in local authority care or youth custody at least for a short time, though obviously they will be released at some point. But most will serve only community-based sentences right from the beginning. These young people still require an education, and, if they are back living with their family, it will almost certainly be in their interests to retain their involvement in their local school wherever possible. There is no automatic assumption that they cannot continue to attend unless, for example, their victim also attends the school and the situation cannot reasonably be managed with appropriate assurances about the victim's safety.

There is a well-established process of risk management, largely managed by the Public Protection Unit, the probation service, the police and the social services (see Chapter 3 regarding inter-agency roles). The education service is not routinely a part of this procedure, which mainly involves adults rather than children, unless there is a perceived risk in an adult's behaviour that relates to a school. Should such a person, for example, start walking his dog every afternoon past the gates at 3.30 or move to a flat across the road from the entrance, the LEA would normally be advised of the situation so that *generalised* warnings can be given to the staff and parents. This does *not* include releasing details concerning the individual to the general public. Child protection professionals, especially the police, would normally rather know where offenders are and assist them in maintaining a low profile, suitably supervised, than risk their going underground for fear of reprisal and therefore being much more difficult to monitor.

If the offender is a young person who is still in education, a multi-agency plan to address their needs and to manage any risk they pose will be put in place. LEA officers *will* normally be involved via the juvenile panel (MARAP), and agreement reached about who needs to know. Disclosure can only be made by the police with the permission of a senior officer, not by any other member of the panel. A headteacher would normally be told about a pupil in their school, but they may be asked not to release the information to all staff, only to those who are best placed to assist with the implementation of the plan. A 15-year-old, for example, who carried out a sexual assault on his much younger sister might be assessed as posing no risk to those of his own age. It may, however, take some time for these arrangements to be formalised, and headteachers may be asked to take interim action on a confidential basis such as agreeing with parents a suitable way of providing the young person's education for the time being, or putting voluntary risk-management strategies in place pending the full assessment.

Young people of this kind are not locked up routinely and for ever. Their best route away from a troubled past is to make the best of their educational opportunity, not to be pushed even further out to the margins of society with all the inevitable consequences. Removing them from the community is appropriate only in extreme cases. Some teachers may be uncomfortable about this approach if it is new to them, but it seems to be working well where required. Reoffending rates are very low because there is positive work being done by the Youth Offending Service and others. Many young abusers are also victims of the abuse of others and may require significant support and help to change their behaviour. The best chance is while they are still young; it is likely to be much more difficult once they become adults.

Complex and organised abuse

Some abuse involves more than one perpetrator or may raise concerns about a number of children at the same time. I once delivered some training in a very small rural primary school, all of us assuming that this was the kind of information that the three staff needed to know but would not expect to use in the near future. Within a month, almost half the boys at the school were involved in an investigation into the father of one of them. Eight of the boys were either his own children, related to him in some other way or had visited his house. Such enquiries clearly have to be handled very carefully and are usually led by the police. These sorts of cases in particular need thorough planning and will usually involve a formal strategy meeting to which education representatives should be invited. The enquiries often take a very long time, and it may be necessary to arrange support and counselling for the children and families involved. Headteachers and designated officers should ask to be kept fully informed of any key developments but will not usually be made aware of all aspects of the case unless they need to be.

Race and culture

Although racism may cause significant harm, it is not in itself a category of child abuse. But the effects of racism may influence the responses of the child and the family to the protection process, and practitioners must be aware of such a possibility. There may be practical issues to be addressed, such as recognising cultural and religious sensitivities, for example in the gender of the investigating officers, or ensuring that information is available in the appropriate languages. The Macpherson Inquiry into the murder of Stephen Lawrence highlighted the need for all agencies to provide a service to people that recognises their unique identity rather than being based on assumptions or stereotypes.

Professionals should also be aware of any religious or cultural factors in a child's life that might affect their safety, or their family's perception of their needs. For example, there has been some criticism of the Laming Report for failing to appreciate that Victoria Climbié's great-aunt, and her immediate community, identified what was happening to her in particular religious terms. Her carers did seek some help in response to her deteriorating condition, not from the health or social services, but from an evangelical church, where her problems were perceived as possession by demons. This dimension was not fully recognised as holding potential both for her protection and for the possibility that it might have reinforced her carers' rejection of her. Professionals working in any particular cultural context that has its own unique characteristics should ask key questions directly related to the setting in which the concerns arise. Otherwise, abuse may be missed or misinterpreted.

The categories and definitions are, however, in themselves all-embracing and designed to protect all children. Behaviours that might be considered acceptable by some of those in certain cultures may still be seen as abuse. Genital circumcision of girls on non-medical grounds is a particular example of an illegal act that is definitely abuse but which might occasionally be seen in a different light by a particular community or family. Similar arguments apply to any evidence of bonded labour, child prostitution or other forms of neglect. This includes a growing awareness of children who have been brought to Britain by traffickers and then abandoned or placed in inappropriate settings. Agencies should not feel disempowered to act in such situations for fear of appearing to be discriminatory.

Children and families who go missing

It is important that schools follow the appropriate procedures where a family has moved from the area at very short notice, especially if there is any concern about a possible risk of harm to the children. Some abusing parents move home suddenly if they think that professionals are becoming suspicious about their activities. Just as social workers and health professionals would now be expected to see the child protection implications in a series of missed appointments or failed home visits, headteachers should ensure that such situations are routinely reported to the LEA for follow-up by education welfare officers, rather than just removing the pupils from the roll. Obviously, this is particularly crucial where there has been any known history of concern, or the children have previously been on the authority's child protection register. Pupils who have gone missing altogether should be reported to the LEA, which will be able to access the national information held under the Lost Pupils Database until more comprehensive data-tracking systems have been introduced as promised. (See also the Education [Pupil

Registration] Regulations 1995 and DfEE Circular 10/99, *Social Inclusion, Pupil Support*.)

School staff also need to exercise caution when one parent suddenly tries to remove a child from the school during the day, especially if that parent is not currently living with the child. It is essential to check whether the person concerned has parental responsibility and that there are no court orders in force that may prevent the action being taken (see Appendix 2 and the Glossary). Ultimately, staff cannot physically prevent those with a legitimate legal relationship to the child from removing them, but any other person with parental responsibility must be immediately informed. Always check the identity of anyone who claims to be a social worker, and if court orders are said to exist, insist on seeing and retaining a copy. If court orders are being infringed, the child is clearly distressed or parents are being entirely unreasonable or threatening violence, call the police.

Pre-birth concerns

It is possible for a referral to relate to a child who has not yet been born, especially in the case of very young mothers, those who are in denial that they are pregnant, and those who do not have appropriate family support or who may be substance misusers. Children can even be the subject of an initial child protection conference before the birth takes place in order to draw up a plan to minimise the risk of future significant harm. Teachers who are aware of girls who may be pregnant, or, in the case of a girl known to be pregnant, have concerns about the likely care that the child will receive, should ensure that such concerns are referred under local procedures. This would be another example where the young person's wish for confidentiality could not be respected in the greater interests of the unborn child.

Chapter 8

Bullying and other child safety issues

Keeping children safe at school

Bullying

Bullying is not usually seen as a child protection issue, except at its most extreme where criminal charges may be appropriate or the young person involved poses identifiable risks to other children. However, schools that are committed to all the procedures we have looked at so far, which are primarily intended to ensure that the staff are vigilant and caring in response to incidents and concerns that arise from within the child's own family, will clearly also benefit from reflection on what is going on within the school community itself. Here as much as anywhere, teachers must show an ability to listen to children and to act on what they hear. They know far more about the school than we ever will!

Many resources are available to assist schools in responding to and seeking to prevent behaviour of this kind, such as the 'Tell Someone' campaign launched in September 2003. HMI 465, *Bullying: Effective Action in Secondary Schools*, is a document that can be downloaded from the Ofsted website at www.ofsted.gov.uk. DfES advice can also be found in *Bullying: Don't Suffer in Silence* (2000). Schools may find it helpful to explore the support offered by ChildLine through its CHIPS programme, a national network of outreach teams. This includes training programmes, conferences, information, newsletters and direct work with pupils. Over 1,000 schools have been involved since 1998. The NSPCC also has a network of education co-ordinators supporting the development of school councils and other services.

Looking at bullying in the context of child protection rather than, for example, as a disciplinary issue alone may bring a different perspective, especially on what it means for *all* the individuals involved. By use of the word 'bullying' I would include behaviours such as:

- actual or threatened violence;
- extortion; theft of money or property;
- coercing a child into doing something they do not want to do;
- ignoring and 'shutting out' a child from friendship groups;
- teasing and humiliating;

- picking on a child who is different;
- racist name-calling and offensive remarks;
- offensive text-messaging;
- spreading untrue rumours and gossip;
- sending insulting e-mails.

Talk of bullying quickly raises issues about judgements, feelings and values. Here, as with child abuse in its conventional sense, we must continue to be careful to distinguish between our personal and our professional reactions. Nobody likes a bully, be they adult or child, but we may still be required to exercise some pastoral care towards them. Teachers are increasingly worried about violence from children, both against other children and against themselves. I bring to this discussion no rosy-eyed belief in all children's basic goodness. It is clear that we are sometimes dealing with highly damaged young people whose behaviour is entirely unacceptable. Some are not safe to have in school at a given moment, if only for the sake of other children. I do not, however, want to see them demonised or simply removed elsewhere, as if that's all that they deserve. *Every* child matters.

A school that is serious about child protection will also be serious about tackling bullying. Bullying is not in any sense trivial or easily excused. Like other forms of abuse, it can seriously damage children's education, threaten their mental health and even, *in extremis*, cause them to take their own lives. No child should have to put up with violence from a peer, any more than from a parent or other adult. A protective school will recognise that bad things happen to children while in our care that can have a devastating effect on their lives. It will help children to access advice, counselling and support, both within the school and beyond, and be constantly listening to their insights into what the school is like and acting in response. It will be improving badly lit or unsupervised areas, providing constructive play equipment and making any other changes that will make the school environment a safer place for everyone. Few incidents take place while children are in the classroom. Protecting children in the less structured parts of the day, or even seeing if we can change the timetable or travelling arrangements in order to reduce the risks, will often make an enormous difference.

But such a school, as well as doing all it can to protect children by anti-bullying strategies and policies, classroom work, building self-esteem, peer mentoring, the use of sanctions, victim support, and so on, will also understand that bullies are likely to be children in need with problems of their own. The staff will seek to ensure that *all* their pupils receive the help to which they are entitled, especially if they have SEN, including emotional and behavioural difficulties. Without such provision, the risks of a child behaving badly are significantly increased. Rather like my approach throughout this book, it seems to me more helpful to focus on what we can do to protect children and to move them on to better things, rather than simply allocating blame to individuals and punishing them as if that were the end of it.

I admit that I am influenced by my own experience. I appreciate that this was a minor incident compared to what some children face, but when I was 10, I was hit over the right eye by a large stone thrown at me in the playground. The injury needed several stitches and I was paraded around by the headmaster in order to impress on the rest of the school how dreadful this action was and that I was lucky not to have lost an eye. Much was made of the fact that had I not been bending down to tie my shoelace, the stone might have hit me a little lower. What the headmaster did not know (and for some reason I saw no need to tell him) was that I was actually bending down to pick up an equally lethal missile to hurl at the other boy, who was just too quick for me! The distinction between those who sin and those who are sinned against is often complex and it is wise to proceed with care.

A tiny minority of bullying incidents, like child abuse referrals, will result in court action or other formal responses. In such extreme circumstances this is the right thing to do. But most of the time in child protection we are talking about more routine interventions: about rebuilding relationships, not ending them, and about how to help people to get on better in the future. The same should be true when it comes to bullying, most of which is low-key and distressing rather than life-threatening and which often takes place between children who in other circumstances might be best friends or who at least will have to continue to tolerate each other for the time being.

The designated teacher for child protection is not officially responsible for dealing with bullying, but I am increasingly convinced that the tasks are probably best done together, and both are best done by the Special Educational Needs Co-ordinator (SENCO). They might also, in their spare time, be the right person to keep an overview of the needs of looked-after children and to encourage home–school liaison! Those who work in smaller schools will recognise that this combination is by no means impossible or unlikely. If it can't realistically be the same person, then the same philosophy of listening to children and being responsive to their needs must be accepted by all those with a more partial perspective on the overall pastoral situation.

Ensuring that the school is proactive in addressing its responsibility to 'safeguard and promote' the welfare of its pupils clearly includes doing whatever we reasonably can to keep them safe in school. At the very least, staff and governors need to work together to make sure that the child protection policy makes some cross-reference to the anti-bullying policy. A school seeking to deal with bullying will not just say that it is against it or that it is not a problem; there will be real evidence of effective practice. Parents in particular can then see that the school is as concerned to ensure that its own house is in order as it is to intervene in theirs.

Child safety and the curriculum

As indicated in *Working Together*, schools can do a great deal to detect and prevent child abuse by creative use of the curriculum. Lessons in personal, social and health education (PSHE), as well as citizenship, can help children and young people to develop responsible attitudes and to gather essential information about family life, relationships, etc. For older children, formal courses in sex education, contraception and childcare that enable them to practise the skills of adult life and explore its complexities will all help in reducing the major risks that are often associated with early parenthood. For younger children, the customary emphasis on 'stranger danger' may need some sensitive adaptation in order to address the fact that the risks are, in fact, much greater from members of their own family and people otherwise known to them. This might be the appropriate subject of consultation with parental representatives in advance.

Many staff may feel embarrassed about talking about such issues, but these misgivings have to be proactively addressed. I was once delivering training in a primary school classroom that had two posters of young children on the wall, a boy and a girl. Each was dressed in a vest and pants and the various parts of the body were identified with labels. Except that there were no names for the parts that were covered by the underwear! What message does this send to the child who wants to tell you something about their vagina, penis or bottom but who perceives this absence of even the right words to use as suggesting that this is obviously not a suitable topic for teachers to hear about? Our reluctance is entirely understandable, but perhaps we need to make sure we have at least put the relevant areas onto the map. Similar issues may arise with respect to disabled children who need specialist communications devices, where the supplied vocabulary often does not extend to what they may wish to say about their own bodies or their intimate care at the hands of adults. Such situations will require careful liaison with the SENCO or the involvement of specialists from outside the school, who may also be able to assist the investigating agencies if required.

Designated teachers may also wish to use the curriculum as a training aid, especially in secondary schools, where not all staff may feel they have a formal responsibility for issues like these. Acting on a concern may mean being responsive to a disclosure that is not made overtly. Children may be observed while changing for PE (subject of course to suitable safeguards), or a conversation about accessing the Internet inappropriately might be overheard while pupils are using IT. A child may write a story, even in the third person, that is actually about themselves, or express their personal pain in an art project. Child abuse can be studied in literature, contemporary music or drama. Concerns might arise in the context of a class about nutrition and healthy eating. It is essential that every teacher and classroom assistant sees themself as part of the protection process. Children often choose the most unlikely sources for seeking help, not just the official pastoral systems.

Volunteers

Not all adults who have contact with children though a school will have received a formal check through the Criminal Records Bureau (CRB). At the time of writing, the CRB has still not cleared an enormous backlog of applications from paid employees, foster carers, etc., and the DfES has softened its previous expectations somewhat (see DfES Circular 0870/2002, *Criminal Records Bureau: Managing the Demand for Disclosures*). In any case, a CRB check is not sufficient on its own, and the following statement is offered as the basis of an agreement between the individual and the school that seeks to ensure a reasonable understanding of the nature of the volunteer–child relationship. I would anticipate something of this kind being in place for anyone who is involved in escorting children on day trips, doing one-to-one or group work in school, driving a minibus, etc.

Safe practice standards for volunteers

The temporary care of other people's children is a considerable responsibility and volunteers may have to deal with a number of situations in which children are upset, distressed, challenging or in need of an adult to assist them. While children are under your supervision, you are acting in place of their parents and as a representative of the school. You should be aware of certain expectations:

- There is a senior teacher in every school who is responsible for child protection matters. If you are aware of a child who has any kind of injury that may be non-accidental or appears distressed by anything that may have happened at home, you must immediately report your concerns to———. Do not speak to the parent yourself.
- Do not get over-involved with the child concerned by asking them too many questions, beyond being friendly and supportive. You do not have to sort the matter out yourself; just pass it on to the appropriate person.
- At all times be aware of anything in your own behaviour that may be misinterpreted or be inappropriate. You must keep to the school's professional Code of Conduct just like any other member of staff. It is acceptable to touch a child in order to keep them safe (such as fixing a seat-belt or stopping them running into the road), or even to comfort them if upset, but be very careful that your behaviour will not be misunderstood. Always use the minimum contact necessary and only if no other alternatives are available.
- It is never appropriate to touch a child in an intimate area of their body or to use any form of punishment that is intended to cause pain or humiliation. No kind of hitting, slapping or shaking, etc. is permissible, and any such behaviour may be a criminal assault.

continued . . .

- Only those persons authorised by the headteacher may use any kind of physical force or restraint. If you are approved for such actions, make sure that any interventions are carried out and recorded in accordance with the school's procedures.
- If you see any other adult behaving in a way that is not in accordance with this Code, you must share that information with————. Doing nothing may place children at risk.
- At all times you must conduct yourself as a responsible and caring parent would do. If an action seems to be needed to protect or assist a child, do not just assume that someone else will take it.

Arrangements for supervision/monitoring/training

Declaration:

I have read the terms and conditions relating to my role as a volunteer with the pupils of ———— School, in accordance with the school's child protection policy. I agree to abide by these conditions and understand that my involvement is subject to review at all times. I have not been convicted of any offence that might make me unsuitable for such a role. I agree to tell the headteacher of any relevant change in my personal circumstances.

Additional procedures would be needed if the individual is largely unsupervised, is in a setting where children are undressing or has frequent involvement with the pupils. It may be wise to obtain specific parental consent for arrangements for supervising children while they are getting ready for swimming – for example, if the person supervising is not a member of the teaching staff. It would be best practice also to obtain character references, ideally from those who have had contact with the volunteer in a similar caring capacity outside school. People who are not formally employed still need to have a clear sense that they are bound by certain obligations and they must recognise that their behaviour in such a role is subject to external scrutiny at all times. Anyone who just wants to be left alone with children should always be politely refused. (See also NEOST 2002.)

Internet and media security

There is an obvious need to ensure that pupils do not access the Internet inappropriately at school, by the use of screening software and 'firewalls'; rules about not releasing personal information and e-mail addresses; teaching pupils to avoid open-access chatrooms; maintaining appropriate supervision; etc. This is clearly a matter for each individual school to ensure that it has put the necessary safeguards in place. Advice can be obtained from the National Grid for Learning at www.safety.ngfl.gov.uk or from a Home Office website, www.thinkuknow. co.uk. A resource from the DfES, www.parentsonline.gov.uk, encourages schools to hold events for parents to discuss how to keep their children safe in their computer use at home. There are, however, some wider issues that are not always as easy to resolve.

School websites

Advice from the DfES on 'Superhighway safety' (online at safety.ngfl.gov.uk/ schools) contains guidelines for developing school websites. Such sites are primarily about the school, rather than the children who attend it. If you are also publishing any information about the pupils, the general rule is:

- If the pupil is named, avoid using a photograph.
- If a photograph is used, avoid naming the pupil.

The permission of someone with parental responsibility *must* always be obtained in each case, before any information is published about the child concerned, even on intranet systems, which are generally more secure and restricted to certain educational users. They have every right to refuse consent and to have that wish respected. There may be family violence or court orders restricting contact, even changes of identity, people living in 'safe houses' and witness protection schemes involved. All these reasons entitle the family to anonymity if they wish it. The parent does not have to justify their refusal and should not be made to feel in any way awkward in doing so. Using photographs of a general kind with captions such as 'Class 6 enjoyed a visit to the zoo' is safer than actually naming the children. If you want to name individual children because they have made particular achievements that deserve wider recognition, ensure that their parents have agreed and then do not also publish an image that can identify them.

Local media

Similar issues may arise in relation to the publication of images of children in the local press, though such information is generally considered less hazardous as, unlike the Internet, it is more limited in circulation and quickly goes out of date. Such publicity is usually very popular, but parents must again give their consent in each case as this too might raise possible breaches of confidentiality. The annual class photograph of the new intake in a nursery or primary school, for example, should not now contain all the names of the children listed from the back row, left to right, etc. A list of the names in alphabetical order would prevent any particular child being identified but just 'The new class at x school' should be sufficient. If a photographer or reporter is visiting the school for a particular event, only those children whose parents have given permission in advance should be featured in any published material.

Videoing school events

There is a story most Christmases about a school banning the use of video cameras at the nativity play. There have also been examples of parents apparently being told that they cannot record or photograph even their own child while the child is taking part in a sports day or swimming gala. 'Ownership' of such images, once taken, effectively rests with the children's parents, not with the school, so common sense needs to come into play here. There should be no problem with parents photographing or recording *only* their own children. But this is often not possible in isolation. Other children's parents may not wish them to be filmed or photographed, especially while wearing sports- or swimwear. Such sensitivities on whatever grounds – personal, religious or cultural – need to be respected and a policy agreed with parents that allows them reasonable access but that also recognises the right of any parent to control what images of their own child are taken by others. If all parents have agreed, there should be no difficulty, but no one should be required to consent to the videoing/photography as a condition of their child's participation. It may be necessary to arrange separate staged opportunities for such a purpose involving only those children for whom it has been agreed that they may take part. Parents should be given the opportunity to give or withhold their consent at least annually.

School trips

The general health and safety of pupils on school trips is an issue of some significance in the light of recent examples where children have died or been seriously injured, but is generally outside my own area of expertise. It needs only a brief mention here to reinforce the general duty of care that staff carry in such situations. Headteachers must ensure that they have referred to the relevant DfES and LEA guidance and that all events are organised, supervised and insured in accordance with both national and local authority requirements. (See, for example, the role of the Adventure Activities Licensing Authority [AALA], set up after the Lyme Bay canoeing tragedy, DfES Guidance 803/2001, *Health and Safety: Responsibilities and Powers*, and DfES 0565/2002, *Standards for Adventure*.)

One area of wider concern is that teachers may be involved in organising activities for children away from home that are not actually official school trips, perhaps for clubs or organisations outside the school or even as individuals. Parents must be made aware that such events are wholly outside the school's control and staff advised that they may not misuse their professional position to recruit for such activities without permission. It must be clear on what basis any payments are made, and to whom. Such trips may not be covered by insurance or properly supervised according to the standards of an official trip. Any specific child protection concerns that arise, including any awareness that certain children, or children of a particular type or gender, are being targeted inappropriately must be referred outside the school for investigation. (See also Chapter 14.)

I am also aware of isolated examples of problems in connection with overseas exchanges. Headteachers must be satisfied that their pupils will be safe if they are staying with families or in hostels abroad. This should be the subject of proactive discussion with colleagues in the country concerned, and with parents, before the visit takes place, in the light of whatever systems are in place there. Most European countries will now have a similar level of awareness, but not all may see the relevance of child protection issues in this context. Staff accompanying such visits should ensure that pupils can contact them at any time in an emergency and should ideally visit where they are staying in person at some stage to see their conditions for themselves. Action must be taken if concerns are raised by a pupil about anything that may be putting them at risk, such as any kind of perceived threat of sexual abuse, as well as basic issues like adequate food, accommodation, privacy, etc. Headteachers must also take all reasonable steps to ensure that those who offer to host visiting pupils in Britain are suitable to do so. Guidance on such visits should be available from the LEA.

Helping children with medical needs

It is not true, as I have sometimes heard it claimed, that since the Children Act teachers cannot administer medication, put on a plaster or help a child with their inhaler as any parent would do if they were there at the time. If someone with parental responsibility has given written consent for another person to act for them, this could not possibly be seen as an assault. The teacher in this position is no different from a foster-carer or even a step-parent, and, if anything, their role is clearer since the Children Act. They have 'care of the child' (s.3(5)), and when in that role, if they have the consent of someone entitled to give it, they may do whatever is reasonable to carry out *that person's* parental responsibility on their behalf, in order to safeguard and promote the child's welfare. This is why it is so important to specify that any form or agreement must be signed by someone who has 'parental responsibility' for the child, not just a 'parent' in the wider sense. (See DfEE Circular 0092/2000, 'Schools, Parents and Parental Responsibility', and Appendix 2.)

Individual teachers cannot be required to administer medication or go beyond what a reasonable parent might do, but, with suitable training, they can agree to do so voluntarily. It is best, if the child has particular or long-term care needs, to ask the parent to specify in advance on the consent form exactly what is needed. Some children may require a formal written plan. School staff and others caring for the child are expected to ensure reasonable supervision and provide first aid if required, but they should not undertake any form of treatment. Support from health professionals should be obtained if needed. Children should, however, never be excluded from school events only because they would pose such additional responsibilities that are not an issue for the others. That would be illegal discrimination. (See any local advice and also DfEE PPY 19, *Supporting Pupils with Medical Needs: A Good Practice Guide* [1996], and DfES 0732/2001, *Access to Education for Children and Young People with Medical Needs.*)

Summary

In a sense, everything a teacher does is about protecting the best interests of all the children at the school, and this agenda can be as wide as we want it to be. As long ago as 1986 in a High Court judgment (*Sim v. Rotherham MBC*), Mr Justice Scott stated:

> The professional obligations of teachers are not confined to the imparting of academic knowledge to the pupils. There are obligations of discipline and care. . . . To fail [to perform these duties] would not simply be a breach of common humanity, but would also be a breach of the professional obligation of the teacher.
>
> (quoted in Blyth and Milner 1997, p. 112)

No one doubts that, at their best, every teacher and school in the country would agree. But we have to make it true, not just assume that it is so, and our concern must extend to every child, even those who are difficult to help. There has never been a better opportunity than there is now with the new section of the 2002 Act and the intentions outlined in the Green Paper *Every Child Matters*. Notwithstanding the workload issue, which is real, if schools ever become places where children come solely for intellectual programming, this whole element of the adult–child relationship that they have the chance to learn there will be lost, and we will all be the poorer for it. If teachers do not have time to do it all or these areas are not part of their designated responsibilities, then other professionals must be employed, and empowered, as part of the school's team. Nurturing children to successful adulthood in the face of *all* the potential obstacles they may face is an essential part of their education. For some, it is the very key to their survival.

Chapter 9

Children in part-time work

A case for child protection and why their teachers need to know

Danger: children at work

Children in the United Kingdom work, and few people realise that it is local education authorities that are responsible for the system of regulation, if indeed they know that such rules even exist. About two-thirds of children will have had some part-time employment outside the family home before they reach school-leaving age at 16-plus. Children have always worked, and for at least the past three generations, much of what they have done has been carried out illegally. Their parents worked illegally; their older brothers and sisters worked, also illegally. Some of what children do is dangerous, inappropriate and exploitative. For children in general, ensuring that their health and safety has been addressed is a 'safeguarding' issue. For an unknown smaller number it is about countering actual abuse according to international definitions, and should be seen as such by those who have the opportunity to challenge it.

Some children are being put at risk just because they are cheaper to employ than adults, and they are expected to do things that are not suitable at their age, like collecting glasses late at night in a dance bar or operating an industrial guillotine. Some are working with people who are unsafe to be with or have given no recognition to their youth and inexperience. Some have even died as a result of adults' failure to meet the requirements of health and safety legislation. Many more will have been hurt at work in some way, or had time away from school with a work-related injury that was probably never notified to anyone as such because the employer did not see them as included in the national reporting requirements.

Consequently, there are no reliable statistics available, but simply asking children easily exposes the reality of what they do. As I have been writing this chapter, a 14-year-old boy has had to have an entire hand amputated after an incident while working illegally at a butcher's shop, resulting in a subsequent fine for the owner of £8,000. Research reported in Lavalette (1999) summarises what little is known nationally. For example, in 1998 O'Donnell and White reported what they knew to be extremely limited figures from the Health and Safety Executive which indicated that forty-seven children had suffered a serious injury at work in the previous two years and that there had been a death every year but one since 1992. In their own study, 44 per cent of their sample claimed that they had been injured at work in the last year. Pond and Searle in 1991 found examples including burns, hand and finger injuries, and broken limbs.

In recent years, children at work have died after having been overcome by fumes in a factory or crushed under farm animals, milk floats or machinery, and been killed or injured in road accidents while delivering newspapers or selling flowers. Despite the supposed duty of an employer to carry out a risk assessment in every case *before* employing a child, and to discuss the issues with their parents, few actually do so or take active steps to ensure that the child is trained, supervised and safe while carrying out their duties. Paperboys and girls, for example, rarely wear cycling helmets, even though serious head injuries are reported on a regular basis, because employers (and indeed parents) do not insist on it. In contrast, hard hats for adults on a building site are taken for granted, and their use is actually enforced if necessary.

Most child workers do seem to combine work and education without too much difficulty, and there is even some evidence that a limited amount of childhood employment is useful in promoting responsible adulthood. I am not of the view that we should seek to ban it altogether. But it is still mostly illegal, despite the fact that hardly any employers are ever prosecuted, sometimes even in response to cases resulting in fatalities. The current law, which dates back to before the Second World War, tends to be equally ignored, whether the infringements are trivial or wholly irresponsible. Almost nobody is interested in enforcing or updating it.

We have known about all this for some time, although governments have routinely argued that there is little or no evidence of a problem and have even denied that many children worked at all, other than in delivering newspapers. Practice is, however, well documented by published studies, especially over the past fifteen years, and does not need to be elaborated in detail here. The description of illegal working has often been mistaken for action in actually doing something about it. The more interesting question is perhaps *why* there has been so little interest in child employment, rather than simply outlining the evidence yet again.

As the opening chapter of this book illustrates, most other areas of children's lives have been the subject of frequent legislation over the past hundred years. This was, at least to some extent, intended to protect and promote their welfare, gradually raising society's expectations about its duty of care towards children and young people. Why is this area so different? The answer, sadly, seems to be that when it comes to children's work, it has suited adults to leave things the way they are. Suddenly we are still entirely content with an essentially nineteenth-century framework designed primarily not to promote the best interests of children, but to ensure that their economic value was not entirely lost with the advent of mass education (see Chapter 10).

Children at work seem to merge into the background as if they weren't there. As individuals, we have not always recognised that it was a child who delivered our morning paper while we were still in bed or who served us in a late-night takeaway or shop. We hardly notice that those who are still at school also work in our local market or look after our dogs at the kennels while we are on holiday. At a corporate level, in their quest to employ staff who are not even entitled to the minimum wage, even major national employers have thought it well worth the bother to issue fictitious National Insurance numbers to those who are too young to have one, just so they can be lost among the adult workforce on the computerised payroll. Despite this anonymity, children rarely receive the same employment rights as the adults. Just taking a week away with your parents or being sick, even from a legal job, may mean it's gone to someone else when you return.

Children form a significant part of the United Kingdom's workforce, and they do not work only at traditional children's tasks, although even some of these, such as farming, still contain obvious dangers, and the regulations about hours are frequently disregarded. A study in a shire county recently found a 14-year-old girl beginning work alone in a paper shop at weekends with the adult male proprietor at 3.30 a.m. (unpublished thesis). Children also work in catering, cleaning, pubs, restaurants, hotels, boatyards, animal care, garages, warehouses, horticulture, fairgrounds, holiday parks, many retail settings and even in industry. Children, still in school uniform, have been collected by coach and driven to work all evening on an industrial estate 20 miles away. Others, from a northern city, were taken halfway across the country to work in a rural turkey-processing plant at weekends. In the mid-1990s children as young as 10 or 11 worked late into the evening on a production line in a market town in the Midlands. There have been examples of child scaffolders, roofers and even gamekeepers patrolling with loaded shotguns. Children still help to deliver milk, even though it is now illegal and there was, incidentally, an outcry when it was prohibited.

Parents, schools and LEAs

Parents, of course, usually know their children are working, even if it's in school hours, very early in the morning or late at night, but often they know little about what they are actually doing and who they are doing it with. The CRB has not included employers among those who are required to seek disclosure before they can have contact with children. 'Disqualified persons' may not work where there are children present, but there is no power for an LEA to check whether a given shop owner or other adult is in that position themself, or is also employing somebody else in their business who is. They may even unwittingly license such a person to employ children without knowing their history.

Few parents know that their signed consent to any legal job is required, and that they are responsible for declaring the child fit to work and for discussing the health and safety aspects with a potential employer *before* it starts. They have generally been grateful for the extra income, or glad to see the child doing something useful, without even worrying, for example, whether the paper-bag is too heavy or whether the bicycle they use is safe, with proper brakes and lights, and the child knows how to ride it safely. Many parents employ their own children in the family business and may act responsibly. But given the way some parents treat their children, even they cannot be entirely trusted not to exploit them, or they may argue that such activity, even to excess, is part of their family or cultural tradition.

Attempts by LEAs to restrict children working are often criticised by employers, the media and other interest groups, so few local councils give the issue any kind of priority. Despite localised publicity campaigns, everyone always claims ignorance of the rules when caught, even where they are part of national organisations with extensive legal and human resource departments that clearly have a duty to know about the requirements. Headteachers often do not know the law as it affects their pupils. The National Record of Achievement folder, for example, asked pupils to record their part-time work with pride, despite the fact that most of what they would have been doing is illegal! (This could also be an issue with any new baccalaureate that takes account of non-academic elements for those under school-leaving age.)

LEAs have seen their resources dwindle for anything other than combating truancy, despite having a statutory duty to do this work. Very few have dedicated child employment officers – usually only small metropolitan authorities. Government departments have all sought to avoid getting involved. This lack of political ownership has undoubtedly contributed to the national inertia on this issue that has always been taken for granted, but in part it simply reflects it. Regulating child employment has long been the poor relation, whoever was supposed to be responsible for it. Rather more is required than just the occasional exhortation to LEAs to try harder when a particular case happens to surface in Parliament or the papers. An inadequate law cannot be adequately implemented.

Why teachers need to know

At first thought, the protection of children in part-time employment might not seem very relevant to teachers. Surely they have enough responsibility, as we have seen, for children while they are at school and for monitoring their safety within the family, without also having to worry about what they are up to while trying to earn themselves a bit of pocket money? It is also fair to say that the current responsibility lies quite clearly with LEAs and not with schools, although the implications of s.175 Education Act 2002 might be taken to include a duty on governors and staff to 'safeguard and promote' the welfare of children in employment as much as at home, if they have information that suggests they are at risk.

However, there are three main reasons why some awareness of these issues at school level is essential if children are to be given the care and information that they need:

1. *There has traditionally been a link between problems of school attendance and child employment.* While I would be the first to question whether this link is entirely relevant in all cases, this is why the duty historically lay with LEAs rather

than with other departments of the local authority. This was originally based on the fear that children might have been working when they should have been at school, and reflects the antiquated origins of the legislation. This will still be an issue for some, especially older children who may be working in school time, but it is now more a case of making sure that children's participation in education is not adversely affected by more general concerns such as getting up too early or staying out too late at work. Does anyone check, for example, whether a poor attender or a child who constantly arrives late also has a part-time job either before or after school? Perhaps there isn't room in their life for both. I have known of several Year 11 pupils who used their so-called study leave to put in a few hours' extra work at the supermarket during the day (probably while their school was marking them 'present')! Education should be a high priority in a child's life, so school staff might reasonably expect to take an interest in anything that might make a good education more difficult or affect their likelihood of eventual successful achievement.

2. *Schools are in the best position to monitor the safety issues with children and parents on a day-to-day basis.* Similarly, does anyone think to ask, if a child has a bad back, a fracture or some other injury causing them to be away from school, whether it might have been sustained while working? This is certainly more common than we ever know about under normal circumstances, and questions might have to be raised before automatically authorising the absence. Schools also have a crucial part to play, as part of both citizenship education and PSHE, in raising awareness of the existence of the regulations. Most children and their parents are not aware of them; some are happy to disregard them until challenged. The legal duty lies with the employer, but teachers are in an ideal position to encourage children into taking greater care of themselves. They can circulate leaflets, organise assemblies, hold class discussions, etc., and support the registration process in partnership with their LEA.

3. *The importance of the school-leaving age.* Teachers are also best placed to promote greater awareness of the minimum age at which children can end compulsory education and to make it clear that the child employment regulations apply up until that date. There is considerable confusion about this, not least among colleagues in other agencies, not helped by the government's habit of referring to '16' without making it clear that is not the sixteenth birthday that is significant but the *end* of National Curriculum Year 11 (i.e. the last Friday in June for the whole year's cohort). Some social workers in particular, whose regulations about care orders are different, or who may use the term 'young person' rather than 'child' at a much earlier age, often misunderstand this requirement.

It has been estimated that up to 10,000 15- and 16-year-olds may not be in any form of education at all, many of whom think they have 'left school' (*Vocational and Work-Related Learning at KS4*, DfES/0514/2002). Many other children, some much younger, live on the margins of conventional society. Some of these will undoubtedly be working in the unofficial economy before they are legally old enough to be employed, or at least unlicensed and therefore unprotected. These children may not be on school rolls so are not picked up as absent; an unknown number will be in settings that are largely hidden and unregulated, often not subject to any safeguards concerning the adults with whom they are working, and carrying out tasks with little or no educational value. This cannot be in their best interests in the long run.

Chapter 10 relates to the legal protection supposedly afforded to all children of compulsory school age as defined by educational legislation, however they are educated (ss.8 and 558 Education Act 1996). For those with birthdays very early in the academic year at the beginning of September, it will be up to nine months *after* they are 16 before they can leave school or work in school hours, at the end of the following June. The early arrival of a National Insurance number misleads many children and their parents into thinking that they can get a job from that point onwards. However, all unlicensed employment of a child *before the single leaving date* is an offence. They only become 'young people' in employment terms once they have gone past this point. As far as the Children Act is concerned, they are all children up to age 18 and are therefore entitled to the protection which that status gives them.

A new approach

What is proposed in this book, as well as outlining the current legal framework, is an entirely new system based on regulating the *employer* rather than licensing the child. The existing system, even if a licence has been issued, offers no guarantee of an appropriate duty of care. It makes very little difference in practice. Typically for its time, the current law regards the child, not the employer, as the source of any potential problems. Children needed restricting at work in order to make sure they did not neglect their education, but not so much that they would be unable to continue providing essential services or get into trouble because they had too much spare time on their hands. Recognising that children clearly want to work and that prohibiting children's work entirely would be completely unworkable, my alternative puts their welfare and protection at the centre, but it does not assume that employment is always inappropriate.

Physical abuse, emotional abuse and sexual abuse may all be a possibility within the workplace, as well as wider forms of harm and neglect, but, as far as we know, they are untypical. That does not mean, however, that we should ignore the very real concerns at the margins, any more than with family life in general. As both the *Working Together* definitions and the UN Convention on the Rights of the Child make clear, society has a general duty to protect its children from *any* injury or the unacceptable exploitation of their physical and emotional immaturity in any setting. There is little doubt among those who care to look that in this particular context the United Kingdom is falling short of where it ought to be.

But that said, LEAs, or maybe some other enforcing authority, do not need to know about every single child who has a paper round as if that in itself is a threat to their welfare. They do need to know that the job is appropriate for a child of a school age and is not interfering with their education; that the hours are reasonable and that a proper risk assessment has been undertaken; that the person employing them is responsible and safe to employ children; and that proper parental permission has been obtained. They need powers that could actually make a difference, like prohibiting a business from employing any children at all until further notice, with an immediately enforceable offence if the direction is not complied with. They need a right of entry to check whether practice is acceptable and a duty to check the criminal record of someone in such a responsible position. None of these powers exists at present.

Parents employing only their own children might be entitled to a slightly lighter touch, provided the times and the places where they work are acceptable, but they too must have some standards by which to operate. There needs to be some relaxation of the law that recognises that children want to work, and will do so whatever the law says, but we must distinguish more clearly between what is acceptable and what is not. We must deal with the ridiculous anomaly of Muslim children not being allowed to work for more than two hours just because it is a Sunday, and we must find a way to be more reasonable about the 15-year-old who wants to work in a seaside shop at 8.00 on an August Saturday evening.

In my view, we should either abandon all attempt at restriction or we should have a proper, modern, twenty-first century framework that recognises reality but that also puts the child's protection and safety at the centre. This issue clearly belongs within the context of child protection, both to promote general good practice and in order to ensure an appropriate response when unacceptable incidents occur. The illusion of a system seems to me to be more dangerous than no system at all.

Children in performances and entertainments

A further issue for schools is that some children of school age (and below) have the opportunity to take part in professional performances that now include modelling, advertising, cultural and sporting activities as well as shows, circuses, cabarets, TV, films and theatres, etc. The person responsible for the performance (not the parent) is required to apply for a licence from the LEA with respect to each child. Most organisations that operate in this area – model agencies, studios, etc. – are familiar with the requirements of the Children and Young Persons Acts 1933/1963 and the Children (Performances) Regulations 1968, and take-up is probably higher than with child employment in general. However, as before, what actual protection the licence affords is an open question. Recent changes provide rather more safeguards, though whether LEAs will have sufficient resources to put them into effect is another question entirely.

These rules relate only to commercial activities such as:

- performances for which a charge is made (but specifically excluding events put on by schools, churches, amateur drama clubs, etc.);
- any professional performance on licensed premises (e.g. a pub or club);
- any broadcast performance (TV or radio);
- any recorded or filmed performance.

Before issuing a licence, the LEA has to be satisfied about the child's fitness and health, but few health authorities will now provide the facilities for a medical as is actually required, and officers have to rely solely on a parental questionnaire. There must be either a parent, teacher or an approved 'chaperone' or 'matron' present to supervise the child. Places of performance may be inspected as regards dressing-room facilities, toilets, etc., and there are various regulations relating to hours of work, meal breaks, etc. that are much more generous than with child employment in general. Work can, for example, be done up to 11 o'clock at night if necessary (e.g. in theatres and night-time filming). Unlike in the case of the rules on employment, this procedure may even include permission for the child to have time away from school, and with no limit on the annual number of performances or absences, provided some alternative educational arrangements are made. (These rules have recently been relaxed under pressure from the British film industry and make an interesting contrast to all the normal concerns about 'truancy' and family holidays.)

While some of these requirements date back to a time when theatres and music halls were considered rather dangerous places for impressionable young minds, the recognition of the risks inherent in, for example, child modelling and photography is particularly welcome. There has been some concern that such activities could easily be misused by those who have an interest in creating opportunities for child sexual abuse. It was always said that children who walked about while modelling were in an entertainment, and so eligible for a licence, but those who sat still were working! (This meant that, until the extension of the regulations, all catalogues showing clothes for children under 13 were the product of illegal employment and consequently unregulated.) Any suggestion that children are involved in 'posing' or 'photographic modelling' should be followed up immediately. Any continuing concerns should be referred under child protection procedures.

The significance of this issue for teachers relates both to the need for reasonable vigilance about any situation that might not be bona fide and to an awareness of the implications for attendance and absence. All such activities must be properly licensed before children are given permission to be absent for rehearsals or for performances, although notice is often very short, especially for work that is 'live'. Agencies, and TV and film companies, etc., are in theory required to give twenty-eight days' notice, but the nature of the industry makes this impossible. Many children are on renewable open licences that simply require the company to give the maximum possible notice for a child already approved to perform.

Requests for absence from school, without prior approval and consultation with the LEA, should not be authorised for such activities. Parents who request leave of absence must be asked first if a licence is required. Leave for other kinds of events, not requiring a licence, is entirely at the headteacher's discretion. Headteachers are of course free to raise objections if a child has already had a lot of time away from school, and in such a situation the LEA may prohibit any work in school time or even refuse to issue a licence at all. Parents should make arrangements with the school about catching up on any work that will be missed, and in some circumstances private tutors may be required. Special regulations apply to schools specifically designed for drama and music students and for children performing abroad. As with child employment in general, these rules do not apply to sixth-formers.

Training idea 4: Part-time working in my school (individual/group)

This is an activity that could be carried out by a group of pupils in a high school with staff support. The results could then be fed back to staff at a training session that also gives them information about the child employment system.

TASK: Following classroom work on the issues, devise a survey to find out the kinds of work that pupils undertake outside school. This could be restricted to one or two year groups. It will need to be completed anonymously with an assurance that no follow-up action will be taken unless the young person wants something done (unless a clear child protection issue is involved). The sorts of questions that might be appropriate include:

- Age, gender, home area, ethnicity, etc.?
- Do you have a part-time job now or have you ever had one?
- How old were you when you started?
- What kind of work was involved?
- How did you get the job?
- What hours did you do (days, times, etc.)?
- How much did you get paid (if at all)?
- Did you receive any training?
- Was the work safe? Have you ever had any injury? If so, what?
- Did the work ever affect school and homework?
- Did the employer have a licence to employ you?

continued

Research what local employment opportunities are available and any particular features of the economy in your area. Ask the LEA for copies of any information leaflets, applications forms, etc. Invite an LEA representative to the school to hear the results of your research. How do the figures fit with the employment known to them?

Encourage the pupils to write to their Member of Parliament saying what they think should be done to protect children in part-time jobs.

Chapter 10

The law on child employment

What children of school age can and cannot do

History

Many people assume that the exploitation of children at work disappeared with *The Water Babies* and boys up chimneys! This is where I start with my own discussions with children, or with images that assume that child labour is a feature only of developing countries in Latin America, Asia or Africa. As we saw in Chapter 1, children have not always been seen as in need of any special protection by virtue of their immaturity. This was nowhere more true than in the workplaces of eighteenth-century Britain, when the Industrial Revolution led to a massive increase in the use of children as cheap labour.

This had always been true in the grand country houses, on the large agricultural estates and in rural and cottage industries, farms and smallholdings, but child labour's increased visibility in towns and cities gradually seems to have raised expectations that it could not be allowed to continue unchecked. Children had quickly become indispensable to the work of lace-making, weaving, silk mills and several other key industrial processes. They kept open the ventilation systems of the coal mines, even from as young as 7, despite the extremely high risk of explosions. Only when it was realised that this job was actually rather responsible for such young children, because miners died if they fell asleep or made a mistake, did people begin to question whether it was right!

Society initially regarded work as a more useful occupation than education, especially for the children of the poor and fatherless, but from 1802 regulations began to restrict their hours and to raise the age at which a working life could begin. It appears that these rules were often ignored, however, not least because many families needed the income provided by older children, but also because those in Parliament and the magistracy were often themselves the owners of the mines, mills and factories concerned. But as some of the manufacturing industries declined, so children were able to access other forms of activity, even if, for some, this still meant only swapping regular employment for the yet more precarious life of an itinerant tradesman.

The 1833 Factory Act introduced external inspections, which significantly improved working conditions; further Mines and Factory Acts outlawed the employment of children under 10, and then those under 13. Changes in production technology also led to a reduction in the need for children. But it was the introduction of more universal education under the Education Act 1870 that eventually led to serious reconsideration of the view of children as primarily economic producers. By 1880, most children were expected to be in school, at least for some of their time, and were indeed attending at levels not very much lower than they are today, if often combined with 'half-time' working alongside reduced school hours. But practice into the early years of the twentieth century was still inconsistent, with continuing concern about work replacing school in a considerable number of cases, especially in large urban areas and in the more remote countryside.

Politically, the Home Office initially won the battle with the Board of Education over the right to regulate in this area, despite the provisions of the Education Act 1918, which ended the 'half-time' arrangement and should have sent all children to school full-time until age 14. However, both the needs of industry, and an eye to discouraging delinquency and social unrest, remained the essential focus. Officials were confident that the worst excesses had been eradicated and that there was a need to provide only an enabling framework, thereby resisting wider reform. Incredibly, the Employment of Women, Young Persons and Children Act 1920, which outlawed work in 'industrial undertakings', and the Children and Young Persons Act 1933, which allowed local authorities to legislate through by-laws and made only minor variations to the requirements of the 1918 Act, still form the core of contemporary legislation.

Since the child employment laws were last substantially revised we have had the invention of television, the computer and mobile phones, the creation of a National Health Service, the growth of teenage culture and the advent of mass entertainment media. People have landed on the moon and overseas travel has become routine. There has been a huge shift towards multiculturalism and a revolution in living standards and the availability of consumer goods. The nature of family and working life has changed beyond recognition. But when it comes to their part-time jobs, our children are still stuck in the age of blackboards, cloth caps and rickets!

As had also happened in 1914–18, the Second World War led to the acceptance of wholesale breaches of the regulations at a time of crisis, especially in rural areas, thereby reinforcing existing bad practice. Rules about attending school were relaxed again, despite opposition from both trade unions and headteachers. But as education returned to normal after the war, it seems that no one was especially concerned to look at what kind of child employment framework would now be appropriate, despite a local government review that recommended modernisation. The Home Office was still primarily responsible at this time and took the view that newspaper delivery and agriculture at least could not continue without the extensive participation of children as before, so it was judged best to leave things alone.

The wartime exemptions did not actually disappear until 1954, with many children still missing school, at least for harvesting, even beyond that. But by then, more middle-class children had also started to work outside school hours, apparently with little effect on their education. This may be a key reason why politicians chose to do nothing, now that the issue was no longer about regulating only the poor and those who might cause problems if under-occupied. As the stigma of working lessened, girls began to work as well as boys, and a general climate arose that saw it all as safe and harmless.

Regulation effectively disappeared until, under some pressure, the Home Office reluctantly sponsored a study by Emrys Davies in 1972 that exposed the reality much as before. An Employment of Children Act, actually passed in 1973, has never been brought into force, but even if it had been, it would have made few significant changes and is no longer sufficient. Responsibility then shifted to the Department of Health, but changes to by-laws made in 1998 in response to an EU Directive of 1994 were almost entirely cosmetic, though they did at least get rid of the 'lather boys' and 'bagatelle operators', still included in some areas until then! However, some local authorities have still not updated their regulations in response to this Directive, and have simply been required to adopt the new model *de facto*, whether they realise it or not.

The current framework

It is difficult to be precise about the work that children do because of the problems of definition and the generally hidden nature of much of their activity. It is also important to draw a clear distinction between jobs such as running errands, car-washing for neighbours, helping around the home, etc. (not 'employment' within the meaning of the word), and those jobs that come within the scope of the regulations. 'Employment' is any work done to assist a *commercial* enterprise or business that is carried on for profit, *even if the child isn't paid*. It's not only about what you do, it's also about who you do it for and what use they are making of your labour. All such work should be licensed by the LEA. If not, the *employer* is committing an offence, even if they are employing their own child.

So, for example, helping your dad to wash the family car is not employment; going with him to the garage where he works and washing the cars on the forecourt is. Mucking out your own horse at the riding stables is not employment; cleaning out the owner's horses or supervising lessons is, even if you don't get paid for either! No child can legally do any work of this kind before the age of 13, and then only once the employer has applied for an individual licence for *every* child concerned, even their own. Everything else carried out by children in commercial settings is illegal.

Babysitting and related issues

The most obvious activity that is excluded from these requirements is babysitting. This is not employment, as it is not done for a commercial enterprise or business.

In effect, children are self-employed in such work and so are outside the scope of the law, as are all those who work for individuals and families rather than for profit-making organisations. This is an area of real concern now that we are aware of the existence of children who are allegedly brought to Britain to act as domestic servants, some of whom may not even be known to the authorities or be engaging in any kind of education. The lack of effective regulation of such arrangements makes exploitation much more likely. Any child thought to be in such a position should be reported under child protection procedures.

There are actually no laws about the appropriate age for undertaking any domestic or caring responsibilities; it all depends on the circumstances, the maturity of the child, etc., but 14 might be taken as a reasonable guideline for leaving a child in temporary charge of other children. (Failure to make proper arrangements can constitute neglect; see Chapter 3.) Parents remain responsible for their children if they leave them in the care of another child, but anyone may do so, provided they are not putting *either* child involved at unreasonable risk of harm.

This also means that there are no controls over the hours children may spend in babysitting, unlike the very strict controls when it comes to employment. It is difficult to see how there could be any kind of enforceable regulation in this area, and babysitting is still sometimes included in surveys of the work that children do, in order to recognise its significance. Despite the obvious anomaly of this situation, as babysitting probably accounts for many of the tired children or empty seats at school the next morning, at least most such activity is relatively safe. There are, however, examples of so-called babysitting as a context for sexual and physical abuse both by adults against children and by young people themselves against younger children. Any concerns of this kind that come to the attention of teachers should again be reported under child protection procedures.

Work experience

Children in the final two years of compulsory education can be given the opportunity to experience the world of work as part of their educational programme. It is supposed to be unpaid (apart from expenses) and supervised. Like babysitting, this also is not employment and so does not come within the scope of the regulations. Children may be able to do things as work experience that they cannot do as a job outside school hours, provided it is suitable and the placement conforms to other legislation relating to health and safety, etc. This can cause some confusion for teachers, employers, children and parents, but the context for such activity is quite different from employment. Work experience is education, monitored by teachers, and intended to be an extension of the school curriculum. School staff carry significant responsibilities for these arrangements and should ensure that appropriate child protection procedures are in place to reduce the risk of anything untoward occurring while the child is in this adult environment. By definition, work experience is intended to give the child a chance to have a taste of a setting that they cannot usually be in; no one ever suggested a work experience placement delivering newspapers!

This means they cannot simply stay on and convert the placement into a job, even if their employer wants them to, unless the work also happens to conform with the child employment regulations or they can do something different within the same organisation that would meet the criteria. Parents should be kept fully informed and given details of placements in advance. If parents have found the placements themselves, they must still contain the possibility of a learning outcome rather than simply be an excuse for making use of their child's labour. It must at all times be clear that children are not being allowed to go to work. Work experience placements should be set in the context of classroom activity, both beforehand and through follow-up, and all pupils should receive a visit from a member of the school staff.

There are no precise rules about the length or frequency of work experience as part of the Key Stage 4 curriculum. In the past, the DfES has considered that more than two weeks is exceptional, but there are circumstances in which extended arrangements or a regular period each week might be appropriate, especially for those who are closest to the leaving age. This is likely to become more commonplace in the light of a growing relationship between education and training and the development of more vocational courses at GCSE. Children should not participate in work experience outside the normal school day unless the particular job requires it. Pupils should be seen as still within the school's duty of care while on placement and so not expected to do anything that exposes them to unnecessary risk. They should at all times know how to contact a member of staff at the school if they have a problem and be given appropriate training, supervision and support by their placement employer.

Legal employment

Most legal work for children is defined by local by-laws made under s.18(2) Children and Young Persons Act 1933 (as amended). These requirements are more standard than they used to be, following the model issued by the Department of Health in 1998, though there may still be some variation between local authorities. A child must be 13 to be employed at all. Thirteen-year-olds can do only jobs on a 'specified list', primarily newspaper delivery, shop work and other traditional children's jobs. The options are only slightly more generous once a child becomes 14. As with the rules about hours of working (see p. 130), they apply to all children still of compulsory school age, however they are educated, not just to those registered at a school.

All legal work must be 'light duties' only, and most children who work legally still do paper rounds. Others work in shops, garden centres and markets during the day on Saturdays or in school holidays, deliver leaflets, do light cleaning, office work, hairdressing, waitressing or work with animals. Unfortunately, many teenagers now look on such work as suitable only for younger children, and by the age of 14 or 15 they are desperately looking for something else more 'adult' and likely to be better paid. Not much else is permitted, though a few children have more glamorous opportunities under other legislation that permits them to take part in performances and entertainments (see Chapter 9).

In general we consider such jobs quite appropriate, and many of them are, but the general climate within which they are carried out is very different than it was when the current law was framed. For example, I am not sure that even the delivery of newspapers is quite the same activity now as it was in the 1930s. Roads are much busier and we know far more about some of the people who might be living at the houses children are visiting. It might be thought that getting up sometime around 6.30, or earlier if you're going to have breakfast first, going out on a bicycle in all weathers while it is still dark during half the year, perhaps getting back in time for a school bus, doing seven hours at school and maybe even another round in the late afternoon, and all before doing any necessary homework, is far too much for a child of 13 or 14. That makes a ten- or twelve-hour working day; more than I am expected to manage! Similar arguments might be applied to the countless children who 'help out' on family farms or in their parents' shop, mostly illegally, because no licence has been issued or the work is outside the permitted hours. Parents must take some responsibility here, and not all jobs are suitable for their child as an individual, even if they are permissible. They should at least take an interest in what the child is doing and ensure that all necessary procedures to protect their welfare have been followed.

But the entirely understandable desire for financial independence, which is now so great a pressure on young people, can lead them into unregulated and unsupervised workplaces that are clearly not in their best interests. No child of school age should be working in a club, pub or factory, on a building site, in a chip-shop, a commercial kitchen or any kind of takeaway, most of which function late into the evening and contain obvious hazards. They should not be using sharp knives or dangerous machines, lifting heavy objects, working with fuels, vehicles, chemicals or solvents, sorting refuse or going up ladders to clean windows or install TV aerials! Common sense tells us that some workplaces are dangerous and that children should not work there, but no one knows how many do, except the adults who allow them to do it.

Hours of working

These are defined by s.18(1) Children and Young Persons Act 1933, although there have been a few minor changes over the years to reflect the gradual increase in the school-leaving age. This perfectly illustrates the problem with the current legislation. When framed, these laws were only intended to regulate the position between the age of 13 and the then school-leaving age of no later than the fifteenth birthday, and sometimes earlier if you had a job to go to. As indicated previously, they now cover all those aged up to 16 years 9 months, many of whom enjoy a lifestyle entirely incompatible with what might be still considered suitable at 13.

But apart from a few small differences, the same rules apply across the board. When you are legally old enough to have sex, get married with your parent's permission, buy cigarettes and National Lottery tickets and can easily get into nightclubs with a bit of make-up, it seems utterly irrelevant that you cannot work for more than two hours on a Sunday!

No child can legally be employed before 7.00 in the morning or after 7.00 in the evening on *any* day, even in school holidays. They may not work for more than two hours on a school day (outside school hours), or for more than five or eight hours on a Saturday or on a weekday in school holidays, according to age. They cannot be employed for more than twelve hours in any week in which they are also expected to attend school (including the weekend). The two-hour Sunday rule still applies whatever their religion or lack of it, despite a slight recent amendment. (Only mornings were permitted until the late 1990s.) A previous Minister in the Department of Health was apparently of the opinion that all children, presumably like his own, should spend the day of rest with their families – this despite the fact that many of those parents will now be working themselves, owing to that same government's expansion of Sunday trading!

These rules cannot be relaxed by local by-laws, only made more restrictive, but they are of course routinely broken in farms, markets, seaside cafés, video stores, corner shops, garden centres, supermarkets and countless other settings. Some of them make sense, especially for younger children. Seven o'clock is plenty early enough to be out at work. But the restrictions at the other end of the day and on Sundays and in school holidays pose a real difficulty. Even responsible employers cannot legally license older children who want to work at such times, even in completely safe activities that would be perfectly legal on a Saturday afternoon or when the issue of school the next morning did not arise.

Registration procedures

Under s.18(2) Children and Young Persons Act 1933, any child of compulsory school age who is employed in a commercial undertaking or a 'trade or occupation carried on for profit' must be licensed by the LEA, even if they work in the family business or work unpaid. It is the responsibility of the *employer* to complete the necessary procedures. This normally involves:

- The completion of a form applying for a licence for each child employed who is under school-leaving age, within one week of their commencing their employment. This form will also normally contain a requirement for parental consent, a declaration of fitness and evidence that the employer has carried out a health and safety risk assessment.
- A decision by an officer of the LEA, based on the information provided, about whether the job, the hours worked, the age of the child, etc. all fall within the regulations. Some LEAs also visit the premises or check each child's school attendance record, but this is far from universal.

- The issuing of a licence (sometimes on a temporary basis in the first instance), which should be kept by the employer, or carried by the child in some areas. About 2,500 children are licensed in this way each year in Staffordshire, for example, but the figures nationally would vary enormously depending on the priority given to this work by the LEA.

The main incentive for employers to go through this procedure is that those whose child employees are properly licensed are more likely to be covered by the firm's insurance in the event of an accident, theft or injury. Unlicensed children may not be recognised as employees and therefore may have no claim against the employer's insurance. Their parents might then be able to take a civil action against the employer in person to recover any loss or damages. In addition, registration gives legal protection for the employer against possible prosecution and entitles employers to expect a degree of responsibility from the child concerned. I have known a case of an unlicensed paperboy who kept the payments he had collected door-to-door for himself (collecting money at the door is in itself a very risky activity, and is illegal for children under most by-laws). The employer had no right to claim the money as the boy was not legally his employee, so there was no proof that the money belonged to him!

Enforcement

Even if the employment would be legal in terms of age, hours, etc., it is illegal unless this licensing procedure has been followed for each child. Most LEAs operate a system of annual reviews in which known employers are required to complete a return indicating all the children currently in their employment. This may enable some children in work to be identified, but can become little more than a paper exercise. Failure to complete such a return is an offence, though the law is rarely enforced. Education Welfare Officers or specialist Child Employment Officers in a few LEAs may also do spot checks or early morning visits to newsagents to verify that children are working within the law. Gross abuses may occasionally result in prosecution, though these are very rare, not because children are not working illegally but because few LEAs resource the work sufficiently and because of the generally antiquated nature of the legislation. Magistrates are still not always particularly sympathetic to the proceedings, even when the abuses are quite significant. Most LEAs rely on persuasion and encouragement, acting on reports from parents or other employers, and seek to work by co-operation wherever possible.

Education officers have no right to enter premises where they suspect that children may be working illegally, but can sometimes work in partnership with trading standards or other officers who have greater powers. The police also have powers under the Children Act 1989 which might be appropriate *in extremis* if there is real cause to believe that a child may be suffering or at risk of significant harm. As with the case of the butcher referred to earlier, it may also be possible to take action under health and safety legislation. This tends to produce much higher fines than infringements of the child employment by-laws, though in most cases not employing children illegally in the first place would have protected both the child *and* the employer from the subsequent offence.

Two powers under the Education Act 1996 may be used more frequently:

- An LEA can, by written notice served on an employer, prohibit the employment of a particular child, or otherwise restrict it, 'where he [*sic*] is being employed in such a manner as to be prejudicial to his health or otherwise renders him unfit to obtain full benefit from the education provided for him' (s.559(1)). This requires the LEA to know of a particular child being employed; it cannot be used as a blanket prohibition on any child. Ignoring this notice is an offence. Sometimes this approach can also be useful where a child is a poor attender at school and where threatening to end their part-time job may act as an incentive for them to improve. Teachers should be aware of this possibility and ask the LEA to consider using it where appropriate.
- An LEA 'may serve a notice in writing on the parent or employer . . . requiring [them] to provide the authority . . . with such information as appears . . . to be necessary for the purpose of enabling [the authority] to ascertain whether the child is being employed' (s.559(2)). This is useful where a report has been received that a child may be working but the employer or parent is not being co-operative. This is the only place where there is an enforceable legal obligation on parents as well as employers.

Summary

In all these areas, LEA officers need the assistance of school staff in carrying out their duties, as part of the school's general pastoral care for its pupils. This is particularly true if teachers are aware of any relevant activity outside school that may be putting the child at risk. The child employment system is fundamentally flawed and in need of urgent reform, but it still provides some protection. Such situations will rarely be covered by local ACPC procedures, but opportunities still exist to take action and they should be used as required.

Chapter 11

Safe at work

A proposed new code of practice for children and their employers

Introduction

In this chapter I offer a proposed new code of practice as the basis for a renewed discussion of how we should proceed in creating a modern framework for the safeguarding of children in employment. It assumes a willingness to change the current approach into something that actually addresses the issues. I am not a lawyer, so of course it needs more work, but I believe it is both realistic and enforceable. Crucially, it also seeks to protect the child's right to education as the main priority in their life and to make their welfare and safety the paramount consideration at work, not the need to preserve their role as a source of cheap labour.

---

1 Summary

1.1 This Code of Practice sets out a framework within which those who employ children of compulsory school age are expected to operate. It takes account both of UK legislation and of EC Directive 94/33 on the protection of young people at work. Commercial employers who wish to employ children within the scope of this Code of Practice must first be approved by the relevant local authority. Employers who persistently fail to observe good practice may have their 'approved status' suspended or withdrawn. It is an offence to continue to employ children once a Notice suspending or withdrawing approved status has been served.

1.2 This approach replaces previous requirements for individual children to be licensed by the local authority. The focus of the licensing requirement is now on the employer and the parents. This includes any local agent acting on behalf of the employer. Certain employment remains prohibited to all children (see list in Annex 1).

1.3 This Code of Practice covers children who are 'employed' in any business or commercial undertaking. This includes working in any enterprise undertaken for profit, including charities, clubs, etc., even if the child does not receive any financial payment. Other than the specified ages and working times, it does not apply to children working for their parents or whose work is undertaken within the family home or those children who are effectively 'self-employed', i.e. where there is no business employer, *unless* such work (e.g. in a factory) is prohibited for all children. (Guidance on such arrangements, including babysitting, is attached as Annex 2.) Separate arrangements exist for children taking part in professional entertainments, modelling, sports and filmed or broadcast performances or work experience.

1.4 'Children' means all those who are still of compulsory school age, whether they are registered pupils at a school or educated 'otherwise' than at school. This includes those who are 16 but not yet able to leave school until the relevant date. Those who are no longer of compulsory school age but remain at school or in further education voluntarily are 'young people' and are outside the scope of this Code of Practice. There is no need for an employer to be approved if no children of compulsory school age are employed.

2   Licensing of approved employers

2.1 An 'approved employer' is an individual, not a business or an organisation. This named person is responsible for the health, safety and welfare of the children in their business and must be personally approved by the local authority for their area before employing any children of school age. The approved employer will be a person such as the shop owner or manager, the local agent for newspaper delivery, the manager of the riding centre, etc. Removal of approved status prohibits that person's *business*, not only the individual, from continuing to employ children in any capacity until approved to do so.

2.2 Where more than 15 children are employed in any single enterprise, such approval will be on a corporate basis, covering a nominated individual designated on behalf of the employer. They will be responsible for practice throughout their organisation. Should this individual be considered by the local authority to be in breach of this Code of Practice, or for any other reason, the corporate employer can designate an alternative person for approval if they wish to continue employing children.

continued . . .

2.3 Anyone wishing to be registered by the local authority as an approved employer must apply in writing according to local procedures. Approval will involve:

- production by the individual of evidence of no convictions that would make them unsuitable to be an employer of children, through basic-level disclosure from the Criminal Records Bureau (paid for by the individual/business);
- character references from any parent organisation or company where the individual is themself an employee, or from members of the community in good standing in the case of those who are self-employed, etc.;
- details of the 'specified tasks' available for children within the business;
- A signed commitment to abide by the requirements of this Code of Practice.

2.4 Under this Code, it is not necessary to inform the local authority of the details of all individual children being employed. Employers (including parents) are required to:

- keep to the specified tasks identified as suitable for children and to the specified hours, etc. as defined in the legislation;
- maintain a written record of all children in their employment for inspection by authorised officers of the local authority;
- supply each child employed with some form of identity badge or card to carry while working.

Persistent failure to observe the Code of Practice can result in the suspension or permanent removal of approved status. Approved status has to be renewed annually according to local procedures; once it has 'lapsed', children may no longer be employed without renewal (within three months) or re-application (after three months).

3 Standards

3.1 Approved employers and parents are required to keep to the following standards in addition to the requirements of paragraph 2.3 above:

3.2 *Age*. No child may be employed before the age of 13. All children up to school-leaving age (not just age 16) must be included in these procedures. Children aged 13 can only do certain designated jobs as before.

3.3 *Specified tasks*. Children aged 13 and over may only be employed on a list of tasks that have been previously approved as suitable (see Annex 3). Only tasks on the specified list are permitted. Some are only suitable for those aged 14 and above.

3.4 *Parental consent*. Employers other than parents must obtain written consent to the employment from someone with parental responsibility for the child. Local authorities must make a form available for this purpose. This includes a statement that the parent is aware of the nature of the employment, hours, etc. and considers the child medically fit. The parent is also required to affirm that the child has no other employment or that the maximum permitted number of hours are not being exceeded. The employer has a duty to enquire about any other employment and may not employ the child if it would take them beyond the permitted weekly or daily maximums. Parents and children must also be informed of their right to complain to the employer's local authority and to see a copy of this Code of Practice.

3.5 *Prohibited times of working* (requires legal change). No child of compulsory school age, whether or not he/she is a registered pupil at a school, may be employed during the hours when schools in the area are open. This includes those children who are permanently excluded, attending special units or educated 'otherwise'. Approved status may be removed from any employer who allows a child to work during school hours. No child may work before 7.00 a.m. or after 7.00 p.m. (Sunday to Thursday in term time) or after 9.00 p.m. (Fridays, Saturdays and school holidays).

3.6 *Permitted maximum hours* (requires legal change). No child may be employed for more than two hours on any day when schools in the area are open; either two hours after school or one hour before and one hour after school. No child may be employed for more than a total of 12 hours in any week in which he/she is also required to attend school. On Saturdays, Sundays and weekdays during school holidays, children aged 13/14 may work a maximum of five hours per day (up to 25 hours per week in holidays); children aged 15/16 may work a maximum of 8 hours per day (up to 35 hours per week in holidays). No child may work for more than 4 hours without a one hour break. A two-week break during the school summer holiday must given for any child in continuous employment during the past six months, with a guarantee of the job being available for them on their return.

continued . . .

3.7 *Health and safety*. Employers must meet the requirements of health and safety legislation for children as for any employee. Persistent failure to attend to health and safety issues is grounds for removing approved status. A full 'risk assessment' must be carried out for children in accordance with the regulations, training must be provided as appropriate and all accidents notified as required.

3.8 *Wages and conditions*. Employers must endeavour to meet the requirements of any recommendations laid down by the local authority regarding the level of wages or other terms and conditions and must publish these to parents and children.

4 Appeal procedures

4.1 Local authorities must establish appeals procedures to deal with disputes regarding the awarding, suspension or removal of approved employer status. Any decision to remove approved status must be subject to ratification by an appropriate committee to which the employer has a right to make representations. Once a decision to remove approved status is agreed by the relevant officer of the local authority, it is an offence for the employer to continue to employ children. Re-application may be made after no less than six months but the local authority always has the right to refuse approval of any potential employer, subject to further appeal.

5 Powers of inspection

5.1 Designated officers of the local authority may inspect the premises of any employer at any time to ensure compliance with this Code of Practice. Complaints by parents, children or others may merit formal investigation. Warning notices may be issued regarding any poor practice that would result in removal of approved status if continued.

5.2 Local authorities retain their power under the Education Act 1996 to request information from any employer thought to be employing children, and where no approval has been given may serve a Notice of Prohibition of Employment. Ignoring any such request or Notice is an offence.

6 Conclusion

6.1 The intention of this Code of Practice is to offer employers and parents a general framework within which they must operate, without requiring the licensing of individual children. It is a deliberate attempt to offer an element of deregulation and reduction in bureaucracy while maintaining reasonable controls and safeguards, primarily intended to protect children from exploitation and danger as the EC Directive requires. Responsible employers should find the system much less intrusive than before, but those who do not demonstrate good practice may face significant consequences. If children are important to the effective running of a business, they deserve to be treated with respect and care. Employers seeking to abuse their position of responsibility, or who are not suitable people to come into contact with children in this way, will not be allowed the opportunity to put children at risk.

7 Offences

7.1 The following are offences:

- employing a child where the employer is not their parent but failing to register as an approved employer as required;
- employing a child when prohibited from doing so by Notice;
- serious breaches of the Code of Practice (employment in school hours, exceeding the maximum permitted hours, etc.);
- employing a child in prohibited settings or other than as described in the specified tasks;
- failing to provide information to the local authority when requested;
- refusing access by an official approved for the purpose;
- failure to notify a workplace accident to a child to the relevant authority;
- employing a child when specifically prohibited from doing so under other legislation (e.g. the Criminal Justice and Court Services Act 2000).

In addition, child protection procedures may be invoked where any child is considered to be suffering or is at risk of 'significant harm' as a result of physical abuse, emotional abuse, sexual abuse or neglect while employed.

Annex 1: Prohibited employments

No child of compulsory school age may be employed in any of the following ways. This *includes* employment by parents (for example, in a family business) even where there is no requirement for the employer to be approved by the local authority.

continued . . .

It remains an offence under other legislation to employ a child:

- in an 'industrial undertaking' (though not if the child is working at home under the supervision of a parent) [new definition required which is less all-embracing];
- in the preparation of food in a commercial kitchen;
- in any cinema, discotheque, dance hall or club, except as a licensed performer;
- in any licensed premises, except when the establishment is closed or in areas where alcohol is not consumed;
- at any dangerous machine [defined];
- in the sale or delivery of alcohol, unless in sealed containers;
- in the delivery of fuel oils;
- in any employment that involves exposure to film, video or publications normally unsuitable for those under 18;
- in the sale of National Lottery tickets or tobacco products (up to age 16);
- in window cleaning or any other work higher than 3 metres above ground;
- in the collection of money door to door;
- in any employment involving exposure to physical, biological or chemical agents (including prescription medicines);
- in any other employment prohibited to children of school age under other legislation or local authority by-laws.

Annex 2: Non-regulated 'work'

Not all work that children may do, even for payment, is 'employment' as covered by this Code of Practice. This regulatory framework does not cover work such as:

- *Babysitting*. There is no minimum age at which a child is old enough to babysit. There is a general duty of care on parents not to expose their children to any unreasonable risk; parents remain responsible for their child while the child is in the care of another child. Parents are advised to monitor babysitting arrangements with care. For all but short periods, it is not recommended that children under the age of 14 be left in sole charge of younger children. Further advice is available from the NSPCC.
- *Work in the family business*. Children may work for their own parent (i.e. someone with parental responsibility as defined by the Children Act 1989 and any other person who has day-to-day care of the child,

but not any other relative) without need for approval, but *only* if the work is on the list of specified tasks for children as set out in Annex 3. Parents employing only their own children in a family business are therefore not required to register as approved employers. However, they are still prohibited under school attendance law from allowing the child to work in school hours or from employing the child in a prohibited employment and must also abide by the Code of Practice regarding hours, etc.

- *Work where there is no commercial employer.* No approval is required where children do 'odd jobs' for neighbours or members of their family, helping around the house, washing cars, etc., unless the work is for a commercial business. If their child is working outside their personal supervision, parents should be careful that the individuals concerned are safe and should satisfy themselves that their children are not being exploited or exposed to any danger.
- *Children who are effectively 'self-employed'.* Technically, a child cannot legally be self-employed, but a child may set up their own arrangements to work in return for payment, for example by caring for a friend's horses, walking dogs or doing gardening. This is outside the terms of the employment requirements unless they are working for a commercial business (for example, at a riding stables, kennels or garden centre). If there is any doubt about whether the work a child is doing should be classed as 'employment', parents and employers are advised to check with the local authority.

Annex 3: 'Specified tasks': sample text for employers (and guidance for parents)

All work by children of compulsory school age must be 'light duties' only. Please indicate on the list below those tasks for which you intend to employ children. Any information given under the 'other' heading may first be investigated further before approval may be given. Approved employers may be inspected to ensure that children are not being employed in illegal occupations.

Please tick the relevant tasks for children aged 13 or over in your business. *Children of compulsory school age may only be employed in one or more of these specified tasks.* Note that some are not legal until the child is 14.

- Delivering leaflets, magazines or newspapers (this does not include collecting cash payments, which is prohibited).

continued . . .

- Shop work: serving, stocking shelves, hairdressing, etc.
- Office work: word-processing, filing, etc.
- Light agricultural or horticultural work.
- Car washing, etc. (by hand).
- Work on a market stall (over-13s only); 'street trading' must be under parental supervision.
- Light cleaning duties (over-13s only).
- In a café or restaurant, serving, washing up, etc. (but not preparing food in a 'commercial kitchen', including chip-shops and takeaways, which is prohibited). Children must be over 13 to work as a waiter/waitress on licensed premises.
- Working with animals: stables, kennels, etc.
- Other: Please give FULL details so that a decision can be made as to whether the work is suitable for school-aged children.

Summary

During recent years there have been some attempts to rekindle a debate on child employment, but with only limited success. Following its own research, the GMB union hosted a consultation, but this has done little more than repeat what is already known about the extent of illegal working. Further initiatives have been taken by a group comprising representatives of the NSPCC and some LEA child employment officers who are part of a national network. Some interest has been shown, but it is clear, as before, that little will change until politicians accept the need for reform and ensure that the whole issue is given a higher profile, not least in Parliament.

The Better Regulation Taskforce, an independent advisory body to the Cabinet Office, issued a report in February 2004, *The Regulation of Child Employment*, that supported the principle of moving to the registration of employers as part of the duties of the new lead officer for Children's Services. This is a welcome shift in thinking (though I do not agree with its conclusion that CRB clearance would still not be necessary), but it will need extra resources, more detailed guidance and a more enforceable legal framework if local authorities are to become as proactive as it envisages. There might be more to be gained by moving the whole issue into the arena of those who already regulate health and safety at work, rather than its being seen as an adjunct to social work that would inevitably still have a low priority. We have to raise awareness, especially among employers and parents, that children are workers in this context, not just another pair of hands; and they are young workers at that, entitled to *more* attention to their protection and safety than adults, not less.

For a country such as Britain, supposedly committed to the best interests of its children, this whole area remains a blind spot which suggests that, at this point, other interests continue to prevail. No doubt in part it is still down to the perception that there is no problem and that therefore nothing needs to be done. For most children that may be true, but I and many others can give the names of those, or their parents, who know it to be otherwise. Those children are just as important as any others whose abuse has prompted major national soul-searching. In child protection as a whole we recognise that extensive systems are needed for a relatively small number of children who are most at risk. Why not here? Accidents and abuses do not just happen to children at work; they are invariably caused by adults, employers and parents who do not ensure that they have been adequately protected. It's about time we started to ask why, and what we could be doing about it.

Chapter 12

Allegations against teachers and other staff

Case studies and how they were dealt with

Setting the priorities

The main text of this book ends where it began: with the issue of allegations of abuse by teachers. This layout is deliberate. While teachers' needs are important, the primary focus has to be on children and the role of schools in ensuring their protection. One of my aims in writing has been to redress what sometimes seems to be an imbalance in perceptions in the education service. Getting protection right for the adults must be subsidiary to getting it right for the children, though I would also argue that there is rarely a fundamental conflict between the two. There is no doubt, however, that many teachers *feel* uncomfortable about this whole area, and unless these feelings are addressed, serious obstacles to best practice may remain unchallenged, especially if the individuals concerned are in positions of senior management.

The anxiety in this area is understandable but often misplaced. Of course the overwhelming majority of teachers are seen as caring and supportive, by both children and their parents. No one wants to create a climate in which someone becomes an object of suspicion simply because of the job they do, and it is sad to see how few men in particular now seem to want to work in primary schools or with even younger children. Given that many children lack an appropriate male role model elsewhere in their lives, this is only reinforcing an already worrying trend. But that said, when it comes to thinking about the possibility that we may be part of the problem as well as part of the solution, as teachers sometimes are, things can suddenly become very tense.

The media, highly influential in forming people's perceptions of an area in which they may not have had much personal experience, are interested in only two things: the genuine tragedies that sometimes result from false accusations, and the even greater disaster of those serious and high-profile cases that are proven to be true. But like child protection as a whole, most cases fall somewhere in between. As illustration, here are three fictionalised examples that reflect the range of possibilities and what was done about the concern once it had been raised. In my experience, these are generally typical.

Donna

Donna (4) is the subject of complaint by her mother to the police about her nursery school. On arriving to collect her after lunch, she says she saw Mrs X 'dragging Donna by her arm along the corridor. Donna was screaming, kicking and banging against the wall.' When reunited with her mum, Donna was sobbing and upset. She had no significant injury but her arm was reddened. Mum did not complain to the school at the time. The police contacted social services to convene a strategy meeting under ACPC procedures (physical abuse).

At the strategy meeting the headteacher gave her version of events, as seen by two other members of staff. Donna, who finds school difficult, cries a lot and often tries to run away. She cannot manage a full day yet. As her mum arrived to collect her, she tried to run the wrong way along a corridor full of older children. The teacher, very experienced but rather traditional, held her by the arm and encouraged to her to go to the correct area for collection. Donna protested, tried to kick the teacher and screamed in protest. She came back to school two days later and is quite settled.

The strategy meeting agreed there was no need for any further action by the police or social services. The chair will write to Donna's mum to say that the matter is closed and they and the police are satisfied nothing untoward occurred. The headteacher will reassure the member of staff and no record of the allegation will appear on her personal file.

Comment

This inter-agency process might have been avoided altogether if the school had a well-publicised complaints procedure or if another member of staff had stepped in to support Mrs X at the time. But parents might still choose to refer their concern outside the school if they feel that they may not get a fair hearing from those who may face a conflict of interest. We may expect parents, and children, to raise their concerns directly with us and even be hurt when they do not. But the perspective of the parent may be very different, especially if relationships have not always been very good in the past.

Donna's mother might have misunderstood the incident because she only saw part of it, or she may have known what really happened all along and just be over-reacting. Either way, it doesn't really matter as long as the process examines all the facts and comes to a reasonable conclusion. Colleagues in other agencies do not assume that parents are always right, but they must give them a chance to make their case. To reinforce the point that the school has not just conducted its own investigation, it was important that the chair of the strategy meeting sent the written outcome, not the headteacher or the chair of governors.

This teacher, while potentially embarrassed at having to account for her action, had nothing to fear. It would have been better for the headteacher to be more proactive in contacting the parent herself to explain the incident, ideally before she had time to go the police. This might have been sufficient for her to have let the matter rest, and no further investigation would have been required as long as the headteacher was satisfied that nothing untoward had occurred. However, once a complaint had been made, the police had no choice but to investigate it.

There was a slight complication in this case as the local uniformed police initially dealt with Donna's mother themselves and did not pass the complaint to the specialist officers for child protection, as they should have done. They were not trained in conducting such enquiries through video interview, and had there been a need to speak to an older child in order to gain their view of the event, they would not have been best placed to do so. No photographs of the injury were taken or medical examination arranged, which might have been critical if the incident had been more serious. Outcomes are not always as satisfactory when the specialists are not consulted.

John

John (10) tells his parents that his teacher, Mr Y, is a bully. He says he shouts at him when he hasn't done anything wrong, grabs him round the neck and says he is 'stupid'. He says that other children too are upset by Mr Y, and alleges that Mr Y once repeatedly pushed a boy in the stomach with the end of a stick and called him a 'fat sissy'. Parents complain to the school. The headteacher is aware that a couple of parents have complained before about Mr Y and that another teacher recently brought her a complaint about his behaviour on a school trip. After consultation with the LEA officer, and primarily because this does not appear to be an isolated example, the case is referred to the social services under child protection procedures (emotional/physical abuse).

The strategy meeting agrees a joint investigation by the police and SSD. There is some concern about Mr Y still being at work and, although this is a decision for the individual head and governing body to make, not for the strategy meeting, the head agrees to take advice from the LEA about possible suspension. (In the event, when informed of the investigation, Mr Y takes leave of absence on health grounds.) On being visited by the police, the parents decide they do not want to make a criminal allegation at this time but they do want to make a complaint under education disciplinary procedures. The parents and LEA are advised accordingly that no further action is being taken under child protection procedures, and a disciplinary inquiry is begun. It is agreed that if further protection concerns about other children come to light, the strategy meeting should be reconvened. Following further complaints raised by other parents, the police were later re-involved at the LEA's request. Mr Y was arrested for two assaults and an advice file was sent to the Crown Prosecution Service regarding possible prosecution. He remained on sick leave pending the outcome.

Comment

There were probably enough warning signs to merit this situation being referred outside the school at an earlier stage. The fact that there was an inexperienced headteacher may have been an inhibiting factor, together with the very real difficulty of knowing when such behaviour tips over the line into emotional or physical abuse. Intimidating and bullying children is not acceptable professional behaviour under any circumstances, but unless it actually causes the child harm by turning into physical contact, it can be difficult for agencies to agree that the child protection process is now required. This would be largely a matter of judgement for the headteacher to make, though in the light of advice and consultation with others.

If the previous complaints included anything that might have been considered an assault, there might be more grounds for criticising the school for not initiating the process earlier. At the strategy meeting it was clear that the headteacher already had grave concerns about the teacher's state of mind. He had become depressed following the breakdown of a relationship and very negative about the children he was working with. He had been seen by other staff to lose his temper and to shout at children, but no formal procedure had been initiated. There were obvious dangers in such a situation, which should not just have been left to drift.

Strategy meetings should always be reconvened if there are new developments. The school and the LEA became aware that other parents had more serious complaints to make once given an opportunity to do so, so it was right to take the case back to the inter-agency forum. Not all the parents wanted to involve the police initially, but all agreed to do so once appropriate assurances about confidentiality had been given and it had been explained to them that the school could not conduct such enquiries by itself. The use of sick leave or 'gardening' leave is open to debate, but can provide an alternative to formal suspension, at least in the early stages. Suspension is more likely in response to serious allegations or if there is a sense that the individual poses a risk either to the proper conduct of the investigation or to the children who continue to be in their care. The police and social services may well advise, but the decision is for the school/LEA, at least until it is clear whether there are going to be any formal charges.

Martin

The mother of Martin (15) finds intimate love letters implying sexual activity by Martin with another person, Z. Martin says they are from a girlfriend but his mother believes this is untrue. When she rings the mobile phone number on the letters, a man answers whom she knows to be Mr Z, a young adult leader of the football club that Martin attends. She talks to some of Martin's friends who also attend the club, even though Martin is not keen that she should do so. They say that it is well known that Martin and Mr Z are 'going out' and that Martin is not the first boy to have had an association with him. Mum goes to the police, who convene a strategy meeting (sexual abuse). Mum tells the police that Mr Z also takes sports lessons in a local high school (not the one attended by Martin), so the headteacher of that school is invited to attend.

At the strategy meeting a joint investigation is agreed. Martin, if he is willing, will be interviewed on video, together with any other young people who have information about Mr Z. Mr Z is currently being employed at the school on a temporary part-time basis to give additional support in football coaching. The headteacher reports that Mr Z was slow to complete the necessary CRB forms and it took several weeks before he did so, but he had no adverse record when it was returned. He works mostly with Year 10 and 11 pupils and is popular, especially with the less gifted boys, who are often difficult to interest. The strategy meeting agrees that if Martin makes a statement, the LEA will be informed.

On interview, Martin discloses some non-penetrative sexual activity that would constitute an offence if true, by alleging that Mr Z has 'snogged' both him and several other boys in the team. After clarification, Martin understands this term to include mutual masturbation. Martin also says that Mr Z has bought him presents, including a phone. The police prepare to conduct further enquiries with other boys, all under 16. Mr Z is suspended from his post at the school and at the football club and arrested. When his home is searched, indecent images of young teenage boys are found on his computer. He is later charged with offences relating to four boys, and others relating to the computerised images. If convicted, he will be required to register under the Sex Offenders Act 1997 and prohibited from working with children.

Comment

Even the suspicion of *any* form of sexual activity between adults and children under 16 in their care is a child protection issue that requires a careful inter-agency response. Hopefully, there should no longer be any examples of individuals just being spoken to in private or moved elsewhere with a glowing reference, as certainly happened in some schools (and elsewhere) in the past. Questions of appropriateness will also arise with respect to those pupils who are between 16 and 18 on the basis of an abuse of trust, though the law is currently a little cloudier. Martin's mother's tactics were somewhat controversial, and parents cannot always be relied upon to take such a thorough approach. There are always questions about whether or not there can be an investigation if the 'injured party' does not wish to make a complaint, but her persistence uncovered several potentially serious crimes.

Children cannot be forced to make statements or to be interviewed on video, and this case might have been left unresolved had none of the young people been willing to talk. There is little or no evidence that children deliberately lie about such things, but they do not always realise that what is happening to them is abusive, or they may fear they have done something wrong themselves. Had this occurred in this case, it would have put Mr Z, the school, the LEA and the football club in a very difficult position and left the allegations as unproven rather than true or false. It is sometimes necessary to make decisions based more on the civil test of the 'balance of probabilities' rather than being able to secure the full legal proof of 'beyond reasonable doubt'.

It is not uncommon for individuals to exploit a number of opportunities to have contact with children or to behave very differently in different settings. Concern may be raised about the personal life of individuals who work in schools but with no evidence that they have ever abused their professional position. The use of child pornography, for example, might not necessarily lead to the direct abuse of children who are in contact with the individual, but it raises obvious questions of risk. Equally, an issue raised in school may be relevant to other settings, unknown to the headteacher, in which that individual also has contact with children, such as a uniformed organisation or club, as well as raising questions about any children in their own family. This is one key reason why such concerns must *always* be referred outside the school for wider investigation if information comes to light.

This case also illustrates the limited value of a CRB check in that it tells you only whether people have been caught and convicted, not how they behave. Other procedures to assess their suitability to work with children will also be required, especially on appointment (see Chapter 14), but no system is foolproof, given the nature of such activity. The football club was weak in its supervision procedures, but the school had done everything necessary. It is always important to ensure that peripatetic and temporary staff are informed as part of their induction that they are covered by the school's child protection policy and codes of conduct like any other member of staff.

Summary

In contrast to examples like these, many people claim to know of cases where all the principles of good practice have been ignored and outcomes were far from satisfactory. Of course that happens, or, with the benefit of hindsight, it is sometimes possible to see a better approach than the one actually taken. But, as with child protection generally, real cases giving genuine cause for concern go on every day with nobody taking much notice. I certainly see more of those than the ones that were entirely without foundation. Where practice works, as I believe it did here, credit should be given where it is due. As ever, when things go wrong, we need to learn from our mistakes, try not simply to blame the unfortunate individuals who happened to be involved and then move on into doing things even better next time.

Chapter 13

Recognising the risk of professional abuse

Managing children and reducing the possibility of false allegations

Facing up to reality

In recent years I have been involved in about twenty to twenty-five child protection incidents a year that involve either teachers or other adults in position of trust in an educational setting. Nationally, teachers and others who work in schools or colleges have been caught accessing child pornography, have targeted individual children and established abusive relationships, have sexually abused pupils on residential visits, or have carried out physical assaults on children at their school. I hope no one still believes that such stories are all untrue. They should remind us of the importance of being open to the possibility that such things can, and do, happen in schools; that teachers and other education staff can, and do, abuse children. Denial that children could ever possibly be at risk in *this* school, or that any teacher we know could ever pose such a threat, would both be equally misguided. This issue is not an optional extra within policies and procedures for responding to child abuse, but an integral part of them.

All professionals must expect to fall in line with prescribed expectations as a condition of their employment. LEAs, governors and senior staff are failing in their statutory duty of care if they do not see their significance. The biggest danger of all is that we keep any concerns to ourselves or define our own standards for what is acceptable, and therefore put at risk any possibility of effective multi-agency practice. All headteachers, governors and education managers need to accept that, whatever their own judgement and values, if an allegation or incident is covered by child protection procedures, they cannot deal with the matter themselves.

We may have certain views about the degree of appropriate social contact between adults and children or what constitutes 'harmless fun', 'horseplay' or 'rough-and-tumble'. We may see the child as primarily responsible for the incident or the teacher as just rather old-fashioned or insensitive. But if an adult in a position of responsibility risks deliberate injury to a child or actually harms them, or if any kind of sexual activity or other abuse *may* be involved, a potential offence may have occurred which must be subject to external scrutiny, just as with the actions of a parent. Such a concern raises wider child protection issues and may also involve other children. Advice from outside the school should always be sought, and at a very early stage.

Risk factors

Facing up to the reality of abuse by teachers and others in a similar position is partly about addressing the nature of the role. Young children in particular, and even their parents, will normally have implicit confidence in those employed to care for them. That trust is occasionally misplaced but is given just the same. It is also about acknowledging that few other adults outside a child's family spend so much time with them in situations where there is also such potential for exploitation or misunderstanding. While the dangers should not be overstated, and perhaps many teachers will never have thought about themselves or their colleagues in this light and will find the following paragraphs rather shocking, there needs to be a clear and self-conscious recognition of the risks. I would identify three in particular.

Power

Teachers still carry a great deal of power and authority over children's lives, and power has a tendency to corrupt. If it is abused, it can act as a potent force for continued secrecy, just as with a parent. It may not always feel like this, but the teacher is still far more powerful than the child. Politicians expect schools to set clear standards of behaviour and allow the staff to impose significant sanctions on those who break them. Other children's professionals rarely expect to do the same. Most children will still do what the teacher says, even if the teacher's demands are unreasonable. Schools are largely hierarchical institutions with a clear pecking order in which the pupils are at the bottom. Education law gives them no real status; it is their parents who are the 'customers', not the children.

Abuse always involves the misuse of power. It requires a dominant party able to exercise control over the other. The more teachers seek to operate in ways that encourage partnership rather than merely the exercise of their personal authority, the less likelihood there is that individuals who rather enjoy being in control of children will be attracted into the role. Examples of both physical and sexual abuse in other institutional settings such as churches, residential homes and sporting organisations have led to a massive re-evaluation of the nature of the training and recruitment procedures that are now appropriate. I am not sure the same is yet true of all schools. Such thinking is sometimes dismissed as rather subversive. In fact, it is essential if teachers want to change the climate away from one that has traditionally placed them as the powerful individual in a wholly unbalanced relationship.

This is why, of course, we will never revert to using physical punishments in schools. The very idea should now be outrageous to most people, many of whom, thankfully, have already begun to think of teachers in a different way. No teacher should actually want such a right, and if they do, I am really not sure what they are doing in the profession. This is not only because it would provide an opportunity to the adult who enjoys inflicting pain and humiliation on children, as certainly happened in the past, but because it is wholly the wrong kind of model for the teacher–pupil relationship. 'Discipline' has its roots in the word for 'learning', not in 'punishment'. Good teaching is in itself good discipline; that is obviously where the emphasis needs to be.

What our children need are positive examples of mutual respect from which they, and their parents if necessary, can learn. Seeking a return to authority-based approaches in which the threat is either real or constantly implied will simply set teachers up for more scandal; either for the few who will go over the top on the basis that they can do what they like, or for the many more who will risk censure because no one could ever be sure about what the rules were. Not being allowed to hit or deliberately cause pain to children *at all, under any circumstances*, is a major protection for the teachers, never mind for the pupils.

Sexuality

Few would dispute that those in the caring professions are at greater risk than others of getting over-involved with children and young people. Working with children fulfils emotional needs in us; that's why we do it. No wonder it sometimes goes horribly wrong. If you have never met a paedophile (and you probably have, but without realising it), do not imagine that they are all cruel and inhuman monsters or pathetic individuals who could never hold down a responsible job like teaching. Many would claim genuinely to love children and to be good at working with them. Like Mr Z in my examples in Chapter 12, the evidence may not all be one way. People maintain their position and status for years without anyone suspecting, and not only because they are very clever or very coercive. But the risks, though real, are often unacknowledged. It is difficult to accept that people can be so devious, and sometimes behaviour is tolerated just because we rather naively assume that everything must be all right really, despite how it looks.

The personal elements of the job may hardly ever be discussed and may be seen as a purely private matter that everyone is left to sort out for themselves. This leaves people immensely vulnerable. Teachers have a difficult enough line to tread between formality and informality, but there is no need deliberately to make things even more difficult. For example, in my opinion the charity calendar that showed school staff apparently naked, if in largely discreet poses, but in their school settings, was most unwise. It surely sends a rather inappropriate signal about how teachers should be regarded that could be open to misunderstanding, even if that was no one's intention. This feels to me like stepping over a boundary.

It would also be foolish to ignore the risks posed by older pupils experimenting with their sexuality and therefore open to exploitation by those whom they see as role models. 'Crushes' have not entirely disappeared even in today's more cynical times, and adolescents carry an attraction in the wider media of music and fashion that betrays a deep ambiguity in many of our society's wider values. They are likely to be flattered by an adult's attention. This does not, of course, excuse abuse, but I wonder how many allegations have been the result of misplaced attraction or misinterpreted friendship? Any sexual relationship with a pupil aged *under 18* (not just 16) is an abuse of trust under the Sexual Offences (Amendment) Act 2000. Other kinds of behaviour may be subject to disciplinary procedures, even if no criminal offence is involved.

An essential element in training for those who work directly with sexually abused children and adults is recognising their own sexuality and how it relates to the job. This can be extremely embarrassing at the time and needs to be done with great sensitivity, far more than I would ever consider appropriate as part of a normal training programme for teachers, but it can be immensely valuable even as a self-discipline. There is sometimes uncertainty in our own sexual experiences and attitudes – 'grey' areas that need to be recognised to avoid us allowing them to influence our judgement. Teachers rarely have the opportunity to go through this process and are, as a result, often not very conscious of the possible impact of any unresolved issues.

Conflict

Some children have been brought up with family and community attitudes and expectations that are likely to lead them into conflict with figures of authority. However much we may regret it, school is an inevitable context for such confrontation. This may sadden many teachers, but there can be no return to a so-called golden age when they were always right by virtue of their position and everyone respected them (at least to their face!). New skills in behaviour management are now required, not simply the assertion of traditional expectations as if that were the end of it. In the end, that will both protect us all from behaving inappropriately and encourage children to see positive examples of how they too should be expected to behave.

Teachers are sometimes required to act in ways that will make children angry or in circumstances where they may be provoked into losing their temper. It is no surprise, or it shouldn't be, that some of these situations result in both genuine causes for concern and false accusations. Clearly, there is much increased potential for physical violence in the face of a child who constantly disobeys you and whose behaviour you feel you cannot control. Many parents are stuck in exactly the same spiral. Children may even occasionally seek revenge against those who they feel have wronged them at school, however unfairly, and goad the teacher into action against them. Even the most experienced and long-suffering professional may suddenly act out of character in the face of such pressure and behave wholly unprofessionally and in a way that is actually an offence, even if they don't realise it at the time. Such risks have to be consciously acknowledged and anyone in such a position carefully removed from any situation that might result in an accusation being made against them or a child being harmed.

Physical contact with pupils

I have lost count over the years of how often I have heard that the Children Act prevents teachers from even touching children or from using any kind of reasonable restraint in response to their misbehaviour or aggression. I have no idea where this idea has come from; probably only from a misinterpretation of the advice issued by the Department of Health to staff in residential children's units, where the context is significantly different from that of a school. It is not in the Children Act itself and is not true. Of course the climate has changed. Children are more likely to resist authority than they were; parents are more able to seek redress, through the police or even through the courts in extreme circumstances, if they feel their child has been assaulted. But touching children is not always abuse, and the Act in no way supports the notion that it is.

The key document for educational professionals is DfEE Circular 10/98 (Welsh Office Circular 37/98), *Section 550A of the Education Act 1996: The Use of Force to Control or Restrain Pupils.* It is only eight pages long and every teacher should have read it, but it cannot cover every situation in detail. There should also be specific guidance available from the LEA aimed especially at those who work in special schools and with children with complex needs, though not all of this will be immediately applicable in other contexts. Circular 10/98 says:

> Physical contact with a pupil may be proper or necessary . . . to demonstrate exercises or techniques during PE lessons, sports coaching or CDT [craft, design and technology], or if a member of staff has to give first aid. . . . Touching may also be appropriate where a pupil is in distress and needs comforting. Teachers will use their own professional judgement when they feel a pupil needs this kind of support.
>
> There may be some children for whom touching is particularly unwelcome. For example, some pupils may be particularly sensitive to physical contact because of their cultural background, or because they have been abused. It is important that all staff receive information on these children. . . . Physical contact with pupils becomes increasingly open to question as pupils reach and go through adolescence, and staff should also bear in mind that even innocent and well-intentioned physical contact can sometimes be misconstrued.
>
> (Paragraphs 33 and 34)

Safe practice guidelines

This advice is obvious and largely common sense. Every professional adult should always keep their use of physical contact with children under constant review. But I have seen enough examples in schools of inappropriate touching, physical intimidation or unwarranted invasion of a child's personal space to their clear discomfort to know that things cannot always be left to the discretion of the individual. If at all possible, staff should ensure that they seek the child's consent before touching them in connection with, for example, a sports activity – such as asking, 'Is it OK if I show you?' or 'Would you like me to lift you over the apparatus?', etc. It may seem rather formal, but it is helpful if it is clear to everyone that the child has some control over whether or not they wish to be touched.

It will usually be best in such a context if there is an agreed whole-school statement about how the adults and the children will relate to each other in a more general sense, that recognises the right of everyone to be treated with respect and courtesy. Schools should always agree clear codes of personal conduct for their staff and volunteers. Such a policy should be monitored and enforced by disciplinary procedures if necessary, as is commonplace in other settings involving adults and children such as voluntary organisations, the Youth Service and 'Connexions'. A protocol might include a range of related issues such as:

- making it clear that adults must at all times be aware of their professional status as a trusted adult and of the responsibility this imposes on them;
- the school's procedure for being alone with a child in rooms or offices or allowing pupils to ride in staff members' cars (both of which will sometimes be necessary and appropriate);
- policy and procedures for dealing with situations requiring physical contact, including the use of force (see p. 157);
- arrangements for supervising pupils while they are undressing or showering;
- policy on giving out personal mobile phone numbers or e-mail addresses, or collecting them from pupils;
- rules about not giving pupils presents or socialising with older pupils;
- whether to allow the use of teachers' first names or disclosure of personal information to pupils.

Many of these activities might be entirely innocent, but they are also a possible source of misunderstanding and misuse by either child or teacher. Some serious investigations begin from an awareness by parents or other staff that an individual appears to be singling out a certain child, or a number of children with similar characteristics. Such behaviours have included text messaging, inappropriate e-mails, calling pupils' mobile phones, use of the Internet to 'chat' with pupils, and meeting up with pupils outside school without parental knowledge. If the behaviour gets to anything approaching 'grooming' with an ulterior purpose, it may itself become an offence in the United Kingdom in the near future, even if no actual sexual relationship results.

If the school has clear guidance in place, as it should, and members of staff then infringe those standards, there must be an appropriate response by managers. Where the behaviour suggests there may be any motive of a sexual kind, child protection procedures *must* be invoked. Where such activities are only due to innocent mistakes, staff must be helped to appreciate that they are putting themselves (and the school) at risk of accusations by infringing the agreed expectations. Very few children make up an entirely malicious allegation, but such a possibility is significantly enhanced if the adults do not act responsibly and professionally. Further guidance should be available from the LEA or there may be a set of locally agreed inter-agency standards. (See also NEOST *et al.* 2002.)

Training idea 5: Avoiding false allegations of abuse (group/plenary)

TASK: Discuss the following advice and its implications for the practice of teachers and schools. (It may be helpful to have a copy of the NEOST guidance available as well, together with any local protocols, etc.)

This is not a strategy to enable abusers to remain undetected, but many allegations against teachers arise from misunderstandings, lack of policy and guidance, or failures to exercise proper management. Being proactive in anticipating possible risks may save someone's career *and* protect children; the two are not incompatible.

- Keep to staff codes of behaviour about contact with pupils. If there isn't one, insist the school creates one for your protection. Expect to see it enforced in practice.
- Witnesses are always useful. Can you work in ways that avoid your being alone with an individual pupil wherever possible (e.g. in cars, in a room) (EWOs, for example, will usually try not to be alone with a child in their house without a parent if at all possible.)
- Keep a written record of anything that might be open to misunderstanding as well as all incidents of the use of force or restraint. This can be very useful if the child's version of events is different from how you remember the incident but there is nothing written down.
- If a child is injured by accident by a teacher, or if physical restraint has to be used against them, parents are much less likely to suspect a conspiracy if they hear about it from the school *before* the child tells them a possibly less reliable version. If the headteacher is satisfied that no one has done anything wrong, they should seize the initiative and say so.
- Think 'How would this look if I saw someone else doing it?' Is an action that is innocent in your mind open to misinterpretation?
- Physical contact can be embarrassing – watch your body language. The prohibition on the use of corporal punishment includes 'any degree of physical contact which is deliberately intended to punish a pupil, or which is primarily intended to cause pain, injury or humiliation' (DfEE

Circular 10/98, para. 2). This can include being physically threatening or intimidating.

- *Never* lose your temper. If you do, get out.
- Support one another wherever possible; senior staff should not allow hierarchies of status to prevent colleagues from questioning their behaviour.
- Do not criticise someone who feels that they need support, advice or a witness that you do not think you would need in the same situation.
- Challenge bad practice if you see it. Report any concerns.
- Working to procedures is better for everyone rather than leaving people to sort it out for themselves (and so carry the can if they make a mistake).
- Training, supervision, management and accountability are not an assault on a teacher's integrity but evidence of professional good practice.

The use of force

The issue that still seems to cause most controversy is the use of force in a disciplinary context. The circumstances under which staff are empowered to use a degree of force or restraint must be clearly defined in *written* policy and procedures in every school, open to inspection by parents and known to all staff, with suitable training as required. Headteachers are required to designate which staff are authorised to use such a response, and all incidents must be immediately reported, documented and proportionate to the circumstances. Children who are identified as likely to need such interventions should have a written plan, agreed with their parents, as part of an individual behaviour management strategy. Circumstances that arise unexpectedly should be dealt with using the minimum force necessary once all other alternatives have been attempted. Again, DfEE Circular 10/98 must be the starting point. (For those in SEN settings, see also DfES Guidance 0242/2002 and 0264/2003 on the use of restrictive physical interventions.)

There are a wide variety of situations in which reasonable force might be appropriate, or necessary, in order to control or restrain a pupil. They will fall into three broad categories:

a. where action is necessary in self-defence or because there is an imminent risk of injury;
b. where there is a developing risk of injury, or significant damage to property;

c. where a pupil is behaving in a way that is compromising good order and discipline.

(Paragraph 14)

In situations such as these, legitimate actions may include:

- having to intervene between two pupils who are fighting;
- blocking a pupil's path;
- holding;
- pushing;
- pulling;
- leading a pupil by the hand or arm;
- shepherding a pupil away by placing a hand in the centre of the back; or,
- (in extreme circumstances) using more restrictive holds.

In exceptional circumstances, where there is an immediate risk of injury, a member of staff may need to take any necessary action that is consistent with the concept of 'reasonable force': for example, to prevent a young pupil running off a pavement onto a busy road, or to prevent a pupil hitting someone or throwing something.

(Paragraphs 21 and 22)

Appropriate actions, even in situations that require some intervention, would clearly *not* include:

- holding a pupil around the neck, or by the collar, or in any other way that might restrict the pupil's ability to breathe;
- slapping, punching or kicking a pupil;
- twisting or forcing limbs against a joint;
- tripping up a pupil;
- holding or pulling a pupil by the hair or ear;
- holding a pupil face down on the ground.

Staff should always avoid touching or holding a pupil in a way that might be considered indecent.

(Paragraphs 23 and 24)

Even when exercising restraint, it is good practice to keep explaining to the child what you are doing and why, and to make sure they still have options available to avoid the intervention. Inadvertent touching can usually be avoided by sensible precautions, and adults must appreciate that there are always reasonable limits. A child or young person's objection to being touched, even if the teacher considers it necessary, should not automatically be dismissed or, worse still, treated as some kind of misbehaviour in itself. They may be entirely correct in their understanding, even if their response is dressed up in the typically blunt style of a contemporary teenager! They may not, for example, wish to attend a school medical, receive immunisation or undress in front of other pupils. No one should ever make them do so under any kind of threat or actual use of physical force.

Any disciplinary confrontation that is escalating into the possible use of force by an adult should be de-escalated again as quickly as possible, if necessary by withdrawing from the situation, even if it means loss of face in the short term. Calling for assistance, admitting that you have made a mistake, are in danger of losing your temper, or asking a more experienced member of staff to deal with a situation for you should never be interpreted as weakness. It is far more of a weakness not to know your own limitations and to blunder on into a situation that is clearly putting both the teacher and the pupil at risk of acting with unacceptable violence. Children should *never* be seen as 'deserving' abuse – physical, emotional, verbal or racist. Staff must at all times be aware that the deliberate infliction of pain on a child is an illegal assault, not appropriate restraint. Again, an active climate within the school that fosters mutual respect will certainly help to discourage pupils, parents or anyone else from acting inappropriately.

Provided all these safeguards are in place and adhered to and if, in the event of an incident, the headteacher is fully satisfied that use of force or any other kind of physical contact was acceptable according to the guidance, no child protection issues should arise. After making initial contact with parents at the time, a written account should follow once the facts are clear. Otherwise it may at least appear that the school is attempting to hide what 'really' happened, even if nothing actually did. The parent or child may, of course, still choose not to accept that the situation was handled properly, but they are far less likely to take the issue further if the school has already been proactive in assuring them that nothing untoward occurred. Many minor incidents can then be resolved very quickly. Child protection situations in which staff did *not* act appropriately must of course be identified as such by the headteacher and referred outside the school for investigation (see Chapter 14).

Staff behaviour on school trips, etc.

Extra care will be needed in situations where school staff are supervising pupils while they are away from home, especially during overnight stays, trips to activity centres and visits abroad, etc. Here, as in the kinds of medical situations discussed in Chapter 8, staff must ensure that appropriate parental consent has been obtained to enable any necessary action to be taken with respect to their child. Forms *must* be signed by someone with parental responsibility for the child as defined by the Children Act 1989, not just by anyone who may qualify under the wider definition of 'parent'. (See DfEE Circular 0092/2000, *Schools, Parents and Parental Responsibility*, and Appendix 2.) This reduces the likelihood of any dispute about whether the teacher will have acted correctly in the parent's absence.

Such visits sometimes raise additional questions about appropriate behaviour and the need to make sure that everyone always acts responsibly. (Other issues about general safety are also mentioned briefly in Chapter 8.) Teachers and any other adults – including, for example, parent helpers and volunteers – should take proper measures to protect both the pupils and themselves from any possible misunderstandings or unprofessional conduct that may occur in this context. Relationships are often more relaxed on such occasions, or opportunities may be presented that are out of the ordinary.

Sleeping arrangements must obviously be carefully monitored and no conduct permitted which might give the impression that a child and an adult should ever sleep alone together. I have known examples where special favourites were invited into private rooms and tents or where an individual helper took a child into their bed because it was said that they were distressed in the middle of the night. If it is necessary to isolate a particular child on the grounds of their behaviour, never do so in such a way that leaves that child and teacher in any position that is open to compromise. Try always to have another adult present in any situation that might be a source of difficulty – for example, if an item of clothing has to be removed after an accident or if a child requires any use of force, or assistance with washing or toiletting. Remember that the need for personal privacy, even from one another, is essential to most teenagers.

A complication might again arise where the child, especially an older child, objects to the teacher's authority. For example, I do not think any teacher would be criticised if, after reasonable persuasion had been attempted first, they had to use some limited force to prevent a young person from drinking too much or going out late at night, even if they protested about it at the time. Parents may have given clear instruction that the child is not allowed to smoke and staff may therefore wish to intervene to prevent it. What must be clear, however, is that any use of any force was not excessive, that any intervention was witnessed by another adult, and that parents were informed as soon as practically possible.

Training

Ignoring such issues and hoping they will go away, or seeing them only as the responsibility of the children and their parents, is as much a failure to act responsibly as failing to carry out the local procedures when required to do so. All these issues should be the subject of both personal training and staff supervision. The ethos of the whole school should actively promote high standards of personal integrity. At the very least, employers must ensure that their employees have actually seen and read the documents that define their practice, such as those on the proper use of physical force or standards of personal conduct; that written records are kept of any incidents; and that everyone is aware of the procedures that apply in the event of a complaint.

I am rather concerned, on the evidence of the numerous training events that I have delivered around the country, about how much of what I say in this critical area appears to be entirely new information, even to those who have been in teaching or educational management for years. I regularly hear stories of events and concerns that were not handled according to the guidance or were simply ignored, such as a teacher deliberately tripping up a pupil who was running in the corridor, flirting with older pupils or using physical and humiliating punishments. In some cases, behaviours that were clearly putting the teacher at risk of acting inappropriately were tolerated and left unaddressed by managers, sometimes resulting in subsequent allegations.

Summary

Surely no school or individual actually *wants* to be the subject of either a scandal or an unnecessary investigation? It must be worth being prepared and making sure that we have taken the necessary action at the time. The litigation culture will catch up with schools eventually, but in any case such things should not be allowed to happen, because they are simply wrong and unprofessional.

Chapter 14

When investigation has to happen

Guidance on the inter-agency process when a teacher is accused

Working Together to Safeguard Children

As we have already seen, all agencies' practice in dealing with child protection concerns has to be evaluated against this national guidance from the DoH, DfES and the Home Office (1999). This specifically includes a section on 'professional abuse' and what must be done when a concern of this kind is identified. This issue will also be covered in local ACPC procedures, which must be used as required. Teachers may not always be aware that this inter-agency framework applies to them, and the possibility should be acknowledged in the school's child protection policy. There is no special arrangement for those who work in education rather than in children's homes or other settings. While there is also specific guidance from an educational point of view, this wider perspective must again be the starting point.

Working Together applies to a wide range of people connected with education, not just teachers, including teaching assistants and other support staff, LEA officers, youth workers, coach and taxi-drivers, escorts, volunteer helpers, governors, residential staff, etc.:

> Experience has shown that children can be subjected to abuse by those who work with them in any and every setting. All allegations of abuse of children by a professional, staff member, foster carer or volunteer (from ACPC member agencies) should therefore be taken seriously and treated in accordance with local child protection procedures. Other organisations which provide services for children (including day care, leisure, churches, other places of worship and voluntary services) should have a procedure for handling such allegations which is consistent with this guidance and with ACPC procedures. There should be clear written procedures in place which are available for scrutiny by service users, and which are supported by training and supervision of staff. It is essential that all allegations are examined objectively by staff who are independent of the service, organisation or institution concerned.
>
> (Paragraph 6.13)

There is really very little room for misunderstanding here, but it may help to explore the implications of this extract a little further.

1. *Children, as well as parents, have a right to make complaints.* This is often seen as a relatively radical idea in education, though I do not see why. The UN Convention on the Rights of the Child, formally ratified by the United Kingdom in 1991, gives children a right to freedom of expression and to have their views respected. The Children Act says much the same. Anything children have to say about their own safety at school, and the action required, is clearly to be taken seriously. Since 1 September 2003, schools have had to publicise a general complaints procedure for parents to use, within which there will need to be a specific process for dealing with those complaints that raise child protection concerns. It is important that these are distinguished from other kinds of complaints about the staff or the school and that they are referred on for investigation under local procedures.

I do not believe that telling children and their parents that they have access to a genuinely independent process for resolving issues about the conduct of staff will open the floodgates of unwarranted accusations. This has not happened in other settings where such expectations have been introduced. Indeed, I would argue that the perceived absence of agreed complaints procedures makes it *more* likely that even concerns that could have been dealt with only as disciplinary matters will end up with the social services and the police because parents were offered no real alternative in which they could have any confidence.

This is not the same as saying that we must always do what children or parents wish. But given that opportunity for complaint is made available, what they say should then be properly investigated, not immediately dismissed as untrue. It is futile to argue either that children must always be believed or generally not believed when they make an allegation. Neither position is realistic. But they must be listened to and their perspective understood. Some incredibly unbelievable stories turn out to be true; some that seem entirely plausible turn out to be a fabrication or a misinterpretation. Only a proper inquiry will resolve the issue, but, either way, the first step is to make it clear that the child has a right to be heard in a spirit of openness, opportunity and empathy.

2. *There should be a clear written policy for dealing with such issues.* This is surely best for everyone, including any teacher who is the subject of an allegation. Policies and procedures should set out the rights of all the people involved, not just the rights of the child. They should contain provision for the resolution of disagreements, timetables for decision-making, appropriate assurances about confidentiality, and clear indications of who is responsible for what, in line with national guidance. Policy should be widely discussed, not just imposed, and, if possible, shared in advance of its being needed so that there can be no accusation of making it up at the time as we go along.

3. *Criteria for decision-making should be open and consistent.* There is a genuine fear among teachers that decisions will be made behind their backs, without their being made aware of what is going on. In the very early stages, information will probably be shared before the individual concerned is made aware of the complaint, especially if there is likely to be any involvement by the police. It is sometimes necessary to control the timing of events for evidential purposes. But once the procedure has commenced, those who are the subject of an allegation clearly have the right to know about it. If professionals being investigated under child protection procedures have been suspended for long periods without knowing why, something has gone wrong. Parents are entitled to information when they are the subject of an investigation; there is no reason for teachers and others to be treated any differently. There should be legitimate scope for challenging decisions, for making representations and for the right to know, at the correct time, what the evidence is. Some of the cases involving unnecessarily ruined reputations appear to have shown scant regard for these principles, which only reinforces how important they are, not that the correct procedure is flawed.

4. *'Whistle-blowing' is a reasonable professional response to bad practice.* It can be very awkward when a junior member of staff feels that a more senior colleague has acted inappropriately or has real cause for concern about their behaviour. I was once told of a male deputy head in a high school, tolerated as being rather eccentric and above criticism by anyone else, who regularly took favoured girl pupils into a stockroom at lunchtimes 'for a smoke' – or that was what was assumed. That kind of behaviour might well have been acceptable in some circles in the past; it is certainly not so now. Staff may witness a colleague losing their temper with a child, overhear inappropriate gossip or even become suspicious about a potential sexual relationship with a pupil. They are entitled to feel that acting in the best interests of children will not be seen by their managers as underhand. Where complaints are against very senior members of staff, perhaps even including the designated teacher or the headteacher, all adults in the school community should feel that the chair of governors or the LEA lead officer is available to them if needed.

5. *Professional supervision should recognise child protection issues.* There is currently only limited evidence that this issue will feature to any great extent in initial teacher training, so it must be part of induction programmes and ongoing professional development. How to handle and relate to the pupils, especially when they are challenging, has to be regularly talked about in staff meetings and INSET. No one should be left to 'do it their way'. Such an approach is courting disaster and is an abdication of managerial responsibility. Staff should expect to be regularly confronted with questions like 'Did you feel you dealt with that situation properly?', 'How could it have been done better?', 'What might have gone wrong?', both in groupwork and in personal observations and assessments, without feeling unduly threatened or defensive.

6. *Specific allegations must be dealt with under the inter-agency procedures*. The significance of this point is explored in full on p. 166 but needs making explicitly here. Co-operation with agreed child protection procedures is a legal requirement in all child protection work. There is no place for special cases or for effectively inventing a way of doing things that does not accord with the obligations which the education service has, along with every other agency. There is, of course, room for discretion where a concern does not meet the child protection criteria, but not when it does.

Education guidance

Advice on dealing with allegations specifically aimed at schools (which includes all schools, however they are maintained and managed) is found in the current DfES Circular on child protection. There has also been helpful guidance from the teacher unions and from the network of DfES Investigation and Referral Support Co-ordinators (IRSCs), set up in recent years to assist LEAs and schools in their responsibilities. There may be a local protocol drawn up between the agencies that clarifies the issues about teachers and others. It will always be helpful to first reach an agreement about what kind of allegation we are dealing with in order to determine the correct response. There is no point in wasting everybody's time when the concern is not about child protection or the incident may not even have taken place at all.

For child protection procedures to be used, there would normally have to be some evidence that a child has been harmed, or is at significant risk of harm, or that some incident may not have been in line with the appropriate force that teachers are legitimately empowered to use. Just being in a confrontation with a teacher that resulted in some kind of physical contact is not sufficient. Disagreements about how a situation was handled, short of an allegation of harm, would normally be better dealt with under complaints or disciplinary procedures within the school. However, if there is any uncertainty about what happened, or the child does have an identified injury, school staff must expect the external investigation process to be followed. Those receiving such information must pass it on to the social services or police under local arrangements.

The IRSC advice identifies four levels of concern and the action arising as a result:

1. Demonstrably false
It is known without a doubt that the allegation is untrue. This position requires strong evidence and must not be based on preconceptions about the child or member of staff concerned (e.g. the alleged perpetrator was known not to be anywhere in the vicinity and the child is not confused in terms of time, place or person). Internal enquiries can be undertaken by the school . . . the LEA lead officer **must** receive written notification of the allegation, the evidence and how the matter was resolved.

2. Unlikely

The alleged incident most probably did not take place (e.g. where circumstantial evidence appears to be incompatible with the allegation). Only clarification of the specific allegation or concern should be sought. No attempt should be made to investigate the matter at this stage. Consultation **must** take place with the LEA lead officer. The decision to handle the matter internally or refer to social services will be made with the lead officer.

3. Possible

There are indications that an abusive incident might have taken place, or little evidence objectively to disprove a child's allegations (e.g. where a child's allegations might be supported by other information, or where it is a matter of one word against another). A child protection referral **must** be made to the social services (or the police). Local ACPC procedures **must** be followed. The LEA lead officer **must** be informed of the case and the action taken.

4. Apparent corroboration

Where an allegation or concern is accompanied by actual or circumstantial evidence (e.g. a child may have a visible injury. The incident may have been witnessed. The member of staff may behave in a way which is consistent with the allegation). A child protection referral **must** be made . . . the LEA lead officer **must** be informed.

As before, this advice must be read in the light of *Working Together*, the circular on the use of force and local ACPC procedures, but it can help in giving more specific examples of best practice as applicable to the education setting. LEA child protection officers and headteachers should certainly be aware of local arrangements where they exist. These may include a recognition that minor incidents can be dealt with under single agency procedures, once the police and social services have agreed that there is no need for them to be involved. What such additional guidance does *not* do, and cannot be allowed to do, is to provide an alternative system for teachers when the concerns *do* meet the criteria for an inter-agency investigation. Teachers feature in these arrangements more frequently than any other professional, but that simply reflects their numerical dominance, and perhaps their general vulnerability, and does not mean that they are being singled out for excessive scrutiny.

Inter-agency procedures

The decision about whether an investigation is required, as with any child protection referral, is made by the social services or the police on receipt of a complaint from a child, parent or other person. In the case of an allegation against any childcare professional, they will usually think it best to call a formal strategy meeting, as long as the complaint relates to child protection at a sufficient level of seriousness. There should normally be immediate consultation with the designated LEA officer and the headteacher or manager of the individual concerned (i.e. the chair of governors if it is the headteacher). Other kinds of complaints may be dealt with by the local uniformed police or referred back to the school and LEA to be dealt with under their own internal procedures.

If an allegation of abuse is made directly to the headteacher, chair of governors or LEA, they should ask for the strategy meeting themselves, which should take place within no more than two working days. Here as elsewhere, delay is to be avoided, and the school and LEA cannot be expected to hold a situation for more than a day or two without clarifying what action may now be needed. As head-teachers and LEA officers cannot investigate these kinds of concerns themselves, systems must be in place to ensure that others do so promptly when required. If the individual involved does not know about the allegation already, it is best *not* to make them aware of it until after the meeting, as this may affect any future police investigation.

At all times there will be three elements of the process to be considered in parallel:

•   child protection procedures if any of the four categories of abuse are involved (largely the responsibility of the social services department);
•   a criminal investigation if an offence may have been committed (solely the responsibility of the police and then the CPS);
•   disciplinary procedures if there may have been infringements of acceptable professional behaviour or school policy (solely the responsibility of the employer – in most cases, the governing body and the LEA).

It can be complicated to hold all these strands together at once, and they often proceed at different speeds, with separate elements taking priority at different times. But headteachers, governors and LEA officers, as in all cases of potential child abuse, are not qualified, trained or legally empowered to conduct investigations into criminal offences or to take their own decisions about the protection of children in isolation, and must therefore be aware of the distinctions. However, there is clearly a need for some initial enquiry into the alleged incident. Often there is no dispute that something happened, just disagreement over the context, motive or intent. It will be difficult for the headteacher or LEA officer to make an effective contribution to the strategy meeting if they have no idea who or what the allegation is about. It may also be necessary for enquiries to be made in order to inform a decision about whether an incident requires referral under inter-agency child protection procedures or whether it is solely a matter for the school and LEA.

Headteachers may naturally wish to take written statements from staff or pupils and to come to a clear decision about what 'actually' happened, but this degree of detail should normally be avoided until *after* the strategy meeting, if one is required. It is acceptable for the headteacher to form a view on the incident as they understand it, but that alone cannot be seen as a sufficiently independent 'investigation' that necessarily closes the matter. That role belongs to the external agencies, once it has been agreed that we are dealing with a child protection issue, not just a complaint of a different kind. Each of the three strands can then be allocated through an agreed process.

If there are statements to be taken in such circumstances, it is best if they are taken by the police, either alone or jointly with the social worker, recognising the strict rules of evidence that apply in all such procedures. Headteachers would do better to confine themselves to gathering confidential incident reports and personnel information, making their own notes of conversations, and making it clear that they are not carrying out a full inquiry at this early stage. If in doubt, they should do the minimum necessary to clarify any misunderstandings and to gather factual information about the individuals involved (career details, dates of birth, addresses, incident reports, letters of complaint, etc.). Then they should wait until after the strategy meeting for clarification of who will be responsible for taking the investigation forward, if indeed there needs to be one at all.

The rights of the individual

If concerns continue no further than the strategy meeting, as in the case of Mrs X in Chapter 12, the individual will normally be told by their manager at that stage that a complaint was made and is now closed. No one else needs to know. For other cases, it is perfectly reasonable to suggest that anyone who is the subject of an allegation is entitled to anonymity at least until such time as they are charged with an offence. Unfortunately, although the core professionals are likely to keep the investigation secret, parents may not do so. The magistrates' courts rules currently allow those who are charged and appear in court to be identified in the press, not just those who are convicted. Sometimes it is colleagues who identify both teacher and child, which is equally unfortunate. Avoiding the allegation altogether by proactive and self-conscious efforts to reduce the risks is always a preferable alternative. It is sometimes too late to do things absolutely correctly, even by the time a complaint has been made.

Suspension or other disciplinary responses are not automatic and are not always used, but should always be considered. There must be some sense that there is a risk to the inquiry, to children, and possibly to the individual if they remain at work. Suspension is more common when someone has been arrested at a very early stage or in response to allegations of sexual abuse, as with Mr Z in Chapter 12. This is a decision for the governors or employer, if acting on LEA advice, *not* for the strategy meeting or other agencies. Of course, suspension is perceived in a negative way even though it is strictly neutral, but it is a routine response for other professionals as well. If there are formal enquiries to be made, it is often in the individual's best interests to be well away from the situation until the outcome is clear. No one, of course, should underestimate the personal stress involved, and every effort should be made to ensure that the accused person is treated fairly. They should always be advised to seek support though their legal or professional representative or association and be given all possible opportunity to present their case at the appropriate time.

LEA lead officers and headteachers or other managers are entitled to some consultation about the progress and outcomes of police and social services investigations, but may not receive updates as often as they would wish. If information is not forthcoming, they should seek to obtain it from either the senior manager who chaired the strategy meeting or the manager of the workers concerned, especially where staff have had to be suspended. As in the case of Mr Y in Chapter 12, it may be necessary to reconvene the meeting in the light of further developments. It will be essential to reach agreement about what the accused person is to be told and when. They should not be left in a vacuum, but cannot expect to be consulted at every stage or told everything immediately. That would make independent investigation impossible and leave them and their employer wide open to accusations of collusion.

Under current police procedures, it may be some time after the allegation before the individual will be formally interviewed or, if appropriate, arrested and charged. It is usual practice to accumulate all the evidence, witness statements, etc. first, which can be very frustrating for all concerned. There is, however, no way of knowing in advance which accusations contain the most truth and so to ensure that only the guilty have to be investigated. Trying though it is, we may just have to wait until the process can provide a satisfactory result, or as good a result as is possible, given sometimes irreconcilable accounts that can never be proven one way or the other. The headteacher acquitted of an alleged assault involving a fish-head was perhaps particularly unfortunate in having to go through the ordeal of a court appearance, but is not entirely typical!

Training idea 6: Dealing with an allegation (group/plenary, ideally including governors)

TASK: Discuss the following case scenario:

1   What issues will need to be considered in this case?
2   How could the situation best be handled?
3   Does the age of the child make a difference? If so, why?
4   Are the necessary procedures in place? If not, what needs to be done?

Try to look at it from the perspective of all those involved:

*   child;
*   parent;
*   teacher;
*   colleagues;

continued

- head;
- governors;
- LEA;
- the police;
- social services.

This could be done by a role-play, or just by going through each participant in turn to understand how they might each see it.

Andrew Jones is a pupil with moderate learning difficulties who often exhibits challenging behaviour and is of mixed race. He 'thinks with his mouth' and has a tendency to irritate both staff and other pupils with silliness and cheek. His mother, who is white, is very committed to her son and can sometimes be pretty confrontational on his behalf. She has come into school this morning demanding to see the head.

She immediately launches into a tale about Andrew being 'assaulted' yesterday by a male supply teacher. She says that he grabbed Andrew around the neck in registration yesterday afternoon, swore at him and then kicked him to the ground as he tried to defend himself. She alleges that Andrew has red marks around his neck and bruises to his legs. She has already contacted the police and they are coming to see her and Andrew later. Andrew is not at school today.

She intends to contact the chair of governors and the local press, and has told the head she expects the teacher to be suspended immediately. The head was not previously aware of the incident, though he/she is aware that not all the staff are very happy with this supply teacher's methods and approach to pupils. The school is two staff down on long-term sick leave.

Reporting outcomes

Following the conclusion of the investigation, there may be action required by the employer, police and social services. As with all child protection cases, whether or not there is a criminal prosecution is not the only measure to be used. Other outcomes, short of complete exoneration, may be appropriate. Where criminal proceedings do result, resignations and dismissals may follow. In other circumstances, written and verbal warnings may be sufficient, or it may be agreed that no further action is needed. It is not appropriate to impose a punishment on a child whose allegation has not been substantiated, unless there has been a serious breach of the school's policy on discipline and their behaviour merits it. Simply being wrong in their claim is not sufficient. As before, all parties should be offered continuing support as necessary.

LEA officers are now required to report to the DfES on the eventual outcomes of all such cases (without revealing the identities of any of those involved). This system of reporting was set up largely as an attempt to measure the effectiveness of inter-agency and LEA procedures in avoiding unreasonable delay while the accused person was still waiting for a decision on their future. In practice it usually demonstrates that any delay is more likely to be because of the time taken for the police to gather evidence and receive a final decision from the CPS about whether a prosecution is to follow. This decision is supposed to take no longer than two months, with an initial response within two weeks. It often takes much longer, or the police may take a long time to send the file in the first place. Lengthy delays in resolving the issues will often therefore not be a problem within the LEA's control. There does appear to be some inconsistency in deciding which cases go forward and which do not, but it is possible that not all the relevant facts are always in the public domain.

CRB disclosure and List 99

As a general preventive measure, schools must ensure that anyone who has regular contact with children is not included on List 99 held by the Teacher Misconduct Team at the DfES. The previous language referred to those who had 'substantial unsupervised access to children on a sustained or regular basis'. This has led to some confusion over who needs to be CRB checked, and at what level of disclosure, particularly as the fees have risen dramatically over the past year. (For more information, see *Child Protection: Preventing Unsuitable People from Working with Children and Young Persons in the Education Service*, DfEE Circular 0278/2002.) Headteachers and managers must obviously make sure that they carry out the necessary checks on all newly employed professional staff, usually through the LEA human resources section, but this may not cover all the possible implications. (See also the guidance on volunteers in Chapter 8.)

Where individuals already connected with education are convicted of certain specified offences, information *must* be sent to the DfES under the Education (Prohibition from Teaching or Working with Children) Regulations 2003. This is usually done by the police, but employers clearly also have a duty to ensure that correct procedures are followed. DfES staff are apparently sometimes reduced to picking up examples from the newspapers because the police, social services, schools or LEAs concerned have not advised them appropriately. The process, including the right to make personal representations if it is requested, should then ensure that those who are unsuitable are not employed in a similar capacity in the future.

For those required to register as sex offenders, it is an offence even to seek employment with children while barred from doing so. Alternatively, if not barred altogether, they may be restricted in some specific way following a risk assessment – for example, in relation to children of a certain age group. There should also be cross-referencing with Ofsted procedures for those in early years provision and with lists previously held by the Department of Health (now incorporated into the DfES) of people who had previously worked in care settings and other voluntary children's services who are judged unsuitable.

Supply teachers whose behaviour has raised concerns, and any others who move frequently between schools in suspicious circumstances, might not be properly identified unless procedures are robust. Sometimes headteachers employ the staff themselves on short-term contracts or use those from a supply agency without the LEA being involved. People may move into the private sector or have missing references and unexplained gaps in service that should be checked before appointing them. Agencies must be asked for the evidence if they are saying that all the required checks have been undertaken already.

It is essential that managers institute other procedures for monitoring applicants rather than relying entirely on CRB clearance, which may not tell the whole story. For example:

- There should be an attempt to assess the individual's understanding of their personal responsibilities as an educational professional and their current level of knowledge of child protection arrangements.
- The applicant's direct interaction with children should be carefully observed, in both formal and informal settings.
- The views of children should be sought wherever possible.
- References should specifically ask for any information that might suggest that the person is not suitable, otherwise referees may just leave it out.
- References should be followed up in person and to ensure authenticity.

There is some concern about the fact that far more people are referred to the DfES than those who are eventually placed on List 99. Many of the others will still be unsuitable for teaching but might not actually be formally prohibited. In some cases, former pupils are now seeking redress for unacceptable behaviour towards them when they were at school, even though many of those cases might not have been dealt with at the time. It is vital that the DfES Misconduct Team is informed whenever resignation or another agreement is reached as an alternative to dismissal, as well as when anyone is cautioned for a relevant offence without a trial (for which a 'guilty' plea is required), in addition to those who are actually convicted.

The case of Ian Huntley and the Soham schoolgirls has also raised important questions about non-teaching staff and those employed directly by headteachers and governors. I can only feel deep sympathy for all those who were taken in by him, but it is right that there should be a detailed investigation into how someone with Ian Huntley's past record managed to obtain a position of trust as a school caretaker. There are always lessons to be learned. He may have taken advantage of loopholes in the system for CRB checks by changing his name and moving areas, but there had been many previous concerns expressed to both social services and the police in other parts of the country that would have obviously made him unsuitable and even dangerous, had the school known about them. There has long been a difficulty over how agencies should respond to information that may suggest someone is a risk to children, but short of actual convictions. People do have rights to privacy, and allegations may not always be as accurate as is claimed.

The best advice, pending any change in the procedures or new legislation, is for all those making appointments to be absolutely rigorous in checking the background of applicants. Ask for original birth certificates to confirm the name being used; speak personally to anyone who is claimed to have employed the individual previously; do not rely only on references that are 'open' and not specific to the post. Anyone in a position of trust must be monitored, and accountable to someone else, and their behaviour constantly supervised. It is impossible always to second-guess a determined liar, but we must be careful not to make it any easier for them. It is sadly true that some people who want to harm children deliberately seek to get jobs where they are in contact with them. Trust and goodwill are not good enough to spot the potential abusers.

Summary

All this guidance, and the consequent procedures if followed, should give as much protection as possible to an accused teacher, but it is impossible to have a system that always ensures that the adult's interests outweigh everything else. There will always be examples that turn out to be misunderstandings, mistakes or misinformation. In my experience, just as in the major national scandals about families, things tend to go wrong more often if the guidance was *not* read and procedures were *not* followed rather than because they were. For example, I have occasionally faced unreasonable pressure from the chair of a strategy meeting to move towards suspending a teacher just because an allegation had been made. My knowing that the procedures do not require suspension in every case, and that anyway suspension is solely a decision for the employer, enabled such pressure to be resisted. Equally, delay in calling a meeting or commencing the investigation should be challenged, and colleagues in other agencies expected to work within reasonable timescales as laid down in procedures.

All such areas of potential difficulty are best defined in shared multi-agency agreements that can then be used to protect the interests of all those involved, including the child and the teacher. This is the only agreed process we have, and therefore we have to use it because it provides some continuity and fairness for everyone. Once things have been properly examined and dealt with in this way, *outside* the agency concerned, they can be considered 'closed' in a way that other kinds of investigations may not be able to deliver. Crucially, it particularly offers closure where the concerns have no basis – an outcome that might otherwise be subject to further challenge if decisions appeared to be in any way arbitrary, incomplete or lacking objectivity.

Conclusion

A glimpse of the future

Getting it right

Protecting children is difficult. No one who knows much about it could ever suggest otherwise. It is especially difficult when it comes to raising the possibility that someone may be harming their own child or abusing their position of trust. Most parents and others would, I am sure, say that they wish to receive the same degree of 'innocence till proven guilty' as should be accorded to anyone who is the subject of any kind of complaint. But equally, no professional would want to be involved in anything that might appear to be a cover-up or a closing of ranks that puts children at continuing risk of harm. Nobody wants anyone to be the subject of an unreasonable allegation, but neither do we want our society or its agencies to be tainted by those who are abusing the goodwill of children, other parents or their colleagues.

The government is clearly right to focus on supporting families before things get to a crisis, not just on dealing with the disasters. That's where the pressure will always be, in any system, but there must also be room for more preventive work. Intervening before it's too late can offer real job satisfaction and significantly improve children's quality of life. The goal has to be better parenting and happier families, not just stopping deaths and serious incidents. But even when something has gone wrong, fundamental change may not be needed, just better practice next time. With the exception of the wholly inadequate law on child employment, it should be encouraging to discover that so many procedures are in place for all those involved to follow and that there is so much advice available on how such complex issues should be handled. We are not simply working in a vacuum, left to sort it out for ourselves. The framework exists to safeguard all children, at least as far as we possibly can.

For things to happen properly, however, we must have reasonable expectations of one another. It all comes down to people in the end. Transforming the children's workforce means helping us all to do a better job, but we cannot work miracles. Social workers cannot solve every problem or know intuitively in advance which concerns are genuine. The police and court services are vastly over-stretched in this critical area. Parents are sometimes under enormous pressure and may suddenly act entirely out of character in a way that no one could have predicted. Some abusers are career criminals who are highly effective in avoiding detection, and we may never get a chance to catch them out. Teachers and LEAs cannot do everything that is asked of them all the time. Children are often a challenge! We are not usually in control of the events to which we are expected to respond, and it is always more complicated to do something with others than to do it by yourself.

We must each take individual responsibility for *our own* behaviour and actions, both professionally and personally, but cannot expect also to tell others how they should understand theirs. I was once asked by a senior member of a high school's pastoral team exactly why I was unwilling to go into a teenage girl's bedroom and drag her out of bed and bring her in. I am sure things have now moved on from attitudes like that, which suggested scant regard for the best interests of either of us! But social workers will not necessarily do what you would have done, nor take exactly the same view of a given family's situation. We cannot do their job for them; neither can we ask them to do ours. It's about working *together*, not in parallel or, worse still, in competition.

Most of the time, child protection referrals have some genuine basis and are raised in good faith. Sometimes actions are misinterpreted or unwise rather than abusive, but nobody can possibly know until the concerns have been properly investigated. Some relatively minor issues are just the tip of an enormous iceberg; sometimes it's the other way around. When things turn out to be a false alarm, when children accuse adults unreasonably, or even when they themselves pose more of a direct physical threat, responses must still be balanced with a broader welfare perspective. They will almost certainly remain a child in need, entitled to support and help, even if not a child in need of protection.

The potential betrayal of a child or young person's relationship of trust with key adults in their life is a very serious matter, and one that cannot always be resolved easily. There may be shortcomings on many sides or deliberate attempts to mislead and confuse. There may be no perfect outcome available. But the way such issues are handled by those who work in educational settings is vitally important both to the child's immediate protection and in the longer term. If we can act effectively when required, we may even be able to mitigate the effects of the abuse over the coming years. We can make a real difference. Equally, professional failure, and an inability to communicate with one another, can lead to the abuse being compounded, to further serious injuries and even to entirely avoidable deaths.

Meeting the challenge

Soon after she was appointed, the first Children and Young People's Minister within the DfES, Margaret Hodge, said:

> We are determined that the needs of children should be at the heart of all decisions that affect their lives. By working together as one body, children's

professionals will be able to pool money and staff and share information to offer better support and protection.

(On launching Pathfinder Children's Trusts, July 2003)

This makes obvious sense, and it is clearly intended that education services will be central to any new approach designed to bring multidisciplinary workers much closer together. I only hope that the needs of vulnerable children in particular, not just saving money, will be their common concern. Just as crucially, it will be essential not to lose touch with the needs of very young and pre-school children, where the risks are usually greater and for whom health agencies are normally far more important. We will be making a very familiar mistake if they feel in any way marginalised. Some would say it might have made rather more sense to place other professionals in doctor's surgeries and health centres, closer to where people actually live and without some of the obstacles to access that many schools present, even if unintentionally. Children's centres may be a more viable alternative but cannot operate everywhere.

But what do these expectations actually mean for schools? My worry is not that teachers are less willing than any other professional to act as they should if a child is in trouble, or that they are more likely than others to abuse their position. I am sure that neither is true. But I am concerned that teachers in particular seem to receive little formal training in these complex pastoral areas. Many have little awareness of the wider social context in which they work, so the vision is often far from the reality. Many teachers have never had time even to see their pupils' home environment or to understand the lives they lead beyond the school gate. Asking them to take a key role in protecting their wider welfare may feel like a massive step into the unknown.

I never cease to be impressed by the efforts that some teachers make to improve the lives of desperately disadvantaged children, but it's hardly a level playing field. Similar expectations of completely different schools are simply incompatible with what has happened in education over the past twenty years, even at primary level, let alone with older children. A polarised service, as education clearly is, cannot easily be used as the basis for a universal system of protection. *All* schools are required to put child protection arrangements into place. But in some it may be a virtually full-time job, rarely reflected in budgetary terms, while in others policy and procedures may remain unused for years. Both extremes are equally dangerous for the best interests of children as teachers risk becoming either exhausted or complacent.

The concept of 'vulnerable' or 'abused' children may be misleading if it conjures up images of helplessness and innocence. Abuse issues do sometimes occur in relation to children who have no other problems, but they are likely to be the exception. The children who need us the most are those who already have no one else in their lives who thinks they're worth it, including sometimes our colleagues and even their own parents. These are the same children who take up all our spare non-teaching time and are never in the right place at the right time;

who attend poorly, stretch the dress and hairstyle code to its limits, underachieve in SATs and examinations, misbehave or require hours of extra support. Their parents owe dinner money, complain about the slightest thing and may well be aggressive and uncooperative, if they ever darken the doors at all. They won't even look at anything described as a 'home–school agreement', let alone keep to it, and may treat a contract or even a Parenting Order with much the same indifference.

Child protection practice will inevitably reflect pastoral practice as a whole. Teachers cannot be expected to carry out these responsibilities in complete isolation from the wider life of the school. But this kind of work may appear to be out of step with all the rest and may therefore be given little priority. If there are accusations to be made – and they need to be addressed to government as much as to employers and individuals – they are largely those of inconsistency, naivety and intellectual laziness. In short, do teachers and governors realise what is now required of them? Do they know what they need to know about their duty to safeguard children's welfare? What about all the pressures pulling in the opposite direction?

The new post of Director-General for Children and Families in the DfES was advertised under the slogan 'Putting children at the heart of everything we do'. The Green Paper is called *Every Child Matters* (Chief Minister to the Treasury 2003). Fine words, but not always reflected in general educational policy, or in the practice of all schools, in my opinion. The level of knowledge and expertise in education about social care in general, and child protection in particular, is historically far lower than among those who work on such issues all the time. Teacher training still gives it little attention (although the government has said that it intends to address this; and see NSPCC 2003). Headteachers, often inexperienced in this area and increasingly isolated from immediate LEA support, do not always seek sufficient advice before taking actions that are unfamiliar. Doing something to protect children has only just become a formal legal requirement. Until very recently we have all been expected to follow other, quite different agendas that have a far greater priority, all of which are still there.

Changing schools?

Recent government thinking, which has moved the DfES to the centre of children's services, and highlighted the role of schools as a result, was prompted by a perceived failure by the DoH to ensure that children were being adequately protected, largely as a result of the Victoria Climbié case. But focusing services primarily around schools may not necessarily be in all children's best interests. Parents are free to educate their children themselves if they wish, entirely outside the school system, without much effective supervision or regulation. Victoria was unknown to her LEA and might have had difficulty accessing a school place, even if one had been asked for. Many vulnerable children are not on school rolls at all or are frequently absent. Now that some parents at least have a wider opportunity for choice, many children attend schools miles away from where they live, perhaps even schools of another local authority. Who will be responsible for them under any new, more school-centred approach?

A child-focused, multidisciplinary approach to children's needs is often in direct tension with the culture of selection, choice, tables and targets that now dominate educational thinking. Even where schools *want* to help troubled children, they may face considerable conflicts in doing so. 'Good' schools are almost always measured by their academic achievements alone, and in such schools attendance and behaviour will also present little difficulty. That's what we have been told to see as success. Few schools deliberately market themselves as specialising in children with problems! They may simply reflect the areas they serve, because they are the only school that's available, but many schools will not be neighbourhood schools at all and will not want to be. Local admission arrangements may mean that those children most at risk are concentrated into a few schools, almost invariably in areas of poverty and social deprivation, and these will probably be expected to take similar children unwanted by other schools as well. Equally, there is a real danger that the needs of vulnerable children in the more 'successful' schools will be overlooked, either because they are so out of the ordinary or because staff will be unable to develop the expertise they may suddenly need.

There is a fundamental uncertainty in education about how we should deal with troubled children and their parents. There is much talk of partnership, but education welfare officers, for example, have recently seen their focus specifically moved away from social work approaches and on to the legal enforcement of attendance, if necessary through the courts. This is often completely ineffective with families in which abuse and neglect have been a feature. Giving headteachers, or anyone else, the power to impose fixed-penalty fines on the parents of 'truants' risks sending entirely the wrong signal about school as a place where they can also expect to find sympathetic help with their children. Many parents already feel unwelcome and inadequate when it comes to education and see school as part of their problem, not as the source of the solution.

Nothing affects a child's life chances more than missing out on education. But exclusions, formal and informal, are rising again, and at ever-younger ages, in part because headteachers and governors have been sent clear signals that it is good practice to remove badly behaved children, whatever their personal circumstances, even though this will often precipitate a family crisis and create major difficulties for other professionals left to pick up the pieces. Not all exclusions are for serious violence, and alternatives are often not adequately explored. Some children are still being excluded in the vain hope that some other way of meeting their needs will be found as a result, when in fact exclusion just compounds their difficulties. A decision of this importance requires no prior inter-agency collaboration at all, even where the parent is the local authority, and where it may even result in the loss of the child's home as well as their school. Some schools are unwilling to offer children a new chance after previous problems, or are even prepared to ignore the Code of Practice on admissions or defy tribunals.

Not all schools have yet appointed a designated teacher for looked-after children or actively participate in making referrals, attending reviews, training, and multi-agency meetings, etc. when asked to do so. Pastoral work in general is frequently seen as low-status and not really what schools are for. This is all very hard to reconcile with an emphasis on putting the child's welfare at the heart of all we do, as the Children Act requires. With so many independently managed schools as the actual point of educational delivery, each subject to their own financial pressures and individual interpretations of their ethos and priorities, there is little feel of a national service with a consistent approach to children's problems. LEAs may plan, but they cannot always hope to deliver.

If we are to work much more closely together, perhaps even based around education services as the 'hub', those who were previously in other agencies but are now our colleagues will also ask what is going to happen during the three months a year that schools are closed and the overwhelming majority of the staff are unavailable. Even EWOs may be on term-time-only contracts. But child protection never stops; indeed, the pressures increase on both families and agencies at weekends and holiday times. If education is to be fully part of these new arrangements, the culture of social inclusion has to be accepted root and branch so that all kinds of children, and their families, can find a place, not just those who are most easily able to conform to our normal expectations. We have to find workable solutions to problems of poor behaviour and even poorer parenting, not just push the children away on to somewhere and someone else.

Schools might have to look very different than they do now. They will have to become even more multi-professional and multi-skilled. Specialist roles other than direct teaching will have to be given a much greater share of individual school budgets, and be much better paid than has so far been the case. The idea that we can meet the complex needs of children who are too difficult for teachers to handle by handing them over to people paid half their salary will have to be changed. This kind of work is just as skilled and requires just as much training and dedication. It should carry just the same status and value as producing a string of A grades with a child who has had every encouragement and advantage. Indeed, you could argue that it's not these children who really need the best teachers, but those who pose the greatest challenge in enabling them to learn.

Making sure that those most at risk are actually here, and then engaging with them, must be a top priority for someone in every school, both for reasons of personal achievement *and* so that they can be protected. We cannot help a child we never see. We may even need fewer actual teachers and significantly more counsellors, home liaison workers and other support staff, because that's what some children need if they are to learn anything amid all the obstacles presented by their wider lives. In the end, such provision makes life better for the teachers *and* for the pupils (both the untroubled ones and the others), but it cannot be done for nothing.

Children first?

All this may sound overly critical of schools and their staff, which is not my intention. I am, at least in part, concerned to protect teachers and schools from unrealistic expectations of what they are currently able to do without radical changes to the way education is organised and significantly increased resources. Most are currently reflecting only what successive governments have asked them to do. But, as well as making sure we have got the basics of child protection right, these are the sorts of practical questions that will have to be addressed if these expectations for *every* child are to mean anything worthwhile. The job was not done with a new section of an Education Act, a change of ministerial responsibility at the top, the abolition of corporal punishment and the adoption of a policy that no one ever reads.

Safeguarding and promoting the welfare of children has to be genuinely placed at the centre of why we have schools at all, not be seen as an optional extra that is not really part of the educational 'day job'. Child protection is only a small part of a much bigger package about meeting all children's needs. The whole approach has to be about putting them first, not just in general or in principle, but in each individual case. Otherwise, we may have to get used to the idea that it will be teachers and schools, not just social workers and children's homes, who will become the object of public criticism whenever a child's life ends in tragedy or serious harm. I am not sure that we are yet up to the task, but I will be delighted if I am proved wrong.

Appendix 1: A policy for child protection

The following is presented with acknowledgement to Staffordshire County Council, Education and Lifelong Learning Directorate. An alternative model policy may be available from your LEA.

In line with the requirements of the Freedom of Information Acts, the existence of this policy should be made known to all parents (and pupils as appropriate).

Introduction

This school/college recognises its legal duty under s.175 Education Act 2002 to work with other agencies in safeguarding children and protecting them from 'significant harm'. The framework for such procedures is defined by national guidance, *Working Together to Safeguard Children* (1999), the relevant Circular from the Department for Education and Skills, and the local [Area Child Protection Committee]. These duties relate to all children and young people under the age of 18.

The staff seek to adopt an open and accepting attitude towards children and young people as part of their general responsibility for pastoral care. Staff hope that parents and children will feel free to talk about any concerns or worries that may affect educational progress and that they will see the school as a safe place if there are any difficulties at home. Children will be taken seriously if they seek help from a member of staff.

'Children in need' and 'children in need of protection'

Parents will normally be consulted and their consent obtained before any referral is made to an agency outside the school under local 'children in need' procedures. However, staff cannot guarantee to consult parents first, or to keep children's concerns confidential, if referral must be made to the appropriate agencies in order to safeguard the child's welfare.

If staff have concerns about any child which **may** indicate

- physical abuse,
- emotional abuse,
- sexual abuse or
- neglect,

they are **required** to discuss them with the agencies responsible for investigation and child protection.

Staff who observe injuries that appear to be non-accidental, or who are told anything significant by a child, **must** report their concerns to the designated teacher. School staff do not, however, carry out investigations, or decide whether children have been abused. That is a matter for the specialist agencies outside the school.

Procedures

All staff will be familiar with the school's internal procedures for keeping a confidential written record of any incidents and with the inter-agency recording requirements of the local [Area Child Protection Committee]. Further information is available on request to the headteacher. Advice may be sought from the Local Education Authority, the Social Services Department or the Police if staff are unsure how to proceed.

This policy will need to be accompanied by more detailed procedures that have been formulated at school level according to local circumstances.

Resources

Child protection is important. The Governors will endeavour to ensure that sufficient resources are made available to enable the necessary tasks to be carried out properly under inter-agency procedures, including attending meetings, staff training, etc.

Curriculum

Child protection issues will be addressed through the curriculum as appropriate, especially in Personal, Social and Health Education and sex education.

You could insert here reference to the school's policy on bullying, the supervision of children on trips away from the school premises, the use of images of pupils on any website and in local media, computer screening policy and any other related child safety issues.

Staff issues

Parents can feel confident that careful procedures are in place to ensure that all staff appointed are suitable to work with children. More informal procedures are also applied to voluntary helpers, non-teaching staff, etc.

Any use of physical force or restraint against pupils will be carried out and documented in accordance with the relevant guidance and policy. If it is necessary to use physical intervention to protect a child from injury, or to prevent a child from harming others, or if any child is injured accidentally, parents will be informed immediately. Children will not be punished within the school by any form of hitting, slapping, shaking or other degrading treatment.

Any complaints about staff behaviour may be made to the headteacher, or to the Chairperson of the school's Governors. All those involved will be entitled to a fair hearing, both children and staff. Complaints that raise child protection issues will be reported under local inter-agency procedures for investigation outside the school.

The designated teacher for all child protection matters in the school is:

The Chairperson of the Governors is:

The nominated officer for child protection within the Local Education Authority is:

ADOPTED BY THE GOVERNORS ON: (date)

Appendix 2: The Children Act 1989 and parental responsibility

Parental responsibility is 'all the rights, duties, powers, responsibilities and authority which by law a parent of a child has in relation to the child and [his] property'.

(s.3(1))

Identifying who in a child's life carries the legal status of parent, and who does not, is essential. This information will normally be requested as part of a child protection referral. All pastoral practice depends on ensuring that these data are gathered correctly on admission, and then updated as changes occur. Parents must be asked to clarify the status of all those adults who either live with the child or may have a legal relationship to them while living elsewhere. They are all 'parents' under education law, but parental responsibility allows the individual person concerned to be involved in the child's education in their own right, without need for anyone else's permission. Parents who do not have parental responsibility do not have this same right automatically.

Married, separated and divorced parents

Both parents have parental responsibility if they have ever been married, provided they are the actual father and mother of the child, even if they married after the child was born, are no longer living together or are now divorced. Legal rights of this kind are not lost with the ending of the marriage or on the making of a care order, unless the child is adopted. Neither parent can deny the other their independent right to exercise their parental responsibility by attending parents' evenings and meetings, receiving reports, etc., unless they are restricted from doing so by court order. All those with parental responsibility must consent before the child's name can be changed. They can each ask someone else to carry out their responsibility for them – during an illness or prison sentence, for example. All such parents should be included on the school's admission register, wherever possible.

Unmarried parents

A mother who has never married the child's father has traditionally had sole parental responsibility; co-habitation did not confer the same legal status for the father as does marriage. This has been amended by s.111 Adoption and Children Act from 1 December 2003, but only if the father is actually named on the child's birth certificate, and the provision is not backdated for children born before that date. Alternatively, the couple can still make a formal voluntary agreement to give parental responsibility to the father, or a court order can be granted to the father if the mother is unwilling, but both are still uncommon even where the parents have been together for some time. Where there is only one person with parental responsibility, that person may legally make all the decisions about the child without consultation with any other parent, including changing their surname, school, etc. Their consent should always be asked for on forms, etc. ('Parent or guardian' should now be avoided. Use either 'parent' for everyone, or, if the signature of someone with parental responsibility is required, say so explicitly.)

Step-parents and other carers

People bringing up other people's children are 'parents' in a general sense, but they do not normally have parental responsibility. S.112 Adoption and Children Act 2002 now enables a married step-parent to acquire parental responsibility, but only by agreement with *all* those who have it already – that is, only with the consent of a divorced father/mother not now living with the child. Otherwise, their involvement is dependent on the consent of those who are legally responsible, and in some circumstances where parental consent is required, they would have to defer to those with parental responsibility. Step-parents may also have parental responsibility if a court has granted a residence order (see the Glossary) that names them as caring for the child or they have adopted the child. These are the exception, not the rule.

Glossary

This is a list of terms that may be used in connection with child protection, especially by those in other agencies. Many arise directly from the Children Act 1989. Terms highlighted in bold are defined elsewhere within this list.

Accommodation   The term used to describe the status of a **looked-after** child who is not **in care** but whose placement away from their home has been arranged through the social services on a voluntary basis (s.20 Children Act 1989). All the parental responsibility remains with the actual **parents** as before.

Adoption   The permanent assumption of parental responsibility for a child through a court. This is the only process that ends the actual **parents**' legal relationship with the child. There are now some examples of 'open' adoption, especially of older children, in which some **contact** with family members is maintained.

Anti-discriminatory practice   An integral feature of social work that seeks to ensure that services are provided in a way that respects differences of race, gender, physical and intellectual ability, sexual orientation, etc. Sometimes called anti-oppressive practice.

Authorised person   A person who is authorised by the Secretary of State for Health to bring proceedings under s.31 Children Act 1989, in addition to officers of the local authority. Currently this covers only certain officers of the NSPCC.

Care centre   A county court that has full jurisdiction in all **public law** and **private law** matters, usually hearing those cases that are more complicated than usual. Most **public law** applications are heard at magistrates' court level in the **Family Proceedings Court**, at least to begin with.

Care management   The process by which a family's needs are assessed and met by a social worker. It may be the term used to describe the local team of social workers in the social services department.

Care order   An order under s.31(1) of the Children Act 1989 that places a child in the care of the local authority. The effect of a care order, which can be made initially on an interim basis, is to give parental responsibility to the local authority in addition to those who may hold it already. Using the right of **independent action**, the local authority is then able to restrict the actions of these other persons in order to promote the child's welfare, such as determining where they will live, keeping them in hospital, etc.

Centile charts A system for measuring children's weight, height, etc. in a way that compares them with other children of similar age. Scores consistently below the norm that have no organic explanation may be an indicator of abuse.

Civil court proceedings Legal proceedings that are not criminal – that is, divorce, **care orders** and other applications under the Children Act 1989 and related legislation.

Complex (multiple) abuse Abuse that may involve more than one child or perpetrator. May also be used in connection with allegations against professionals.

Contact The replacement for 'access' under previous legislation, and broader in its intention. Contact is any arrangement by which a child is enabled to see, visit, telephone, write to or be contacted by a **parent**, sibling, relative or other person. Orders are usually made only when there has been some dispute. Most family situations are not defined by any court orders but are left to voluntary arrangements to be sorted out between the **parties**.

Contact order An order made under s.8 Children Act 1989 that requires the person with whom the child is living to allow them to have **contact** with another person as defined on the order. If there is no order, all reasonable contact is permitted.

Custodian of the register Not now a universal term, but may be used to refer to the person in the social services department who is responsible for maintaining the child protection register.

Direction An instruction from a court, or written into an order, that certain actions must, or must not, be taken.

Directions appointment A preliminary court hearing intended to reduce delay in applying for orders, fix timetables, sort out any disputes, etc.

Disclosure A child telling an adult that they have been harmed. Often used in relation to sexual abuse in particular.

Ecomap A diagram used to show a child's relationships to people outside their family such as school, friends, significant adults, etc. May be used as part of an assessment under the Assessment Framework.

Emergency Duty Team (EDT) Social workers who deal with emergencies, including child protection and mental health, outside normal office hours. The likely place for a referral if concerns arise outside the working day.

Encopresis The passing of faeces in inappropriate places. May have a dietary or emotional explanation.

Enuresis Bed-wetting, usually mentioned in the context of children who are over the age where accidents might still reasonably occur. May indicate other problems, either physical or emotional.

Evidence in chief The statement a child has made for a court, either in civil or criminal proceedings. It will often be pre-recorded as a **video interview**.

Ex parte A court hearing held without some of the **parties** present, usually in an emergency.

Fabricated and induced illness (FII) The up-to-date term for 'Munchausen's syndrome by proxy' in which adults either feign or induce symptoms in their children in order to receive attention from medical or other services. Such behaviour may involve actually injuring the child deliberately and, at its most extreme, responses may include the use of covert video surveillance in order to gather evidence.

Family proceedings Court proceedings defined by the Children Act 1989, including almost all decisions relating to children. Technically, child protection procedures are not family proceedings, but the same principles usually apply if court action is necessary.

Family Proceedings Court The court at magistrates level which hears most applications about children, at least in the first instance.

Female infibulation The correct term for female genital mutilation or circumcision, which is illegal in children except for specific health reasons.

Foster carer The preferred term for foster parents (as most children still have **parents** as well). Foster carers are **parents** for educational purposes.

Frazer guidelines The court ruling of 1985 which held that children of sufficient age and understanding, even if they are still below the legal age of majority, can give or withhold consent to medical interventions. (Formerly known as 'Gillick competence'.)

Genogram A diagrammatic way of showing a child's family relationships and history. May be used as part of an assessment or to help the child to explore their feelings about family members.

Gillick competence See **Frazer guidelines**

Grooming The preparation of a child for potential sexual abuse; an adult establishing a relationship with a child for an ulterior motive. It is planned to make this a specific offence, including using electronic and Internet communications as well as direct contact.

Guardian Someone who has taken over parental responsibility for a child under s.5 Children Act 1989, because those who held it previously have all died. Despite its prevalence, 'guardian' should not be used on forms as meaning the same as **parent**.

Guardian *ad litem* (GAL) An independent person appointed to safeguard a child's interests during **family proceedings**. A national shortage of GALs is a major factor in causing delay in making decisions.

In care Children should only be described as 'in care' when the local authority has assumed parental responsibility by virtue of a **care order** under s.31 Children Act 1989. Both these and other children who are provided with **accommodation** on a voluntary basis are included in the term **looked after**.

Independent action The right of any person with parental responsibility to exercise it, without the permission or involvement of any other such person. Most (but not all) decisions about children can be made by one such person acting alone, but as either person may decide if there is more than one of them, arrangements should be as even-handed as possible.

Independent chair A term that may be used for the person who chairs a child protection conference and reviews children who are **looked after**.

Injunction An order made under the Domestic Violence and Matrimonial Proceedings Act 1976 that restricts the rights of an individual in some way, possibly changing arrangements for **contact**. A **Section 8 order** under the Children Act 1989 may also have a similar effect.

Life story (book) A way of helping a child to make a record of their life through pictures, letters etc., especially where they have experienced a lot of changes.

List 99 A list of those known to the DfES to be unsuitable for teaching, or restricted in some way from professional contact with children.

Looked after The generic term covering both children who are **in care** and those provided with **accommodation** through the local authority. All schools should have a teacher with designated responsibility for any such children.

Multiple (complex) abuse Abuse involving a number of children as part of the same incident or inquiry.

No order principle A fundamental requirement of all proceedings under the Children Act 1989, and therefore of social work practice, that court orders should be made only when to do so would be better for the child than making no order at all.

Notice of hearing The requirement to inform all those with a right to know of any court hearing for a child for whom they are responsible or with whom they are living. Such people then have a right to apply to become a **party** to the proceedings if they are not one already.

Organised abuse Sexual abuse that involves a number of perpetrators or a number of children, or that has required an element of deliberate planning. This may include paedophile 'rings' or even some element of 'ritual' abuse, though the extent of such abuse is a matter of some dispute.

Paramountcy principle The principle inherent in the Children Act 1989 that the child's welfare is the paramount consideration in any proceedings.

Parent In its educational definition, this term includes those with parental responsibility (wherever they live) *and* those who have day-to-day care of the child (even if they do not have parental responsibility). Other agencies sometimes use the term as shorthand for birth parents only. (See also Appendix 2.)

Party A person or agency with an automatic right to attend court hearings relating to a child and to have their views represented. Those who do not have this status automatically, such as a grandparent, may be able to apply for 'leave' to be joined as party where they can demonstrate an interest in the child's welfare.

Permanency planning The term used by social workers when discussing long-term plans for children.

Private law Family issues that do not require the intervention of the state, such as matrimonial disputes and questions about children following divorce or separation. **Section 8 orders** are primarily used in this context.

Prohibited steps order An order made under s.8 Children Act 1989 that restricts the exercise of parental responsibility in some way.

Public law The law that regulates the intervention of the state into family life, especially child protection and care proceedings.

Residence order An order made under s.8 Children Act 1989 that defines the person with whom a child shall live. Any such person who does not already have parental responsibility for the child in their own right acquires it for the duration of the order.

Schedule 1 offender A person who has been convicted of an offence against a child under Schedule 1 Children and Young Persons Act 1933. This includes both sexual offences and others involving cruelty or neglect. Anyone with such a conviction would not usually be suitable to work with children in a position of trust. (There are also Schedule 1 sex offenders under different legislation.)

Section 8 orders Four types of orders under the Children Act 1989: **residence order** (the replacement for custody); **contact order** (the replacement for access); **prohibited steps order** and **specific issue order**. These orders resolve particular disputes or issues about a child and normally apply only until the child becomes 16.

Sibling abuse The causing of harm to a brother or sister.

Special review cases A formal review under local ACPC procedures where a child dies or is seriously injured. Also known as Part 8 reviews, referring to the relevant chapter of *Working Together*.

Specific issue order An order made under s.8 Children Act 1989 which resolves a particular dispute about the exercise of parental responsibility, such as choice of school.

Sudden Infant Death Syndrome (SIDS) The sudden unexplained death of an infant, or 'cot death'.

Supervision order An order made under s.31 Children Act 1989 that places a child under the supervision of the social services department (or, in other contexts, other agencies).

Threshold criteria The criteria for deciding whether sufficient grounds have been established to be able to justify agency or court intervention to protect a child.

Video interview Procedures for recording a child's **evidence in chief**. This is done by social workers and police officers in accordance with detailed guidance at particular centres (video suites), which should be as child-friendly as possible.

Ward of court   A child who is under the protection of the High Court and about whom no decisions can be made without the court's consent.

Written agreement   An agreed basis for the provision of services, including **accommodation**, between a local authority and a family.

For further reference

Government documents (chronological order)

All recent DfES documents can be downloaded from the DfES website, www.dfes.gov.uk, or through teachernet.gov.uk. A copy of the Children Act 1989 can be downloaded from www.hmso.gov.uk/acts.

Department of Health (1995) *Child Protection: Messages from Research*, HMSO, London.

National Commission of Inquiry (1997) *Childhood Matters*, 2 volumes and a Summary, The Stationery Office, London.

Department for Education and Employment (1998) *S.550A of the Education Act 1996: The Use of Force to Control or Restrain Pupils*, Circular 10/98; Welsh Office Circular 37/98, DfEE, London.

Department of Health, Department for Education and Skills, and Home Office (1999) *Working Together to Safeguard Children*, The Stationery Office, London.

Department of Health, Department for Education and Skills, and Home Office (2000) *Framework for the Assessment of Children in Need and their Families*, The Stationery Office, London.

Department for Education and Employment (2000) *Schools, Parents and Parental Responsibility*, Circular 0092/2000.

Department of Health (2002) *Safeguarding Children: A Summary of the Joint Chief Inspectors' Report on Arrangements to Safeguard Children*, The Stationery Office, London.

Department for Education and Skills (and Department of Health) (2002) *Guidance on the Use of Restrictive Physical Interventions for Staff Working with Children and Adults Who Display Extreme Behaviour in Association with Learning Disability and/or Autistic Spectrum Disorders*, Circular 0242/2002, DfES, London. Specialist advice but with some wider general implications.

Department for Education and Skills (2002) *Child Protection: Preventing Unsuitable People from Working with Children and Young Persons in the Education Service*, Circular 0278/2002.

Department for Education and Skills (2002) *Criminal Records Bureau: Managing the Demand for Disclosures*, Circular 0780/2002, DfES, London. Issued in response to delays in the procedure but also contains a useful factsheet about CRB procedures and some practical examples in a school context.

Department for Education and Skills (Children and Young People's Unit) (2003) *The Children Act Report 2002*, DfES Publications, London.

Ofsted (2003) *Bullying: Effective Action in Secondary Schools*.

Department of Health and Home Office (2003) *The Victoria Climbié Inquiry: Report of an Inquiry by Lord Laming*, online at www.victoria-climbie-inquiry.org.uk

Department of Health, Department for Education and Skills and Home Office (2003) *Safeguarding Children: What to Do if You're Worried a Child is Being Abused*, Guidance and Summary.

Department for Education and Skills, Department of Health and Home Office (2003) *Keeping Children Safe*.

Chief Minister to the Treasury (2003) *Every Child Matters*, Green Paper on the future of children's services.

Department for Education and Skills (2003) *Guidance on the Use of Restrictive Physical Interventions for Pupils with Severe Behavioural Difficulties*, Circular 0264/2003.

Department for Education and Skills (forthcoming) new guidance to replace Circular 10/95 and its Welsh equivalent. Due for publication in June 2004 to coincide with s.175 Education Act 2002.

Training resources

NSPCC (2003) *Learning to Protect*, NSPCC. A flexible resource package for use in initial teacher training, covering both core subjects and more specialist areas. Much of the content could also be used to support school and LEA induction and retraining programmes. The NSPCC also produces *Educare*, a distance learning resource for educational professionals.

Other (alphabetical order)

Aries, P. (1973) *Centuries of Childhood*, Penguin, Harmondsworth, UK.

Baginsky, M. (2003) *Responsibility without Power? Local Education Authorities and Child Protection*, NSPCC.

Blyth, E. and Milner, J. (1997) *Social Work with Children: The Educational Perspective*, Longman, London.

Carr, J. (2004) *Child Abuse, Pornography and the Internet*, NCH, London.

Lavalette, M. (ed.) (1999) *A Thing of the Past? Child Labour in Britain in the 19th and 20th Centuries*, Liverpool University Press, Liverpool.

National Employers' Organisation for School Teachers (NEOST) *et al.* (2002) *Guidance on Conduct for Teachers, Education Staff and Volunteers* and *Guidance on Preventing Abuse of Trust*.

Pierson, J. and Thomas, M. (2002) *Dictionary of Social Work*, HarperCollins, London.

Reder, P., Duncan, S. and Gray, M. (1993) *Beyond Blame: Child Abuse Tragedies Revisited*, Routledge, London.

Index